OUR COMMUNICATORS
AND
THEIR
"WORDS OF WISDOM"

A RECORD OF THE PSYCHIC TRANCE COMMUNICATIONS

CON-PSY PUBLICATIONS MIDDLESEX

First Edition

© PAUL & ELLEN
1998

This book is copyrighted under the Berne Convention. All rights reserved. No part of this book may be reproduced or utilised in any form or by any means, electronic or mechanical, including photocopying, recording, or by any information storage and retrieval system, without permission in writing from the publisher. Except for the purpose of reviewing or criticism, as permitted under the Copyright Act of 1956.

Published by

CON-PSY PUBLICATIONS

P.O. BOX 14, GREENFORD, MIDDLESEX, UB6 0UF.

ISBN 1 898680 17 5

CONTENTS

DEDICATION
Page 4

PROLOGUE
Page 5

CHAPTER ONE
INTRODUCTIONS
page 6

CHAPTER TWO
WORDS OF WISDOM
Page 17

CHAPTER THREE
PSYCHIC WAYS
Page 264

CHAPTER FOUR
THE LEARNING SYSTEM
Page 268

DEDICATION

TO SEEKERS OF KNOWLEDGE,

THIS INFORMATION IS

WILLINGLY PASSED ON.

WITH GRATEFUL ACKNOWLEDGEMENT

TO OUR BAND OF

COMMUNICATORS

WITH WHOM NONE OF THIS

WOULD HAVE BEEN

POSSIBLE

PROLOGUE

These writings are the true record of the communications with our group of friends from the World of Spirit. In particular the 'Words of Wisdom' chapter is a direct transcription from the tape recordings of the communications. It will, therefore, be evident that the grammar and use of words and phrases are rather different from standard English. We have chosen to leave the words as spoken, as there is a real danger in using other words and phrases that would possibly lose the true meaning. The characters of our spirit communicators are often portrayed in the phraseology used and their manner of speech. We are aware that this is lost in transcription but we hope the reader will gain an insight into the characters by the descriptions given in 'Introductions.' As we know, spirit communication is normally on vibrations that the medium decodes, however, there is always a possibility that the best word is not known to the medium or simply does not exist in the English language.

'Words of Wisdom' is a record formed week by week of questions answered by our communicators. This work has been recorded in chronological order therefore the subject matter does not necessarily maintain a structured format. The 'Questions' are generally responses to particular points raised by the sitters. As the sitters become more knowledgeable the questions tend to become more involved.

Within this book we wish to share the knowledge given to us from our friends in spirit and hope that it will stimulate the reader's search for truth.

We are both fully aware that we are privileged to be given the chance to understand the true meaning of existence. We have no right to keep this knowledge to ourselves but to make it available as best we can to other seekers of spiritual knowledge.

Readers are advised that if they seek any type of psychic/spirit communication it is vital they ask for the protection of spirit before commencing, preferably in prayer format. Remember it is also important to close communication with spirit with thanks and a prayer.

This book is provided as guidance and as such should not be considered a 'handbook' for spirit communication. Individuals wishing to develop their communication abilities with spirit should study under the supervision of experienced tutors.

PAUL & ELLEN

CHAPTER ONE
INTRODUCTIONS

Both Ellen and myself were brought up by families who had a deep knowledge and understanding of the ability of our friends and companions in the world of Spirit to be able to communicate in many ways. We regularly became involved in the "Spiritualist" movement which in Ellen's case related to both her Father and brother being Practicing Healers, and her Mother being actively interested in the workings of spirit. In my case both my Father and Grandfather (Fruin), were speakers and clairvoyants in the churches and deeply involved in organisation of various facets of the Spiritualist movement and it's Lyceum organisation for the furtherance of spiritual knowledge. Grandmother (Fruin), or as she was always referred to as Nan, was always there to support the family in their Church and Lyceum work, and was particularly involved with fund raising. My Mother was also deeply involved in Church and Lyceum matters, with a special interest in writing and publishing articles and booklets relating to spiritual and character building subjects, often aimed at a young reader. Just to empathise the deep involvement my Grandfather, Father and Mother, were all Ministers of Religion of the Spiritualist National Union.

Over the years we have been involved in various churches as committee members and in Ellen's case a Lyceum conductor for a number of years. Although we sat in various development groups our ability to communicate directly with Spirit seemed to evade us. I have been told that as a child I played with a young girl from spirit and relayed this to my family, who of course were able to understand, but when I was probably 5 or 6, I clearly remember seeing two spirit forms at the bottom of my bed and being frightened, and that was the end of my natural communication with Spirit for some 45 years.

In the early 1990's we were invited to join a Healing Development Circle, run by a couple of friends we had known for many years as healers and investigators and speakers on the scientific approach to psychic matters. We trained as healers and eventually became qualified healers able to practice in accordance with the constitution of The Surrey Healers. As the circle developed it became more and more a Physical Phenomena Circle with table and trumpet movement, production of aromas, spirit writing, tappings / bangings on the floor and walls, ringing of bells and playing of a drum, spirit lights, and on a few occasions direct voices. This was coupled with one of the communicators speaking through the body of the medium, who was in deep trance. All the communication being generally fully understood and in reply to our questions. During this time both of us began to develop firstly in a small way our own ability to communicate with Spirit. Ellen discovered to her amazement and delight that she was able to draw pictures of faces and emblems with her left hand. At this stage I should explain that Ellen has never shown any particular artistic ability, she is right handed and did not see the face clairvoyantly. We both developed the ability, working together to demonstrate Table Phenomena, this being the movement of a table by Spirit to communicate either by signals that we recognised or by words being spelt out by the movement of the table in response to the reciting of the alphabet, numbers or yes / no questions. With patience and care detailed and accurate communication was possible. In 1995 Ellen found herself going into a trance state and the many family and communicators were able to talk direct without the restrictions of the table. I have also been privileged in the right circumstances to receive spirit communication.

There is a growing team of Spirit Communicators who come to teach and reassure us and others who sit with us. Where possible we have endeavoured to understand our spirit friends and their background, in the same way as we get to know our friends on Earth to build up a mutual understanding. In some cases we have been able to visit the area they lived when on Earth, and in the case of Running Bear he led us to his old hunting ground in New England, and told us afterwards. I have tried to describe some of our more regular communicators who come with philosophy and guidance rather than personal visits from friends and relations.

MAFRA is Ellen's protector or door keeper who not only controls proceedings but will when asked answer questions on spiritual matters. Mafra (pronounced Mafwior) was his surname and he was a Grandee gentleman with a port business in Oporto Portugal, the time was before Columbus and he supplied the court of King Louis of France with port. He was proud of his brand of port which included the local brandy from the Franciscan Monks. In January 1996 we visited Oporto and crossed the river Douro to the area of wine lodges known as, Vila Nova de Gaia, and there we were able to place ourselves in the spot where Mafra described the location of his business on the waterfront.

During May 1997 we paid a further visit to Oporto and travelled up into the area in Douro valley where the grapes for the port wine are grown. While in Portugal, Mafra came to talk with us and told use a little more of his earthly life. He lived in a large house in Oporto in a main square near the royal palace and the custom house, evidently the house is still there, but considerably altered today. The house had many servants and during the winter months the family came to the city from their home in the country. Mafra had his business on the other side of the river and crossed by boat, because the rope bridge was too rickety. At the time of the English war with France he was officially banned from using French brandy in his port sold to the English market, however to ensure the high quality of his port wine he obtained the best brandy made by French monks, but that was his little secret! He was able to speak English and Latin.

BEDA was the first communicator to make herself known and comes to bring us joy. Her mother was French and she was born in 1606. She was married to a Count ('Chi-coffer-chiev' this was spoken by Beda but we could only guess at spelling) who at some time was the ambassador, for the area we now know as Russia, to the French Court, around 1630. She was therefore a Countess, and was part of the aristocracy She was very fond of dancing she performed folk dancing with a group to entertain at the various functions held at the time. She tells us that it is her influence that makes the table "dance". Reference books refer to Tsar Mikhail the First of the Romanov Dynasty engaging a dancing master Ivan Lodygin. Also the revival of a type of dance called Trepak involving much stamping of the feet. It therefore seems that folk dancing by the aristocracy was the "in thing" around the 1630's.

BROTHER JOHN when on Earth was a Friar many years ago at the Greyfriers Abbey in Coventry, he always comes through with the hands in the praying position. His role in the Abbey was to pray for peace for as long as he could remember, as such he had taken a vow of silence. Other friars attended his physical needs, provided his food and took every worry from him. He entered the friary at a very young age and used to go and visit the sick and if they were very ill bring them back to the Abbey Hospital for special attention. Then he was drawn into the Abbey learning the chants, eventually he took further vows to allow him to concentrate on prayers for peace. Others told him what prayers were required and he became totally isolated from the world outside.

JOHN LYON was the founder of Harrow School for Boys and is a distant relative of mine on my Mother's side of the family. He is another powerful communicator providing teaching on a wide range of topics. He helps me personally with logical thought and I suspect educational activities in my employment.

KIMYANO is a lady from Japan, brings colours for help with healing the body and mind which includes things like depression.

RUNNING BEAR as the name suggests is a North American Indian who brings strength which should not be confused with power. He helps with strength of conviction and is an extremely powerful communicator. Running Bear is Paul's doorkeeper.

ROSA this lady was skilled in the use of natural remedies and lived high in the mountains of what we know today as Andorra, between France and Spain. She helped people who would come to her home for advice on medical and other problems and she gave help as the "wise old lady", they in turn gave her food and other essentials of life.

GEORGE or to give him his full name George William who is Paul's paternal grandfather, passed to the higher life in 1941 after being knocked off he bicycle by a lorry. Now George, to put it in his own words did a bit of "ducking and diving". He was a mechanic by trade and worked in garages on car maintenance, but he was also on the stage in a semi-professional way. He toured the clubs and public houses as a comic and sing along man, around the Tooting area of South London. Once he tells us he "got lucky", and he was at the variety theatre in Kingston. He communicates with a great deal of humour, often singing or whistling his stage signature song "Daisy, Daisy give me your answer do" (Daisy, or as he calls her Dais' was his wife who he talks about with great affection). George and Daisy had five sons, my Father Leslie Charles, being the middle one, of the family. George has the ability to communicate on any level of understanding, often acting as the go between for others to communicate by passing on their messages, all with a generous measure of well meaning fun. His work in the Spirit World, is helping people who have recently passed to come to a realisation of their new circumstances and opportunities that await them.

CHURCHMAN OF MALMESBURY at the time of writing we do not have a name for this friend. He tells us that he was a country parson in the Malmesbury area who then went on to become a tutor in philosophy in a college for the Church of England trainee vicars in the South of England.

NANDAD, Albert Edward passed to spirit in 1969, being my Mother's Father. He was a medium, speaker and healer while on Earth, together with having a very active involvement in the work of the Spiritualist Lyceum Movement. He was also a transfiguration medium over many years. He is often with us and we sense his presence, also he normally opens up when we sit with the table for communication.

GRANDFATHER, William John passed to spirit in 1949, being Ellen's Mother's Father. He was a originally a driver of horse drawn trams and then became a storekeeper for the predecessors of London Transport. He was one of the first communicators that we had through the table, and brings support for Ellen.

PATERNAL GRANDFATHER, John Thomas passed to spirit in 1936, being Ellen's Fathers Father. He was a Policeman firstly at Bow (London), then at Isleworth (Middlesex). In his case he shows himself in his policeman's cape and brings protection to us during psychic work.

MOTHER, Doris Ruth passed to spirit on the Tuesday 12 March 1996, although she was in a state of a coma from midday on the previous Saturday. On the evening of the 12 March 1996 she made herself known in a circle we were attending at the time, (we are given to understand that this was a " piggy back ", communication with another spirit friend showing her around). Within a matter of weeks she was communicating directly under her own "steam", bringing a knowledge of her progression, who she had "met" and with words of guidance to our sitters. Together with a very clear indication that she knows exactly what is happening with her family and other matters that interest her. It should be explained that my Mother had a very clear understanding of spirit and had no fears or qualms about going forward to her new phase of life, she would have liked a little longer on the Earth plain to finish off the many jobs she had planned, but it was not destined to be.

DOCTOR this man was a medical doctor and surgeon who had his surgery near Bath he trained at Oxford and became a doctor c1750. He has not been able to give his name so far. It seems that he had a country "practice", and dealt with most problems himself although he was happy to have the help of lay people to tend the sick and deal with childbirth.

DAD in this case Paul's Father who passed into the higher life in 1986, following the side effects of Alzheimer's Disease. In his working life which he somehow managed to fit in with his extensive church committee and church platform work, he was a Group Station Master on the London Underground. He is a regular communicator and is still involved from the Spirit Side in Church matters, giving a nudge to those making decisions.

SISTER CECELIA while on holiday in Malta in late September 1996, we were maintaining our usual Sunday night sitting in the relative quite of our hotel room when this communicator made herself known, for the first time. She told us that she was a nursing sister working with the "Order of the Hospital of St John of Jerusalem" or as we know them the Knights Hospitallers or Templers. She worked in the hospice in Valletta tending the sick who had been brought to Malta from many other lands. The medicines they used came mainly from Greece This would have between 1530 and 1800, probably towards the latter period as the Hospice still stands in Valletta and the Knights moved to Valletta from Madina to be on the coast, some years after becoming established in Malta. She told us that her language was a mixture of Latin, Arabic and Greek, today the language of Malta is still a mixture of many other languages with some native Malatise words. Sister Cecilia tells us that she worked with Ellen's father, (who was a healer), assisting with matters that involved the nerves, their control of the body rather than nervous conditions of the mind. She now assists us with healing work with the same speciality as she helped Ellen's father. As we had been near her place of work / involvement while on Earth she was able to make the link.

SISTER CELESTE she tells us that she was a serving sister in a Catholic Church in Paris near the River Seine (St Denise). Her function was to look after the Holy Fathers, look after the church including the candles, undertake vigils when the deceased was laying in the church overnight before funeral service. Her main role was to prepare and sanctify the church before mass. She did this by praying with her rosary in various parts of the church. Her role with us is to prepare the room we are sitting in prior to communication with spirit. She does this wherever we are communicating with spirit. Her service is one of love and duty carried out in a humble manner.

'CHEE FO SO' (Translation said to be Wise One)
This communicator was the elder of the village in a Chinese Island, Chang Fu Su (phonetically spelt) This island was said to be very beautiful with many flowers. His role was to listen and speak few words. He was a healer and dispensed Chinese medicine. He had the power to look at body and see where the problem was and direct energy to that point. This knowledge had been handed down from his father to him and has been handed down through his son to his ancestors today. It is unclear at what time he was on earth but he tells us that the silk trade was good but the opium trade was bad. Today he works with us on our healing work.

E-OM-BA, (meaning wise one), This man when on earth came from the land we now know as Ethiopia, but known to him as Abyssinia. He was the warrier of a tribe that roamed looking for fertile land. When on earth he tells us they had knowledge of spirit, they acknowledged spirit, they danced for spirit to welcome spirit. They used this to create energy for spirit. The following were his words, "not bad spirit good spirit, difference, we gave thanks to spirit for gifts from spirit we linked with spirit for our good, crops, we not go hungry, we would dance special dance for food. Spirit would send blessings for us, respect spirit. We spoke to spirit through a wise one, go deep into meditation, we would dance, create vibration, he go, spirit talk, spirit of ancestor, mighty one, strong one, give words of wisdom".

His role is to bring wisdom. Although he tells us he has joined our group for mutual learning.

Subsequently, Paul's grandmother (Ruth), told us that E-om-ba worked through her husband with his healing activities and public speaking. E-om-ba regularly transfigured on Albert's face while he was demonstrating transfiguration. It's a matter of the continuous system of working through ancestors.

JULES, This man had a family vineyard near to the city of Marseilles in Southern France. He was a devout Roman Catholic and worshipped in the large church in the centre of the city.

Clearly he was an educated man and tells us he sold his wine locally. He joins us to learn and progress.

GEORGE "MAN OF LETTERS", This gentleman introduced himself as another one of the band of spirit friends who comes to learn with us, but he also has a role in recording events. He has told us a little about his life when on earth. He had a legal business in Winchester in a large house with steps up to the door. He undertook the work of a solicitor, swearing oaths, covenants, business transactions, transfer of money and as a Commissioner of Oaths. He used a quill pen to write. His style of clothing was to wear high collars, long coats and foot leggings to protect his shoes. At the time he was in the body men had long hair as did he. He travelled about by horse drawn coach. He tells us it is good to keep records. He takes account of what occurs, there are no records like ours in spirit but a certain amount of order is necessary to ensure everything is in it's due course. Everything is for a purpose, happening at it's appointed time, he oversees what occurs. He is learning also, as others talk he listens, as Mafra co-ordinates.

SOPHIA, This lady is a helper, who helps with our thoughts transmission towards others. She lived in Italy when on earth. Ensuring that we are on the same vibration when linking with the mind, rather than by speech. Prompting can be done by the mind without conscious reasoning.

BROTHER STEPHAN - Was a fellow friar at Greyfriars, Coventry at the same time as Brother John. He helped with the sick creating their own medicine, they grew plants in the friary garden. These were preserved for use throughout the year and were administered to people in the surrounding area. They treated injured people and ensured that their family were taken care of whilst the injured person was unable to work. If the father of the family was injured and had to rest until the injury was healed the brothers would ensure his family did not go hungry and their farm. small holdings or businesses were looked after. It was just not the process of tending the sick but looking at the whole family. There were also sisters if the mother was ill, the sisters would assist with the running of the home, these sisters were not from Greyfriars but from another religious settlement in Coventry. There were also sisters who taught in a school at Gloucester. It was a service to the community not just within closed walls. They would not take payment for their services but they were looked after. They were self sufficient in their grounds, they had vast grounds where they grew vegetables and kept livestock but those whom they looked after were not asked for payment. When thankful they would give what they could afford in the way of their produce and if the brothers did not need it they would pass it on to others who were experiencing hard times. They would look after their buildings themselves, there were brothers who would do brickwork and carpentry. They were self sufficient. There were people who would come and give to the church in gratitude. They were thankful to the brothers but they would show their gratitude through the church and in turn the church would be able to use their donations. Some of the wealthy residents of the area would give monetary donations to the church which would enable the brothers to erect new buildings or create another room for patients to come and stay. They relied on these donations for such works. There have always been those who have more than they need and there has always been those who have less than they need and the brothers felt it was their duty to administer where it was needed. Those that had money would look after their own servants but would give to the brothers to enable them to look after the remainder of the community. Their donations were not for the brothers but for the glory of God. There were other settlements within the town not just Greyfriars. Greyfriars was on the edge of the town and had much ground this was a friary, the big church in the town had it's own monastery different from Greyfriars. This monastery did not serve the community, they attracted more nobility.

Records and accounts were kept but these have been long lost. Account was taken of all that came and all that went. No profit was made but they had to account for themselves, especially after the change in circumstances of the Church of the Country. This was the time of upheaval with churches, churches were closed, so those that were still in existence had to keep good records to show that they were of service to the community. The had to prove their worth, to give education, succour to the sick. Records were kept and these were examined by those who were in high authority who came to Coventry.

It was a time of great change and many brothers in other communities were not able to exist. This was why Joseph and his brothers from Gloucester came to Coventry, others went across water for some years returning later, some went to Ireland, France and other countries where they settled in communities and came back later. Some stayed in their new homes and did not return.

ROSEAH Introducing herself to us for the first time, " I come, I'm here now, I have come for a short while, to experience the body. I have often sat with you and listened with you, I have worked with you, I have so much to learn, there are many of us you know, who come and sit, not sit as you sit but come. I have come because I want you to be my friends. You see I have no one on earth that I could talk to, because they are of a different belief, and I am not able to talk to them, so I am happy if you will let me talk to you. By talking I learn, and I share, so you see I talk to you with voice but I also talk to you on another level, and this makes progression easier for us all. I was on earth a long while ago in your time, and I have been finding so much to learn in what you call spirit. It is wonderful what progress there is for everyone, once they accept that there is more than just sleep. I believed we slept, I was of Church of Rome, They now say I must give you name so you know, Roseah, it was a name I used when I had body, it is a name of years of your time gone by. I go now, someone says you must not confuse me with someone else who has a name similar, (Rosa) not the same not same vibration. I must tell you one thing, I was a Sister. Blessings my friends, I have friends yes" 27/4/97

HANNS Introducing himself tells us that he was a German chemist who is a visiting helper, not permanently attached to our particular group, visiting from another group with compatible vibration. He worked with medicines, science, formulae, lots of numbers, figures and bottles. He comes to talk of work to be done. In his work it was important to have system, columns of figures must balance, must plan next step, mind must be in order. This is important with our work we must have system, must have ideas which plan, must work to plan, must be organised. Know where we go. Must have system, have faith and pride in work. It will work if we think through step before we take step. Have faith that the plan will work if we plan. He told us that we will recognised him if we see him as he wears small glasses.- 6/5/97

GOLDEN RAY explains her link with us. "I have been here for a while but I have not spoken. I have been linking with you on another level and have been waiting for you to reach this stage in your progression when we are able to make a stronger contact. I have left my earthly conditions well behind and I have been in spirit through many changes of existence, through many changes of levels of progression. I entered spirit world from human world at a different level of vibration and I have travelled through what you call spirit world, through levels. There is no word to explain, I cannot say time because it is of nothing. If we measured time it would take one of us a short while, another a long while but there is no difference for us, we are progressing. We do not wish to recall your earth life. I must give you some name by which I can be known. I am trying to give you a vibration which you link with me. There is no word I can find which will describe a spiritual definition. Just call me Golden Ray because I come that vibration, I come with learning and I come on a vibration, a ray. I am not giving you a name I am giving you a vibration.". - Mafra then came and explained that it was necessary for the medium's vibration to be lifted and the communicators vibration to be lowered until the two vibrations merged and it was therefore necessary to protect both the medium and the communicator by this process being carried out slowly. (13.05.97)

HANNAH This lady lived in Whiteleaf a small village outside Princes Risborough where she ran a Dame School for young children. Her work in spirit is with animals and when she comes to talk with us she brings her dog Patch.

THE COMMUNICATOR or Mr Go Forward This gentleman was in public service when on earth and works with a number of groups to promote progress. In his words his status when on earth means nothing in spirit, and he does not want to be thought of as someone special.

MICHAEL or My Call This visitor is from the higher realms and comes to give advanced teaching. His actual name when on earth is long forgotten and the name depicts his calling.

K-CHEE is a Japanese gentlman who comes with a deep knowledge of spiritual matters, speaking through Paul.

This is just a few of the ones who we know, but we are aware of many more some in the background others who are linked with our group of sitters who communicate with us.

CHAPTER TWO
WORDS OF WISDOM

This chapter records some of the words of wisdom given by our communicators, they are in no particular order, except to follow our development and deeper understanding.

QUESTION 1 - *answered by Mafra regarding the sometimes confusion that is found in communicators giving their names ?.*

There are no names as such, and those in spirit know or recognise each other by their vibration, which seems to be unique. When they communicate they may have disregarded their Earthly name, especially the surname. They can recall important things and experiences that were of great significance. When they communicate they search the medium's vocabulary (in the brain), to find the right word and if that word relating to the name they were known by cannot be found they may use a similar word or even a connection. For example a person who was a doctor may have been a "Doctor Jones" but in the mediums brain there is a prominent "Doctor Smith", therefore that doctor gets recognised and is given by mistake.

QUESTION 2 - *answered by Mafra regarding how table communication works ?.*

Regarding your table, it is a table which you usually have standing on it's own. This table is used shall we say as an ornament, it resides in one particular place and it is stationary nothing happens. If you wish to move your table you pick it up and move it to another position. Why then when it is in this room, at this particular time does it become mobile? If you touched it at any other time would it move? You bring it into this room with an intention within your mind and as you know, when you instigate an intention this makes thing happen. The table does not take on a personality of it's own and decide to move, something has to ignite the movement. You already have your intention, you sit with this in mind but this is not necessarily the formula. Another group of people may sit with the intention of moving a table but this will not happen for them. So intention is not enough, it is part.

You then sit, you then enter into communication with each other, you talk to each other this sets up a link between you all. As you know you communicate on more than one level, you open yourself up to each other and communication is starting to work. You then open up your communication with Spirit through prayer and dedication. You welcome Spirit to your group, you invite then thus opening the door for them. Through your many weeks of sitting you have built up a communication which is two way. You cannot work with them and they although they can communicate on their own level cannot communicate with this group without your help also. So now you have a link between yourselves and Spirit.

Your energy is now directed at one particular focal point in your room, that is the point in the centre of your little group. Placed in the centre of your little group is your table. Your table is an object which doesn't usually move but when you link with Spirit things begin to happen. You have built up a form of energy, all of you, and this shall we describe as a ball of energy, I am trying to put it in a function which you will understand. Your energy coming from all of you is focused on one particular point. You now put your hands on this object, you are thus directing your energy at this object and you feel movement. Now this movement is obtained by Spirit using your energies, you have formulated, you call them rods for want of a better description but this is not a physical rod, it is a source of energy coming from you which Spirit are using. They are gathering this energy into a formation, a formation which can attach itself, in this case to the table, and they can then move the table in the direction they desire to make you aware of their presence. As I have said, this is a two way process, you are not able to move the table without Spirit, Spirit are not able to communicate on the table without the energy you have produced. (you note I say through the table not through your mind) for this is physical phenomena not a mental one. Spirit can communicate through your cerebellum without this help you are giving but to actually move a physical object, because it is a physical object which is on your earth they need a physical contact they need a physical energy which is made from the physical person.

You have built up communication and you now know the signs of the table, who comes, in which direction the table moves, in which way it reacts. It is like a persona, a finger print, of a person. The table reacts with the wave length of the Spirit entity who is trying to communicate. If this Spirit entity is a gentle soul the table will move gently. If this one comes with a lot of energy and a lot of enthusiasm your table will take on this energy and enthusiasm. So a certain amount of spirit personality will come across and after a while you begin to recognise who your visitors are by the way the table behaves. It is not the table that is behaving it is the direction from Spirit using your energy to make the table move.

At this point a question was asked by a sitter - 'Is it always necessary to place our hand on the table or could we just place our hand on our laps and direct the energy?'

It is possible for the table to move without physical touching, some of you here have experienced this, you have seen a table move without touching. So it is not necessary to touch but it depends on the amount of energy produced. I do not want to mislead you if I say the more people there are in the group the more energy there is directed at the table the more easier it is for the table to move. This is in fact true but there is a drawback with too many. If your group is in harmony and your thoughts are for Spirit and for one another and for the good and for truth, it is an ideal situation. The bigger the group the more thoughts there are to distract the energy. If the group is big and are all of one mind that is good but if it is not it is better to have a small group and to direct your energy with physical touch rather than mental touch.

The more you sit together the more your link builds up and those that come to you are of varying degrees of advancement. You have those who perhaps are coming for the first time, or perhaps are of a quiet personality and need support, but you have those that are experienced souls. They were aware of Spirit before they came to Spirit and they come back with a wealth of experience and as you perceived with Wendy's mother, (Wendy was one of the sitters present), she needed you obviously here to provide the initial spurt energy but she is quite capable of making herself and her presence known without a lot of assistance. It varies a lot on who the communicator is.

You must remember you are working as a team, a team here but also our team as well, two teams linked to make one team. We are a team, you are a team. We have introduced ourselves, shall I call us our basic team, we that come and talk to you, make ourselves known on your table and through the voice but we bring others in on our energy to communicate. We would not let anyone in who was not of the right level. We would stand and protect. It is good that you ask for protection, you open up the channel and if you do not go through the right channels you can attract the wrong vibration. You are doing well, you have learnt how to protect yourselves, we would not let anything but good come to you.

At this point a sitter asked a question - 'If we used a different table would it still have the same effect or this energy which has been built up in this particular table?'

No, it is not anything to do with the actual table, it is your energy you have built. You have got used to the feel of this table so if you used another table it may take a few minutes of your time, not long to acclimatise to the feel and the way it moves. You may have to say to Spirit 'show me what a no is, show me which way you want to move' but this is only a few minutes of your time. It is your energy which is creating the catalyst to build up the Spirit communication. It is possible to put your hands beneath your table and the table will rise into the air. You can achieve success without complete darkness but the darker the room the greater the success.

QUESTION 3 - Kimyano regarding the use of colours in healing?

Colours are vibrations and of an infinite range of tones. Spirit colours are more vibrant than that perceived by the human eye. Although we may say that projecting the colour blue while sending out healing thoughts, that actual tone of the blue colour needs to be compatible between the healer and the patient. In some cases one healer may not be able to project the exact frequency of the colour vibration or the patient may not be susceptible to accepting the healers thought waves. By trial and error if the patient is not responding to the particular healers work then another healer should take on the patient. This does not mean that the first healer is no good but it's a simple "fact of life", that some people are not compatible with others. We all need colours to give us vibrant energy. Dull or negative colours will depress the human spirit.

Colours are also important in giving the right conditions for communication, the colours need to provide a peaceful environment. Pastel shades therefore put you in the right frame of mind to feel relaxed and not threatened. Therefore the environment is more conducive to good communication.

QUESTION 4 - combination of various communicators, does the environment really matter for communication of any type to happen ?.

Yes, to an extent hostile surroundings either physical or mental will require more energy to overcome the surrounding problems. It is therefore important to put on the "cloak of protection", (This is a technique to be mastered by all persons seeking to develop psychic gifts, to protect against interference from undeveloped spirit enterties and other undesirable influences, once learnt it becomes an automatic function when communicating or undertaking healing work. However, during the opening prayer or thoughts the cloak of protection should be requested for the protection of the medium and sitters.), before undertaking any communication. There are souls who are on a low vibration and although they can do no physical harm to the medium and sitters, they may not provide the level of communication strived for.

QUESTION 5 - combination of various communicators, do all persons passing to spirit progress in the same way ?.

No it depends in a way, as to how the mind has been conditioned during the earthly life. For example if someone truly believes that on leaving the earthly body they will await Gabriel's call on "The day of judgment", then they will remain in that state until they are coaxed to progress by members of the spirit realm who undertake this work. Children on the other hand who pass to spirit at an early age have no preconceived ideas as to the future, and can therefore progress with ease.

QUESTION 6 - answered by Mother a few months after passing, what is it like in the Spirit World ?.

I am free of all constraints, there are things that I would have liked to complete, but others are more capable of completing these tasks. I am happy and contented. I can be in more than one place at a time. I have to consider that I no longer own things that were mine around the house, but I have no hold on physical objects. I am able to urge and hint others and in a way warn. It is not our place, (Spirit), to change a persons destiny. I am able to visit places with you, when you go to places of interest and see sights that I did not see while on the earth plain even experience flying in an aeroplane. I know what's going on and can link with other members of the family and friends, even join them on holiday!

QUESTION 7 - general question to a number of communicators, you often use the term "Code Of Practice", when answering queries relating to matters that would not be in our best interests to be answered fully.

The term "Code Of Practice", has been used when it is clear that there are things they cannot talk about because we are not yet ready for the true answer and would get confused by a reply that required an degree of background knowledge, and would therefore not be in our best interests. They must not tell us things that would cause us to change our "Paths Of Destiny". However, they can advise on how to get over problems, or make the best of life's experiences. Telling the future by precognition is understanding and decoding energy fields and other clues by a "sensitive", rather than in general from the spirit communicators. This also applies to healing where the trained healer will be drawn to the root cause of the problem by developed instincts, and the association of "hot spots", on the patients body. Spirit, of course are still urging and hinting the sensitive healer, to direct the healing energy to the best effect.

QUESTION 8 - We understand Mafra that to communicate with Ellen for example that it is vibration decoded by the brain, you just said to Wendy about talking back to those in spirit, does the action of saying something actually send in out in telepathic manner as well or does there have to be an intermediary in the spirit world who has to convey the message to others?

Just let me clarify one point before I really answer the question, you are speaking of the spirit world as if it were another country where you travel to speak another language, and have an interpreter. Your spirit companions, shall we give them the name companions, are not in another world they are with you, they are not even in another room, they are with you. So you do not have to go through intermediaries. Your spirit friends in the spirit world as you call it encompass your world as yet another dimension of your world. You are not tuned in to absorb their energies in your usual mundane existence. When you sit here of course it is slightly different you are tuning in but in your ordinary mundane life when you are in your material world doing your material actions and earning your crust shall we say, or surviving it is not the time to link in with spirit. You are of this world, this earthly world and that must be your main priority, you are here on earth and you must live your earthly life.

Having said that your spirit companions are ever near within their own vibrations existing on their own vibration but there is always a link that can be made, you use the expression telephone, they can always be called upon and the actual connection is just a thought wave to link with them. There are those who spend too much of their earthly life linking with spirit and this is not good because you are not spirit you are mortal and you have your world to live in. There will be time enough when you are spirit but this does not mean there are not times when you can link the two worlds together. When this is necessary it is just a step away, you just link on your thought wave and there is no need for an interpreter, no need for someone to do this for you. I am talking of you personally, you within this gathering. Others that are not aware of their spirit companions will not find this so easy. There are those who are naturally attuned to spirit, they may not realise they are but because they are old souls and know of spirit from other existence it is possible for them to attune to spirit but most of your fellow companions on your earthly journey are not of this category. They need someone to assist, this someone could be yourselves or could be another mortal who is walking the path with them and quite often they are not aware they are linking with the third party. We will take you for example as the middle party, that fellow mortal I have used the word 'mortal' to differentiate will come to you with a problem, they might just come and have a moan about their conditions they are going through at that time. Now because you are attuned to spirit, because you are trained to attune to spirit without thinking about what you are doing, there may be a loved one of theirs or a companion in what you call the spirit world who is very eager to assist that one but cannot make the link so that spirit companion will put thoughts into your brain and then you will decode those thoughts with your voice to that fellow mortal. So you are the intermediary without even realising what you are doing. It is so natural, this ability is not unusual it is a natural ability and you can do this without sitting down and saying I am going to tune in with your loved ones and I am going to get you an answer. That would probably frighten the one that came to you. It is so very natural, it is a natural function.

QUESTION 9 - Is it better when asking a question of spirit to send a thought or speak out loud? Answer by Mafra
It does not matter if you are in a position where thought is the only way of functioning, thought is O.K. To be more positive it is good to voice because by voicing you are making a positive statement, it is like with the moving of your table the thought is in your mind but by singing and talking you are creating energy so by voicing your thought you are making a more positive statement. There are times when you may do this and you think you are not getting an answer, do not doubt it may not be the time for you to get the answer. It may be you have to do more work on your earth before the answer is given to you. You see we are not permitted to alter your destiny. When you perceive an idea, vision or whatever, feeling, sense from spirit it will be good for your own reasoning to write down what you have perceived and when, so in future days you can look back and you will be able to see a pattern how you are progressing and how spirit are so close to you.

QUESTION 10 - To Running Bear 'Would you like to contribute some words of wisdom'
I give encouragement, I give strength, I give power. You should look to your mother earth, observe the ways of mother earth, everything is natural. Treat with respect your mother earth she will treat you with respect, same with spirit you treat spirit with respect spirit treat you with respect. Treat each other with respect you will have respect returned to you. What you give you receive. Every child of the universe is different do not expect the same from each child of nature, each travels their own path, each goes their own journey through the forest of life but each comes to the same clearing. Your group walks together - good. Must not take different paths, must walk together. If one is slower others must wait. You have duty to each other, each will perceive spirit in a different manner no right, no wrong, each to their own - good. Encourage much. Much love - good.

QUESTION 11 - When we are sitting in this circle environment we are told that a lot more is registered in our minds, can you explain what the nature of this learning is? The information which we gain whilst we are sitting this environment, we don't actually hear with our ears it goes straight into our mind, is this pure spirit knowledge or is it education as to how we live our lives, how we should act upon your hinting and urging without necessarily realising this is happening? Answer by John Lyon -

As you sit here you are within a human frame, with a human body, a human brain, a human thought process. Now not only are you of a human body you are also of spirit and your spirit components are built up from past knowledge of your existence before you came to this earth but as you know while you are in your earthly body there is much you cannot recall from your previous existence in spirit or other lives. It would not be good for you to know everything that went before, you are here to live this life and to learn this life's lessons and when you return home to spirit what you have gained here in this existence will be added to the knowledge that you already have. Having said that, when you sit here in this vibration you are opening up channels which you would probably not use in your ordinary mundane existence and as these channels are opening up you are homing into some of this knowledge which is normally locked away. One of us comes to speak to you and to give you the benefit of wisdom from spirit, you perhaps ask the question you have formed within your human brain and we endeavour to answer your question, As we are answering your question to a human situation and we have to come through a human body to do this we are using words that can be found within this one's vocabulary and store cupboard. Also words that your brain can understand on your level of existence. So this is what is happening now, you have asked a question and I am answering it but at the same time your spirit brain is open to perception. Although through the human tongue we are very likely answering the surface of the question there is a lot more depth than what I am actually speaking. The answer I am giving is very shallow compared to the depth of the question there is a lot more which the human brain would not understand. If I were even able to give it to you through direct voice, if I were able to speak direct voice through your trumpet, and give you wisdom from spirit your human brain would not be able to absorb all the depth of the question and the answer. So what is happening now, having asked the question you have opened up the channels for us to instil knowledge into spirit brain and that is stored until you reach such a time in your level of progress when it is needed and can be absorbed. You perhaps in the past, in this life have asked a question and you have not been happy with the answer, whether it is an answer given from spirit or an answer you have read in a book, or heard from a speaker, whatever. The answer has not made sense to you but perhaps a few years later another situation arises and you hear a similar answer and then that answer makes sense. This is because it has already been stored for you, perhaps you ask a question of yourself and you answer yourself with an answer and you wonder where that answer has come from. This has come from the perception you have had before but it was not until this time in your existence that you were ready to accept it.

You don't breath the same air as we do, is man and spirit the same?

We are an essence, what you perceive is what you decode. When you perceive spirit you perceive our essence our being, our spirit light. If you think of us as a light, a ball of energy, a vibration that is what we are but we can be whatever we wish. If we wish to show ourselves with a body we can. You perceive our energy and you decode our energy different people decode in a different way. One person may decode the energy and visualise a body, a picture of what I used to look like, another person may perceive my energy and perceive a colour vibration of me, another person may perceive my energy and they may perceive an aroma of perhaps something that was connected with me. If I was a person who smoked they might perceive cigarette smoke, or if I was a female and had perfume they might perceive the perfume, or if I was a gardener who worked with tomatoes they might perceive the smell of tomatoes. It is how you decode, if you imagine us as a ball of energy, a lively ball of energy, pure spirit, that is how you perceive it. I have explained I could have a body if I wished but why would I want a body? You would decode me, you could not imagine me as I was if you had not seen a picture of me or know me personally. I would have to show myself as I was. I would have to instigate the decoding if you do not know what I look like but if it was your imagination that was imagining me you would perceive a different form to myself. In my ball of energy is the embryo of what I was. You can take that and it can grow into what my body used to look like. Your energy would link with mine and you would visualise me as I was.

You are learning well. As I tried to explain the more you store the more easier it will become for you as you progress. You do not have to start from scratch. If you on your earthly world read a book which is perhaps a bit difficult for you to read, not that you cannot read, but the subject matter is a bit deep you will read the book and you will think 'I understand part of that but not all of it but is was a good book, it was interesting'. Then perhaps two or three years later you will pick the book up again and you read it again and that book makes a lot more sense to you because not only have you travelled a bit further along your pathway and become hopefully a bit wiser but also the subject matter is already locked away within your brain. You have had time to digest the subject matter and it now makes more sense to you. This is similar to the education which spirit try to give. We do not expect you to learn all at once, it is not possible. A little at a time and do not get distressed if you do not remember because it is not lost it is still there and when eventually you go home to spirit, spirit existence will be a lot easier for you to come to terms with because of the knowledge you have learnt.

QUESTION 12 - Rosa would you like to contribute to our 'Words of Wisdom' book?

Rosa say - what can Rosa say which hasn't already been said? Rosa was on her own but Rosa was never lonely. People came from village to see Rosa, people would tell me their tales, Rosa would listen, Rosa would give them something good and send them home. Then Rosa on her own but Rosa was not lonely. Rosa had the mountains, had the birds, very close to spirit. Nature as you call nature, being plants, things that grow all around Rosa. Rosa would look at these, touch these, look at sky, look at clouds, look at sun, and at night look at moon and stars. Much to link in with, much wisdom, much to learn. You look around at nature it is there always, it was there before you came, it is there after you go. The earth brings forth each year new life whatever befalls, whatever the weather, whether the sun scorches, whether the snow freezes, new year will grow again. Much to learn from nature, much is needed now that is not from nature. You cannot live without things that are not from nature, Rosa lived without these things Rosa was content. Much knowledge if you look around, if nature can replenish itself when it has been through the drought, been through the hurricane. If nature can do this so can you. Man can do this, man can survive whatever befalls, man's spirit is stronger than nature so why should man be afraid?

They used to think Rosa silly, silly old lady. Rosa knew more than they knew. Their problems seemed so big to them but when you are up high on a mountain and you look down you realise how small people are compared to the world around them and if people are small how small are their problems in this vast universe that we have. Everyone is important, everyone is in their space on earth for a time, for a reason and everyone is important. Do not forget that. Not just those with big names or much money, those that are quiet and say nothing they are important, perhaps more because they think more. The more that is thought the more that brings forth.

QUESTION 13 - the Doctor telling us about his work when on earth, and his continuing interest in medical matters.

I was a doctor in the area round Bath, I was a surgeon, that does not mean I was surgeon who performed surgery in a hospital and that was my only occupation. When I was on your earth, I was a doctor who held my own surgery and part of my duties were to perform operations. It was a task that which doctors undertook at that time, (c 1750), there was not the divide that there is in your world today. We looked after our patients, from cradle to the grave, we knew their families, we visited their homes, those in farms we would visit. There were many, you understand that did not have medical treatment, they could not afford medical treatment, but there were many who could. So the way I worked, was that those who paid, paid well, but those that needed treatment I would give. There was much travelling involved, I would go to their farms or their homes if they could not get to me. In those days there was many, you would call them "lay, people who would administer to the sick, they did not have qualifications, but were very skilled. In your world today, it would not be allowed to carry out the work that they did in those days, but they worked for love, with their neighbourhood, it was one caring for the other. There was a sense of neighbourly duty to each other, if a family had a member who was unwell, a member of another family would call in and look after the one that was sick, and look after the family also. Today, it is the duty of the state to look after people who are sick, and those who are in the vicinity are too busy with their own lives, it is not good, one should help each other, but your lives, routines have changed.

QUESTION 14 - *Question to 'Running Bear' regarding a soldier who had been perceived in spirit form coming to the group around Armistice Day (who we could not identify)*

'Time in your year when you recall. One of your group has been sending thoughts and these thoughts have been registered, this one comes looking for one who sent thoughts but not here.' This was later identified by a member of our group who had been selling poppies that day and had been thinking of a member of his family who had served in the first World War. The soldier had been drawn to the members of the group who had been sitting that evening in the usual environment. This signifies the importance all members of a group working together to form a harmonious team.

QUESTION 15 - *Question to 'Rosa'* - *Why do we get so many types of phenomena?*

You are all different, everyone has got their own way. Let's not talk about spirit communication, let's talk about the ordinary things you do everyday. Everyone has got their own way of going about whatever it is they do everyday. We are all different. To give an example, if you go out in your garden to do a bit of gardening you would do it one way and Jack would do it another. Jack might go out there and start tidying up, pulling some weeds up you might go out and start nipping the buds off the roses or whatever, you all work different but you all get there in the end. You have all got your own way of going about things. It is the same with spirit, you have all got your own ways of decoding and some of you hear, some you see and some of you sense by feeling vibrations, some of you see colours. There again us in spirit, we also have got our own way of nudging you and communicating with you. So it is a mingling of the vibrations. Some of us are not very good in communicating in some ways. You will have some spirit people who will never come and talk to you but they will bang or knock on your table because they get on better that way. You get people like your George who likes to come and talk, he is much better at doing that than he is at doing anything else. It doesn't mean they don't love you any more or are not with you any more but it is the way they are happier with. If you have got somebody on your earth who is a bit shy they would just be quite happy to sit there in your vibration and be with you, they might talk to you if there was just two of you in a room but once more people come into the room they sit in the corner and join in the conversation but do not come forward. This is the same when they get to spirit. They are happy to take a back seat but it doesn't mean they are not with you any more, they are still there but the others that are stronger or others who have got the gift of the gab, they let them do it. Like me I can talk can't I? I am behaving myself now, I am not talking rough like when I first came, you see I have learnt I have got to be good if I want to come back to talk to you again. Of course there are different ways we like to communicate. Sometimes you get somebody who likes to show you pictures, perhaps on earth they were somebody who liked to draw and paint so when they come and see you they give you a picture to look at or they may be somebody who liked to move things around so they come and start banging and knocking but you know it would be a funny old world if we all did the same thing. You have been told so many times that when you go to spirit you don't change, you are not going to suddenly become a little cherub you know. It would be a boring life wouldn't it? You have got to think what abilities you have got here, what you are good at and what you are developing. If you are developing what you call clairvoyance, seeing clear, well you will attract people who like to communicate that way but it you like to hear things you will pick up the vibrations of hearing. It is like on earth just because you are good at one thing it doesn't mean you can't do the other things as well, you are just not as good at them, the whole thing goes to make one over all communication. That is a good word for Rosa, Rosa is learning since she first came it is not just the other folk that are learning, Rosa is learning as well.

Rosa was then asked to explain how Mafra organises who comes to speak.

Mafra clears the vibration line for me. Sometimes when you sit your medium will say to you there are a lot of people about, she can sense there are various people, perhaps she can hear them or perhaps she can sense their vibration but she doesn't know which one is coming and there are a lot of people who always want to come and talk to you, there is always a lot but it is not possible for them all to come. My friend, Mafra he sorts who is to come and he links our vibration with Ellen's vibration so we can come and talk but sometimes you have got somebody that is a very similar vibration and they slide in as well but if it was wrong Mafra would step in and say 'No. stop'. You see sometime someone comes in and says I have come in quickly, that is because they are on a similar vibration and they have come as well but because we are all in the same family, spirit family, we are all on a similar vibration. If it was somebody who wasn't it wouldn't be possible. I am talking to you but if Mafra decides you have been talking long enough Rosa he would withdraw my energy, he would stop the energy flowing and I would have to leave, he would stop it if somebody was unhappy with the conditions they were bringing. This would have an effect on your lady and this would not be good so he would stop it, he wouldn't allow it to continue.

QUESTION 16 - John Lyon answering questions on trance communication what it is like for a spirit entity talking through a human body.

It is unlike anything we experience in our world you imagine you are in the same shell that you left but of course you are not and this can be a little perplexing.

The question was then asked 'Is this then why a medium may give the condition of the body at the time of passing when he/she describes a spirit visitor?'

That is correct but if the, you call the term medium, the intermediary is fully trained and developed this should not cause a problem. This one does not feel conditions of body only at very extreme and then you have the knowledge to ask for it to be taken and it is. She gets the sensation of physical attributes to the body, not disease, the tightness or the flabbiness of the skin, the alteration of the features, growth of hair whether on the head or the face. Also apparel but this is not of discomfort, it is a decoding. The one whom returns is remembering what their condition was like and it is decoded. The voice is obviously altered but it is not possible to have the same voice which we had when we were in our own bodies because each human has their own vocal cords, their own voice box, their own way of speaking but we bring with us perhaps our own dialect if it is recognised within this one's function. If it is not one which that one has experienced we are unable to portray it. It is different of course if it is a direct voice but this is not what is happening. We tend to control the breathing, I do not mean we are actually using the organs, the thought process and thus we are speaking in a way in which we would have spoken. The voice is affected by breathing and the way the air flows through the passages in the head as well as of course the amount of air that is exuded from the lungs but course these sounds are in the framework of this one's body. If for instance, our nose was a different shape, our voice would have been a different form. The shape of the mouth and palate alters the sound of the vowels, so much is involved in the actual art of speaking. Speech is indicative to genetics because the body is inherited from the genes of your ancestors so there is often a likeness within a family of a voice but this can alter partly when you speak you copying sounds you have heard without realising. This is why you have dialects in different parts of your land. This is why it seems strange when you have people of a different race who's native tongue was not yours but they still have your local dialects.

This is just one way in which you influence each other. You influence each other in the sounds you make and without realising it you are copying another. So take this a step further, if a voice from another can influence how can their thought process influence without you realising? This is why you have to be on your guard and you are all educated in this area but there are cases where your adolescents are easily influenced without realising. They are not trained to be so perceptive and are not aware they are picking up vibrations from others. Your fellow countrymen are very aware that your young generation are easily influenced by what they watch, what they see, what they read and there is a lot of effort being put forward at the moment to try and educate your young that they are not influenced in this way but the powers that be do not realise they are also influenced on another level with the thought power. Young people are very perceptive, this is not realised and can pick up wave lengths which they do not know they are picking up because they are young and bright, their energies are vibrant. They are very perceptive, they work on a very quick vibration and this quick vibration attracts many influences. They have not had the schooling so much in your world today as previous generation to educate right from wrong, they are encouraged to experiment with themselves to discover for themselves so their minds are trained to reach out and experiment with whatever vibrations are within their area. They are not trained to shut off against influences that are not so good for them. Life is an adventure and they are eager to experiment, which it always has been and always will be. This is part of growing up but unfortunately there has not been a previous foundation laid morally. Your teachers in your schools are not allowed to teach religious subjects and morals as was so very important previously.

It was then commented upon that there seems to be a move toward moral education now.

There is nothing new these cycles have gone on through generations and it will always be so. It is part of your civilisation. There has to be a balance, a seesaw, one swings one way then it swings the opposite and the wheel turns round and it will come again. There is a thirst for knowledge at this moment in your time, a lot of stretching out for knowledge, a lot of seeking which is good. It is the time for philosophy to be taught but it has to be taught in a way that can be understood to a different generation. It is no good talking of what has been. This is why you have an upsurge of what you term alternative therapies, these are so similar to your traditional therapies but are dressed in a new fashion. The new name your young are keen to learn. If it was in the same guise as previous generations' experience they would not take note but it is new, it is vibrant which is good. The remedies we used could well be used today but given another name. They have to be administered under supervision and guidelines to make them authentic and to make them recognised. A lot is thought of little bits of paper which give authority and credence. Accreditation is a word you use today? It matters not what you call it. It only matters that your world is advancing and recognises it. Let them think they have discovered something new and beneficial as is their privilege. What is really happening is they are being brought into contact with these new therapies but deep in their storehouse of memory genetically these are being recognised as having been used before but of course they are not aware. So because these are recognised as something that has been used before it is stirring up a thirst to seek further.

A question was then asked whether spirit are able to draw energy from the cats (that were in the room at the time).

They are on a different vibration, they have their own vibration. They give love and companionship, walk alongside the human race but when they return home they are of a different family. They share your lives, they share your existence as they are sharing with us as a companion. They seek comfort from humans but they seek comfort from spirit as well. They recognise that we are here and this gives them security, they become aware and they at first sense the different vibrations in the room. At first this disturbs as they are not too sure what is happening to them but once they resign themselves to it is a vibration of love not hostility they are content.

They do not have language as you have language so they rely on their vibrations, their sensory ability to sense whether there is danger or whether there is the opposite. So in some ways they are more developed than you are. They know who will do ill to them. Animals cannot pretend, they cannot pretend to like you but a human can pretend to like you. They either show love or they show fear.

QUESTION 17 - We are having a number of unrecognised visitors, answered by various communicators.

We have had a number of communicators talk to us, and they seem to have no direct connection with the group either as friends, relatives or advisors. These visitors are not "earth bound", but spirit forms who are seeking and wish to progress. They come and listen to our questions, in the precious time we communicate with our teachers. They are drawn by the "light", and will stay with us a short time before progressing. They are able to relate to our questioning, which tends to be more practical and "down to earth". They tell us that when they come to spirit it is not easy to be conscious of what is happening. There are those who come to help, but find it difficult to come close because of their lack of understanding. By listening in to our questions they are able to understand, especially if they did not have the opportunity to consider spirit communication, while on the earth plain. They are able to become stronger by taking part in our communication sessions. The numbers of visitors who join us varies, but clearly there are considerable numbers who also listen and learn from our teachers.

QUESTION 18 - From Mafra to Paul - Do you know why you are here, what is your purpose in life ?. I am not able to tell you, but I am able to confirm if your perception is correct, You must voice your perception to me.

This was done and confirmed. The strong links with communicators who are clearly talented in appropriate skills, now makes sense. My perception was as an educator and this is reflected in my business life as well as spiritual matters. The communication skills of my grandfather Albert for philosophy and George for presentation assistance. John Lyon for his views on education and Running Bear with his knowledge of natural law and many others who willingly give help. We only have to ask for guidance, and it will be given.

They tell us that they will always answer our questions by the one who is communicating at the time, who has "broken away", from the group energy. However, if they are unable to answer our questions they are able to link back into the group energy and draw on the collective knowledge and get the "specialist", answer through the one who is communicating at the time.

QUESTION 19 - *What are your tasks in the Spirit World. A question to Aunt Annie.This was the first communication with this lady and after some adjustment she was able to converse with ease. The lady concerned was a great great aunt of Ellen's who is the aunt of grandfather William Kane. She was in service as a lady's maid and was a very devout Roman Catholic. Her reply demonstrates that our way of life and convictions held while on the earth plain follows through to life in the spirit world.*

I direct prayers out where there is need. This is something I did whilst on earth, I lit candles in the church and paid money for the Father to say prayers for those in need but I now realise I can do this for myself. She was then asked if these prayers were directed at those on earth or those in spirit. Especially those who are in lands across the sea who are in great need where our missionaries work and serve. There are missionaries in your world today but their role is different than when I was on earth, they are there to assist, they of course do teach religion but they are also there to help, give support and love where it is needed. Having no family as such of my own I am free to do this of course I am interested in William's family and I am also able to help others. You understand this was my job on earth, I looked after other families that were not my own, I was in service it was my job to look after the lady of the house and her family so this is my vocation to serve. I have learnt to serve in other ways.

QUESTION 20 - *While in discussion with Mother, she was asked if she would like to contribute to these words of wisdom, the following is her response.*

Life is onward and I have proved it. The hard thing is trying to explain to you what it is like because your mind can't understand. I thought I knew but I didn't, it is very difficult to explain what it is like. You have to shut out what it is like really because you have to live in your world, if you start thinking like we think you are altering the way that your brain works and that causes damage, it is a different concept. It is not thought like you have thought in an earthly brain, it is the mingling of energies. It is not so much individuals as you are on earth with an individual body we blend with others but you are still yourself, you are still an identity on your own. All your memories, all the things that have happened to you and made an impression on your spirit, it is not the events that occurred but the result of the events that occurred that makes an impression on your spirit. All the things that happened to you that are not important don't stay with you but all the silly squabbles you have you can recall them but they don't stay with you. Nothing that you have been through in your existence is forgotten it is there but it doesn't make the impression on your spirit, it doesn't make you grow your spirit grows by the obstacles that you overcome as you go through your life and your spirit grows. So you don't necessarily remember what made it grow but that actual art of expanding and growing makes an impression on you. If you want to you can remember the event that made this occur but you don't carry this with you all the time. It is something that you can tune into if you want to, if you want to relive something you can. A kind of memory but not the kind of memory you have in an earthly brain, it is more a feeling, a wave length, a decoding of a wave length. It is not good to keep reliving and reliving an event you should let it go, don't hold the event. This is where a lot of people have problems on earth and in spirit they won't let go of something. They have an event which has made a big impression, it could be a happy event, it could be a sad event, it could be something that they have gone through but they won't let go of this event. You can't let go of the effect it has had on you, that stays with you forever, the impression it has made on you because that has altered you. You have come through it as a different spirit, your spirit has altered through having this event so you can't let go of that part as that is now part of you but the actual story of what happened is'nt any good to you any more. So let that go. There is no point in keep going over and over it again that is not doing anyone any good. Let it go and just be glad you had the experience whether it is a good experience or bad experience be thankful for it because it has helped you grow. Accept that it has helped you grow and let go of the story part and don't keep going over it and try to get sympathy from it. This is what a lot of people do on earth they keep going over the story and think they can get sympathy, you don't want sympathy, you don't need sympathy, you need to stand on your own feet and grow. You don't want to draw from others. While you are drawing from others you are not growing. We all have times when we lean on each other and we are grateful for the help that others give us, it is a hard lesson to learn that we aren't independent and we need other people's help. This is a difficult lesson to learn but we have to learn there are times when we need to lean on other people but we have to learn there is a time when we let go, we don't need their help any more. There are times when you are so independent that you don't want to accept help from others but there are times that you must accept that you do need help and you merge with the other people's love and support but you must not keep draining them. Once you become stronger you stand on your own feet and if they need help you help them. If they don't need help you give your thanks and you then go off to your next stage of existence. If you don't you keep going through that problem over and over again because you haven't let go of that problem. You must let go or it will come back to you, you haven't learnt. Unless you learn from it you are going to keep going through it again and again with another set of people. You are doing them no good and you are doing yourself no good. It is the same in the spirit world because they come here and still are reliving what has happened to them on the earth, they won't let go of it. They relive it over and over again and because they are doing this they are not progressing because they haven't learnt. Also they are taking energies from others, stopping others from progressing but if you have got some you love and they are in trouble you try and support them, regardless of whether you are on earth or you are in spirit it doesn't change. Even though in spirit you are a bit wiser and you know you are not doing them that much good you still, because they are yours, you love them and try and support them. So you are being held back and they are being held back. It is good to try and make them realise that they have to let go. This is what it is wise to try and do. Instead of bombarding them with sympathy try and make them realise that they have finished with that problem, it is gone, let go of it. It is difficult to do that.

THOUGHTS ON WHICH TO PONDER

These words of wisdom are only a small sample of the communications received in the last few months. We have had many visitors, often it seems just popping in for a friendly chat. Many of the communications are of a personal nature with words of encouragement and guidance, which would have little meaning if heard out of context and without a detailed knowledge of the recipient. They are therefore not recorded in this chapter.

What is quite extraordinary is the speed of improvement in the communication. It is less than two years since the communicators were able to communicate through Ellen but we have been trying for the last thirty years or so.

The communications through the table have progressed from a very limited and time consuming communication, with names and words being spelt out. Often for some reason getting the communication slightly confused. We now have the table flying around the room and spirit working with us towards direct voice through the trumpet.

We have witnessed our communicators growing in their ability to communicate from their first faltering steps to providing answers to our most searching questions in a way that we can all comprehend.

We have gained an insight into life in the Spirit World and began to understand how close they can be. Joining in with our special events and giving us a nudge in the right direction when needed.

Who knows what is in store for the future ? With our dedication and our spirit friends seemingly inexhaustible abilities, anything and everything is possible.

The important thing is that we grow in knowledge and share that knowledge wherever it will be accepted.

The Christmas Circle included a number of extra sitters and the spirit children were invited to attend, with the accompanying tree and sweets. We had quite a surprise when another medium in the room went into trance and we had the experience of two spirit friends talking to each other. This was a rare event as of course spirit communicate with each other on vibration links.

QUESTION 21 - In discussion with Rosa about singing songs of a happy nature to manufacture energy the conversations then progressed onto concentrating on colours and their effect.

If you all thought bright colours that would make bright energy, you see music and colours have same energy. If you knew about music, you would know that certain notes, bring to mind certain colours. So colours and music go together, so if you think when you hear music and close your eyes, do you sometimes see colours ? Is the colour different for whatever tune you hear ? If you are listening to a slow tune is it a soft colour, a bright tune is it a bright colour? You experiment and see what you see. You see some music makes you "tap toes", some makes you sit still and close your eyes, has different effect, you want music that makes you "tap toes", that's the music that makes the energy that we need, "not go to sleep", energy, no good that. We want lively energy. It does not matter what words you sing, it's the intention in your mind, which makes the vibrations "dance".

A question on the different colours to concentrate on.

Red gives energy, but can also make disharmony, it can be colour of anger. If it's a red with a pinkie shade that's is better, that is calmer not so angry. A bright green is better than a dull green. You see sometimes when you sit for what you call transfiguration, you sit with red light but if you perceive the energy, some of you may be able to see colours, spirit colours, and when this is happening you see green around the one that is transfiguring. You see colours are different for different things. Blue is healing, yellow is learning, when you see yellow it symbolises learning. Green can also be healing, but it is more healing of the nerves. Gold is good, gold is a good colour, bright gold, an orange gold colour, but not what you call old gold, this gives lots of energy.

QUESTION 22 - *As background one of the sitters whose wife is in spirit had just had a new granddaughter, the previous week he had been told that her spirit name was "ROSE OF WISDOM", and this was shown as a pure white rose. (unbeknown to us the child's surname is also Rose !). The following was given by Rosa in answer to a question as to if the sitter's wife was able to know the new baby in spirit before she came to earth ?*

Yes she knew spirit and babe knows her, when babe grows and you talk of lady (wife in spirit), show pictures she will know, she will not say I know lady but it will be easy for her to understand, what you say to her, because she has knowledge in her spirit. She has a lot of lady in her, she has wisdom of lady in her, Lady taught her, lady taught her spirit. You see before you come to body you have to be prepared for body, and some loving soul teaches you, what you have to expect, when you come to body. Grandmother did this for this one. You were all prepared before you came, although you perhaps think you were not prepared for what you have experienced, that is because you do not carry that knowledge with you, but it's there before you come and when you go back. You will know what happened and why it happened, and what you learnt from that experience and why, and why you learnt.

QUESTION 23 - *E-om-ba giving details about his life on earth.*

He gave a chant, which he interpreted as 'call together'. We used this way of chant when we gathered as tribe and worshipped ancestors. Called spirits of ancestors. You do not do this, worship is tradition handed down your tradition is different from my tradition, still communicate. My tradition used to worship ancestors through nature in open not in buildings. Used our feet to stamp ground and chant, used instruments made from from hollowed out wood, blew through. Drums and animal skin over frame which beat, not always as drum sometimes it was frame with skin tied and we would beat sideways not as drum down.

We had sense of humour not always straight face, happy tribe. Worship with happiness, make happiness, lift spirits, happy people. Your religions are too serious no lightness too heavy, need upliftment, smile on face, too many straight faces. When we worshipped we were part of nature, we would paint face and body with paints made from natural substances. We would then be part of nature, we would then have part of nature on us. Earth, mud, part of plant roots. We touch ground we part of ground as one. Similar to your big man (Running Bear) not same but similar, he also worshipped nature, different from my tribe but understood the importance of nature, respect nature. When you live close to nature you learn to respect nature it is forceful, it can cause many dangers so you learn to respect, treat with respect, not take from nature without first asking and return to nature what comes from nature. Respect animal kingdom, treat as brothers.

You have anything you wish to ask E-om-ba? Paul's reply, 'we have difficulty getting the spelling right for your name'. Answer - I am only used to sound not writing. Our names, our language carried on through generations, one to other. Paul asked whether they drew pictures to leave messages. Answer - We would leave signs, mark trees when on travel we would mark route so others could follow. Paul asked the time E-om-ba lived on earth. Answer - I know not your years, we saw no white face. No permanent buildings, our buildings were moved, rebuilt, we would roam where there was food. They say we savage, not savage. We learn, you say morals we had morals we would treat with respect others, we would look after others if member of tribe was ill medicine man look to that one. If that one did not survive rest of tribe would look after those remaining. We would fight with other tribes if they encroached onto our territory. This was survival. We had to live by our skill, we hunted to survive not for fun as you would today. We would make use of animals we came across on our travels, we travelled many a long way, we would carry with us what we could but it was survival. Each to their own, we had to sometimes be fleet of foot, could not take any companions that would cause us to hold back. Those that were not strong did not survive, you may think this hard but this was our way. The elders were cared for, we would find ways of transporting, we strong we carry. There would be groups of strong young warriors that would carry elders. We would have carriage made of animals skins tied to strong poles and this was carried on shoulders of young men and wise elders were carried aloft on these or when they tired were carried but a group would carry not just one. It was respect for the elderly, we would respect elders, go to elders for advice. They were very wise, much wisdom from age. Our women folk would weave when we were in one place for a long while we would be able to establish a community and then we would gather whatever animals were in area and would use their fur, or wool if it was animal with coat we could use without killing animal. Our women would weave from this, make cloth. We did not have names for animals as you have names they were just beasts we shared our existence with. We would of course learn from very young age which animals were dangerous to us, and those which we could approach. We would light fires to keep away fierce beasts especially in hours of darkness.

Our young learnt from early age to be independent, how to protect themselves, how to hunt, how to survive. All life from young age were taught to look to those elders and respect. When you reach maturity you still did not proclaim that you knew all answers, you still asked elders, you learn you ask, you did not take responsibility on shoulders you would go to elders. Young would go to next generation and that generation would go to older generation all the way through to most senior. They would take responsibility for all and that would be handed down to generation to generation until it got to the tiny ones. We would teach our young ones, take to one side and teach group of young ones to respect their land and how to use their land and how to look after themselves and their family. Brothers to look after their sisters and mothers, when head of family was away hunting young boys would have responsibilities for their mothers and sisters but of course there was always elders to oversee. Family unit very strong.

We did not need your paper that you need today to bind man and woman together, we had own ceremony and took ceremony seriously we did not need paper to make legal. Families had to unite, it was not just man and woman, family and family had to agree. Man did not choose woman, woman did not choose man, family agreed. Union not marriage. I had large family, more than one wife, that was common. It was survival, when one too old to bear child take another who bear child, live as one family not divide as you would divide. Eldest first born would be next to take my place. First wife senior wife, when take next wife first wife would instruct second wife and first wife would have respect from second wife. First wife would not be thrown to one side. This is hard for you to understand. We not take women for fun, take for reason, and there would be a system, which we would have to live by. We would not take woman from another man, unless other man died, then we take in woman, in our family. If brother died we take in his family, as our family. Then another wife, and take her children, as my children. You would not wish this ?, but you see your women to be self sufficient, they would look after themselves, our women had not been taught this. Our women had been taught to look to man, for respect. Man take care. So I can not tell you how many children, because I took brother's children also, and my children accepted them as brothers and sisters.

I tell you for reason, bond between groups are important, bond between your group is important. It is not same way as I have just told you but for other reasons, look to each other, be each others strength when one is weak, others support.

QUESTION 24 - Mafra answering question on the power of the mind versus psychic phenomena.

The mind is very powerful there are many depths to the mind that have not been researched. You must be aware that when you sit you are trained to know when spirit are with you. When things happen when you are not expecting them to happen this can not be your mind but this is why we say to you do not concentrate too hard on a certain occurrence because you put a barrier. Not only can you put a barrier you can also force things to happen so we do not allow it to happen. We want you to experience pure spirit, we do not want you to experience your mind making things occur so when things occur when you concentrate too hard this can be mindful actions. When things occur when you are not concentrating this is not of mind this is of spirit, I am talking of this group here. There are many groups which sit for phenomena, some are very sincere groups and work with sincerity and like yourselves receive from spirit. Some are very sincere and believe they perceive from spirit but do not understand the strength of the mind and there are a few that do understand the power of the mind and unfortunately work on this. It is not for me to condemn those others actions but just for you to be aware of what can occur. Be aware that when things occur to order this is time to question. When things occur spontaneously without too much effort this is evidence of spirit with you. It is not intentional fraud that is happening with some groups they do not understand when you sit with group you know that before you sit with any new visitor you talk, explain, of procedure. Some do not do this they have groups with a visitor, that one comes not aware of what is going to occur, their mind is in a state of quandary, it is a state of turmoil wondering, apprehensive of what may occur. They are not put at ease and this condition of the mind is creating an energy, an anxiety, it is questioning, could be excitement depending on the personality. One person may be excited looking forward but another my be anxious, fearful. This is all energy that is created and the creation of this energy can then be used mindfully and manipulated for events to occur. It is good that whenever you sit you sit quiet and explain to people what you are about, put them at their ease. Do not draw their expectations too high telling them what they will see, what will occur. Explain to them it is an experiment you cannot guarantee spirit will come, you cannot guarantee movement, sounds, perfume or whatever they must come with open mind. They must accept and relax not to be fearful. Their mind is then on an even vibration, it is not causing a disturbance.

QUESTION 25 - *Another question for Mafra relating to compatibility of the medium to the person communicating.*

It depends a lot on the personality, personality is not a good word it should be vibration but I use personality because you understand 'personality'. If it was a person, I give an example your friend GEORGE, he had no problem communicating not only through this one but through others before. He had not passed to spirit very long before he was making himself known many years before this sitting or this one was even born (many years before the medium being used was born) because he had an outward vibration, outward personality. When a spirit comes for the first time it does vary. They have to get used to being in a body, now to be in a body is a very strange experience for us. We are not used to being conditioned to earthly vibrations, we feel heavy, we feel as if we have got a heavy cloak on which holds us down as we are free as a vibration, as free as the air. Then when we realise we are in a body we then take on the body, we take on the condition which varies. Once we are in body some who come would want to experience the body condition, they would want to experience to breath again and some just sit and breath for a while just to experience breathing. Now, I do not do this as I do not need to, it is of no use to me to breath I just use this one's mind and send signals to the mind to speak but we are different. Perhaps the first time I came I may have done this because I wanted to experience. I remember being in a body and I wanted to be the same but I realise now I am not the same I am spirit talking through body, I am not body but because I returned to body for first time my consciousness remembered when I last had body I went through same procedure. I thought I had to breath and experienced the lungs filling with air. Then the spirit returning for the first time might want to experience what it is like to raise hand or move leg but everyone would be different. I have been listening to your discussion regarding voice, when one comes for the first time the voice is a lot different to medium's voice because they talk in the same vibration as they remember when they had body. When your African helper comes he chants and make unusual noise, this is what he did when he had body so he thinks he should do this now but as time goes on he will forget that and realise he is here to talk to you wisdom and will just talk wisdom but at present he is remembering what body was like for him. So when someone comes for first time they will get the feel of the body and maybe take on part of their personality they left behind but the more they come they will come as pure spirit. The more times they visit they will shed their body conditions and just control mind and voice. Having said that, not always as Kimyano has come many times but still likes to use feet and hands. (Being Japanese her feet were bound in the traditional manner and she used her hands artistically to demonstrate her feelings). You see we do not change when we become spirit we are still individuals even though we are part of group we still have our own spark of individuality.

QUESTION 26 - Jules discussing how spirit learns while they are visiting our group.

I join in your teachings. Many come and learn and listen. You hear voice talk to you when, say Mafra talks, also you are receiving other teachings not aware and this is where we listen for these teachings not for your world but teachings that you need for spiritual progression. So this is what we partake of. It is not necessary for us to listen to words about your world that is of no use to us but you receive other knowledge without your physical body being aware. We partake of this with you. It is good. You see you question why we do not have these teaching when we are in spirit, why do we have to sit with you? I use the word sit but that is to try and explain. It is because when you are here you generate energy for your helpers to use and this enables them to speak to you and sets in motion a string of teachings. Because you are absorbing what is being spoken of your brain is generating a frequency which stimulates learning, you are absorbing and because you are absorbing you are giving off an energy. This energy assists us to learn also. You must think when you are sitting listening to say something, perhaps I say your word television, a programme which is light hearted you just sit and absorb but if you sit and listen to a programme which is more in depth you are listening in a different way so you are making more stimuli in your brain. This is generating another kind of energy. No energy can you keep to yourself whatever you generate you have to share. You would damage your brain if you kept energy within, you have to release energy, vibration whatever you give name to. This is then absorbed into the atmosphere around and this in turn can be used to generate more energy for more use. This sets in motion learning, and learning, and learning as one person learns the next person learns. Like in a schoolroom a pupil who learns, part of that knowledge is shared with another who might be listening and that one will listen and absorb what they wish to absorb and pass on to another, and so it goes on. There is not a beginning and an end, it is a continuation. So when you are spoken to, say by Mafra, you absorb and what you absorb creates an energy within your intellect which is released into the atmosphere and it is gathered by a sensitive. A sensitive human or one of us and it helps us to absorb also. Not with your brain but with the vibration because we are vibration, we are not body we are a vibration so we link with the vibration which is partaken, we learn. It is difficult to explain how spirit learns. We do not have a brain as you do we have to learn through vibration.

QUESTION 27 - Rosa firstly talking about George - MAN of LETTERS, then Jules and the groups training responsibilities.

He is learning about spirit, sent to us to get in contact with earth again and be reminded earth is different from Spirit. He will be very useful in Spirit, when he has learned more, can do lots to help. Important for progression to learn before you go to spirit. Different religions teach different theories. Some do not realise they are in spirit, not what they have been taught. Have big job to tell them they still have existence. They must learn to help each other not just themselves, they come to spirit used to just looking after themselves, have to learn to be part of group. This is difficult for them to understand. Rosa was on her own, when I came to spirit had to learn to be part of our group, better now I have learnt to share. Good to have own thoughts, but good to blend with group of own kind. Part of group but still individual. You can share vibration but experience has made you what you are. Others experiences have made them what they are, but still blend in with the group, but come and talk as an individual, all contribute to the group. Those that want to learn, bring them into group to learn, some will stay, some will go on to other things, some will work with other groups. Come to your group (circle), to learn how spirit communicates with earth. When they have learnt they may go onto another group and communicate with them. Rosa say, they are a group who teach us but also teach spirit. Like a school when they have reached a level they can stay and work with us but may find another group to work with

Rosa explain, we have drawn spirits that want to learn. When some have learnt through watching us they come and talk to you, to gain practice in communicating. Jules very good, now talks well. He is learned and capable, he may wish to stay with us, but may wish to draw others who are learning and take them to another group of earth people. He may be part of that team to teach them. He is capable of leading a team, he is a teacher, just as Mafra looks after us, he could look after another team.

The basic team is always with us, others come and learn, practice with each other. We are very fortunate because we are part of an important team, others learn from us, because of this the work will carry on in the future though learning together. It is a school, pupils from the school will work for spirit in many places on earth and in spirit. Some will return to earth others will progress in spirit through learning, not all will do the same thing.

Important group chosen by those on higher levels to be part of this plan, we are fortunate to be part of this plan. Team is special team, very important team, much to learn for spirit. Spirit learning now in preparation for what's in future, special team for learning.

See Chapter Four - The Learning System

QUESTION 28 - Kimyano talking about colour
There are many colours in your room tonight, many colours like paintings of spirit with their vibrations they have painted your room with colour, red, blues, pinks, mauves, gold, yellow, green, clear sparkling white

very pretty. Lots of energy, lots of energy around all of you. Come from all of you to us like rainbow, very pretty. Our colours are so different to yours, our colours are alive, you touch our colour you feel our colour it is alive. It moving it is all around you. Your colours in comparison are flat, it is like looking at a painting and looking at a 3D image, our colours stand out, more energy We transmit on colour you see our vibration, we are colour, we link with colour, send out our love on colour to others. It is living to us colour, our colour is like you breath your air your oxygen we live with colour, we need colour to exist as you need air to exist.

Kimyano was asked where do spirit draw their colour from - we do not draw it is there, it just grows. If we need a colour say for healing the energy is absorbed into the colour we need and that colour becomes more vibrant. If it is needed for a nervous condition the colour will be more green than blue because you just have colour but we have colour with so many shades. You know a little of what I say because you have a paint box with say five or six blues or five or six greens but our colours are more different, many, many more colours of blue or green or yellow than you will ever imagine. Every colour has it's own energy although energy different. We are all different, as you here on your earth are all different so we in spirit are all different and we each have our own colour slightly different. You think if you were spirit what colour would you like to be? and why would you like to be that colour?

Kimyano was asked whether she could see our auras - I can sense. An aura as you can understand is not as we understand it is only something that you can perceive when you are in body. Others who are gifted to see what you call aura have this ability, although it is a spiritual ability it is still linked to your physical sense so it is, I say, flat. It is a surrounding of colour but what we perceive is movement, vibration, colours not one on top of the other, mixing and blending and all the time swirling around of you, not something that stays the same. Changing all the time as your thoughts change so your colour change. When they say you have break in aura this is not so, you have movement in aura. Your aura is moving all the time it cannot break because is part of you, it just is always changing. It changes with your thought, it changes with your bodily health condition, it changes if you are asleep or whether you are busy, with what your physical mind is doing and your spiritual mind, so many things.

QUESTION 29 - The Doctor was asked if the medical condition of the medium has an affect on the ability of spirit to communicate.

We do not over strain the body, what we do is not physical only mindful but having said that if there is a physical condition it means that one's energy is reduced both physical and spiritual. One cannot work without the other. So if there is a weakness we try to compensate, if we take energy we replace. Of course when I talk of physical condition if it is a mindful condition, anxiety or stress that is something quite different. The mind has to be in a subdued episode for us to take control. If there is anxiety this causes tension, this causes a high frequency in the working of the brain which does not bid well for our occupation of the cerebral function and it is difficult for us to make ourselves fluent. You see we occupy the cerebellum and we instruct the voice to say words, sentences without a thought process. The words are directed straight through the body without going through the thought process. If the one we are occupying is anxious this disturbs our system. Mindful reasoning interrupts our transmission, we are using the body as a transmitter on a frequency level without the organisation of the mind or brain but if the one who's body we are occupying mind is not still, subdued, frequency cut across our transmission and cause a disturbance as is the frequencies on your radio transmitters. Sometime when there is a storm or a high frequency in your weather conditions your radio picks up disturbance, this is a way which I can describe that you can understand. So as we are transmitting there can be a disturbance from the mind of the body of the one we are occupying which crosses our transmission lines. So we are not able to give pure transmission from spirit, it is tainted with the interference from a mindful reasoning. Also you see, when a physical body is not functioning as in perfect condition it also makes a difference in the thought process to a certain extent because your body is balanced to behave in a certain way and if for some reason it is out of sequence the whole vibration of the body is upset.

If you have a cold infection it does not just interfere with your breathing it often causes a problem to other parts of your body, not perhaps at the same time but at a later date because your body is out of balance. I don't mean you are mentally out of balance, the working of your body, the metabolism, the system in your body which works without your instruction which continues to carry out the functions that you need to exist is also affected without you realising. One thing cannot be a problem on it's own it has to counteract all through the body, if one part of the body is weak another part of the body will try to counterbalance and become stronger and this is making that part of the body take on more stress. If this continues too long that part of the body will become over stressed and there will be a problem with that part of the body. If you have a cold your breathing could be affected, if your breathing is affected this could affect your heart rate, it could affect the flow of blood around your circulation. If the cold was within your head and your bronchial tubes and upper respiratory tubes are blocked this causes pressure in your ears, or in what you call your sinuses, which therefore will give you a pressure within your head and cause you discomfort and pain in your head. So unless the whole body is working perfectly there will always be a problem but spirit is quite capable of overriding minor problems. We take the body and we look after the body, we de-stress the body, we bring a calming effect on the body and this in turn assists the body in it's recovery because the body is at rest and is repairing itself.

This is just for minor conditions when it is something major problems it can be different but it depends if whatever this condition is affects the reasoning, if it causes anxiety. Also you see, if it is something which is being treated by your medical people there may be treatment which one in undertaking which also affects the mind state and can interfere with our transmission. The body is a very complex piece of machinery for you to understand, it is not like a piece of machinery where you can take one part out and replace it without affecting the rest. This is why after surgery the body needs time to recuperate, not just the part that has been treated but the rest of the body also. If we waited for a body to be 100% fit we would probably very seldom speak to you because your world is full of infection and the older you get the more wear and tear there is on your organs so you are always going to have a slight problem. This is no problem to us. Problems which cause anxiety are the condition we have a problem overcoming because anxiety causes a frequency which interferes with transmission.

When you start talking of illness in the body it is difficult to define, you talk of one area and it leads to another, it is multi-layered. Your physical and mental together and of course your spiritual also. Your endocrine system with it's hormones making mood changes and various glandular changes, this is another function that causes a disturbance in frequencies. If the condition is one where it affects the heart rate, the pulse, the circulation of the body we tend to lower the heart rate when we take residence because the body is as at sleep. So if medication is being taken to control heart you have to be very, very careful. Spirit of course, take as much care as is possible but there again, with the drugs that are in the body it is difficult to overcome. If it were just the body we were coping with we could control but it is difficult for us to overcome the effects of a foreign body comparable to a drug, narcotics or unnatural substance. There again, also when one returns it could be shock to the physical system, we leave as gently as we can and return the body to the condition that we found it but if anxiety is in that one this can cause a problem.

QUESTION 30 - Mafra responding to a question regarding spirit returning as children.

You are all children, I in jest call you my children because I think of myself as your father. You are all children at heart. When you are sitting quiet you can return to any point in your existence, you can recall what happened to you when you were quite small at your parent's knee. You can relive that experience in your mind and that experience has stayed with you all through your many years on your earth world, you can still recall what it was like to be a child surrounded by a loving family and having enjoyment at a happy time. When spirit returns as your brother Alan has his helper his little boy Peter, he is a very wise mature spirit but he returns as a child. This is a phase in his existence he is attracted to. He is comfortable and happy in that phase and he would return as a child but he could very easily talk as a man and give very advance knowledge. He has returned at a stage of his existence which he was happy in and is comfortable in returning as.

Your spirit children who come at your Christmas time these are souls that went home to spirit as children on earth. They have grown in spirit to mature spirits and have learned lessons but when they return to earth by vibration they take on the persona of a child as this was their cloak when they were last with you and they come back on that same vibration. It is an innocent vibration, a happy vibration, they were not tainted with the earth world as those of you that mature. You have your problems that dull your spark, your spark of spirit is within you and is bright but the more knocks you have, the more problems you have the more your light is dimmed until at last it is released and then of course it is bright again. These spirits have a very bright light and they return to your world with that very bright light and take on the form of a child, the innocence of a child, the happiness of a child. As you go through life in defence of yourself you take on attributes that are not always good, you become suspicious of others, you question others, you doubt, you fear and this is as it should be because you are walking a material life. Remember these souls haven't been tainted by these attributes, they are pure spirit and they return as pure spirit, as children. They come back in the vibration that they left and they are happy.

QUESTION 31 - Mafra responding to a question on how we find the spirit world when we return home.

When you return to spirit you return as a spirit without a body, without an overcoat but you can create whatever you wish as a spirit form. You can create your surrounding, if you wish to exist in a beautiful garden you have a beautiful garden. You create this with your vibration and this is the level which you are on and you are happy there. You can stay at this level for as long as you are happy. This is how you can exist in spirit for infinity if you so wish. If you stretch your spirit a little more you can stretch to another level of existence where you do not need any attachment. Your existence in spirit is on vibration, you do not need to eat, you do not need to sleep to exist as your human body does. It does not wear out as your human body does so you can exist for infinity in this state. After a while you realise that although this existence is fine and good, as you shed an old coat or an old garment, you may wish to shed some of this which is around you to become more spirit and rise above to another level. On this next level you can communicate with others just on vibration. When you return home to spirit at first you will have to learn how to acknowledge you are spirit, have to learn who is with you in spirit and for this you put on your spirit body so you recognise each other. You recognise who is with you as if you were still had earthly body but after a while you do not need to look at a spirit body to recognise you sense. You do know a little of this in your earth world. You can sense your children, you are in a room and one of your children walks in and you would know without looking that one is there, you can sense. This is what I am trying to explain what spirit is similar to. You will not need to see because you have not got eyes as you have eyes here but you perceive and your perception is of a different level, a different vibration. The more advance you become the less you will need to visualise, not with your eyes you have now but a spirit sense, the forms and shapes that you will at first need. For example you may wish to give your spirit loved one a flower and you would visualise the flower and give it to the spirit loved one but after a while you would only need to think of the flower and your energies would mingle, it would not be you and them. As you see the mist swirl this is how spirit is we swirl and we mingle. We keep our identity yes, but we blend with each other. I would not stand one side of the room and you would stand the other we would mingle as one but I would still be Mafra and you still would be yourself.

QUESTION 32 - *Discussion with Mafra regarding spirit occupying medium's body and spark of spirit.*
When we first return to a body we transcend into the earth's vibration which is so different from spirit's vibration. It is much heavier much denser and when we enter body we decode we are in body and we perceive we are in the body we last felt comfortable in. This is why when we come for the first time we are much different from when we have been back several times, we are more ourselves and we do not take on the body we are in we are remembering what our body was. So the more we return to you the more we are comfortable in the body we are occupying and we step into

that vibration. You will perceive we do not have same accent or same manner as when we first visited but we still do have some of the character which we had when we had body.

So what I was trying to say, as E-om-ba as an example, but of course this can be any one of us. You perceive when he talks that it is the E-om-ba who was in body and that is his personality but this is what he brought with him to unite with that body. So it goes further than his last life on your earth.

We use word again character. Now character - when we had body, body was flesh, blood, bones, organs which we occupied. We inherited from our ancestors certain features, habits and abilities but added to that we also brought with us the spark from spirit. That spark from spirit mingled with the earth matter which was our overcoat. Before we took on body we had to find a compatible body for that spark of spirit to reside in, for that spark of spirit to progress and to grow so we had to find a compatible body with similar characteristics (the components of the spark of spirit). So when that was in body of human it was able to mingle with the human characteristics, that one had inherited from it's ancestors.

When does the spark of spirit join the body? Do you choose the parents who have the desired characteristics to create the baby? At the moment of conception the spirit enters the dividing cell so the spark is there from the beginning. The sperm joins the egg and then when the egg divides from one cell into two cells that is the moment when life begins and this is when the spark of spirit is ignited. So it is there from the very beginning. It has been said ignorantly that those who are born in your world that are not of great intelligence do no have spark of spirit, this is not right. They do have spark of spirit it is inside and sometimes shows itself more than in what you would call a normal child because there is no pretence, there is no inhibitions, they are very outward going and do not worry what others think of them. Whereas your little ones quickly learn to be on the defensive side and cover their feelings and act as they think they should, not showing to the world their true self.

QUESTION 33 - Grandmother, Ruth Fruin, talking about how spirit people think.

Spirit does have the ability to 'think'. There has been some confusion over this as spirit's communications have been misinterpreted. People on earth have become confused with spirit's explanation and once it has been accepted as a fact it is difficult to alter. You have the experience with many who come to talk with putting words to what they are trying to explain because in spirit there is no such thing as words we work on vibration. So we go above language. What is a word? It is just a sound, a sound to express a thought. You have the thought before you have the sound, so we don't need the sound. We have the thought and it doesn't matter about language because sometimes when you are in your ordinary world you want to explain something and you can't find a word to describe what you want to explain. That happens to you in your ordinary world, in your ordinary country, in you ordinary language. So think how difficult it is for spirit to try and explain something in another language in another body they are not used to. We need to find a word that describes the feeling of what we are trying to say. I will try to explain, a word has a feeling a sense to it, you think that word will describe something but it might not necessarily describe what you want it to describe, it is not the perfect match. Colour is a vibration, look how many colours there are, you think how many words there are which we think match but don't match, very close but not the right one. When somebody is fumbling about trying to find words and then just one word is wrong and instead of questioning it is accepted as truth and once it is accepted as truth the whole history is written. That has happened in many of your books, in the Bible and in books of other religions too, just a word makes so much difference. Sometimes when you get a little bit forgetful and you can't think of a word it doesn't mean you don't know the word you just can't find it. This is what spirit is like, they want to explain something but they can't find the word that matches. They find one near but that is not the right one.

I listen to what other people say, and they tell me about these clever people who know lots of languages but you can't translate one language to another. You can't translate word for word, you have to take the whole sentence and turn it around. You are only comparing the languages in your close countries, when you start to think about countries like China and the Arab countries who use a totally different language. It would be a lot easier if everybody just used thought and didn't try and find a word to fit but you are a long way from that yet. They are very clever and put words into a computer and it comes out in a different language but it doesn't always mean what they want it to mean. The more you put into something yourself the better it is. You think of my sewing machine, there was all clever electric ones but the old one was better because you could do more things with it if you knew how to. Sometimes your world gets very complicated.

QUESTION 34 - A Sitter asked John Lyon his views on the new age of Aquarius.

Your learned people on your earth now have been saying for many years 'you are now entering the age of Aquarius'. It is not this decade, the decade before, the decade before that they were announcing the age of Aquarius. It is a name that has been given to a new awakening. There has been and there will continue to be a new awakening, a thirst for knowledge, a thirst insight into the depths that have not already been investigated. It is time for your world to look deeper than the obvious. More and more questions have been asked and there are many more that will be asked about the meaning of existence, I do not mean the existence of one person on your earth, I mean the existence of the universe, the existence of the worlds you do not know of, the depths of spirit world. There is much thirst but with this thirst there comes a warning that there are many on your earth that do not understand spirit and they purport to know of great wisdom and can have ways of manipulating minds for their own benefits. They have homed into a source and they find there is much financial benefit to be made from this thirst and as there is no definite proof of what they say is right or incorrect they cannot be disputed. Having said, and warned of this malpractice there is much truth to be sought.

You have been told your group here is a group which is part of a vast plan. We are preparing for this thirst of knowledge, we are training teachers. You will be teachers and also others who join you from the realms of spirit are also training to be teachers and as your years on earth progress and more wisdom is sought there will be more groups searching as you are searching. Spirit teachers will be in great demand and this a preparation that is taking place now. You are one of several groups that are sitting uniting with spirit and learning in preparation and from these groups is a vast source, if it was an earthly situation it would be a university and your graduates would leave and go forward to open colleges of their own and teach. This is what you have been called here for, this is part of your destiny, it goes even deeper, it is a calling, it is what all your experience, all your problems and what not only this life but all your lives before have been in preparation for. It is the accumulation of all you have learned so far. You have been prepared for this awakening and you are to be instruments in this quench for the thirst so you are very special people. You were spirit before you came and you are here to go through the ordeals of an earthly existence and through these ordeals, there are also pleasures your life has had pleasures also, but through these experiences your spirit within has grown. Through the experiences you have gone through and are going through your spirit is able to assist others. Through the knowledge you are gaining because you have reached a point where you are more aware of the closeness of spirit and you are aware spirit have told you of many things that are new to you. You are now stretching your mind, your spiritual mind, you are becoming much much wiser, this is good. When you return home to spirit, it is home because that is where you came from, you will not be in the beginners class you will be able to assist those that are in spirit and are searching. I will not go any further as some of you when you return to spirit may wish to return to earth, not in body, but return to earth and give wisdom yourself. Some of you may not wish to do this, the choice is yours. You are not forced in spirit to take any path you do not wish to pursue. There is free will even in spirit, even more in spirit than there is on earth because on earth you are confined to your body, you are confined to your surroundings and the restraints of your country and your fellow men. In spirit you do not have these restraints and you have more freedom of choice.

Another sitter asked the reason for symbols. - What is a symbol? A symbol is a sign which you perceive to be for a purpose. Once you have this symbol in your mind that this symbol portrays whatever that is a fact. It is like a child when you are taught that the straight line means a number 1 and the figure that looks like a swan's neck means 2 and through life you are always surrounded by symbols. You learn very early what the symbol of your name is, these letters of your alphabet mean you they don't mean the person next to you unless that person shares the same name as yourself. The way that is written in your hand writing is not the same as the person next to you who has the same name, so that symbol is you. You see if you look at your life your life is full of symbols. If you have this symbol on whatever surface and you earnestly believe this is for a purpose your instinct which goes deep within you accepts this and it will work for this purpose. If another person ridicules this do not be upset they have not accepted this. If another person believes another symbol should be put in it's place that is good for them because their reasoning is different from your reasoning.

John Lyon talks about communication - What is language? It is the tongue which you speak in whatever country you are born, whatever surrounding you have but there is a common factor 'thought'. A thought is formed within your conscious reasoning, you wish to express that thought to those whom are around you, you are quite capable of doing this without uttering a word. Your instinct, your primeval ability enables you to transfer your thought to others but this is an ability mankind has lost as you have progressed through the existence of mankind. Going back way before myself, going back many generations there was not so much need for spoken word. Your thought which you wish to express to others in your vicinity is put into a word so it is thought before it is word. When you communicate with spirit you do not need language, you are capable to communicate on the level which goes beyond a language. You have many who come to speak to you, to communicate with you who come from countries who's mother tongue was a lot different from your own but they are able to make themselves known. Either through the voice of this one or through other means. This is because they are not using language they are communicating through a different vibration, a thought vibration.

They are not thinking in French, they are not thinking in English, they are forming a vibration in their mind. If they are a person in your world with a body they wish to express through, they find a word from their language to express that thought. The thought is there before the word is there. If you go back to when you first enter this world from spirit and you come into a body of a little one, you do not speak, you have not learned the language of your country or of your parents but you are able to communicate with those around you. Yes, I understand you are thinking you are able to cry but there is other communication which is silent. Mother can look at a child and know what that child needs, that child is able to communicate and as this child grows and learns a tongue whatever language this instinct for communication abates because the child becomes more reliant on the spoken word. You see there is no thinking in French, or English, or Chinese, or Arabic, thought is a vibration and in spirit we communicate on vibration. We are vibration and if I wish to communicate with Mafra I communicate my vibration to Mafra and our vibrations mingle and become one, we are together as one and we have conversation. I use conversation because that is a word you understand but we share thought.

QUESTION 35 - Rosa talks about music performed live in concert

We like music that is happy. When music is happy it sends up vibration and that attracts spirit not just yours but many there had spirit with them, you are not the only ones who have spirit with them. There was so much energy, so much music. If you could see when music plays, I do not mean music on recording but real live music it makes lots and lots of energy. If you could see colour, you would see lots of colours all in your room.

Question - Is this because of the vibrations of the instruments making the vibration in the air? Also the mind of the one who plays music because what has just been said to you, it is in mind before it is in words so music is in mind before played on instrument. All those who play, they like you they all unite their thought as one. We say to you 'you must unite your thought as one to create vibration'. This is what your people do who play instruments they unite their thoughts. When you have recording you do not have the vibration of those who are actually playing music, they are not there. It is like having a real flower which you can feel the shape, the smooth or the rough and having picture of flower and it is flat, no smell. It is still a colour on paper and still has a bit of vibration because it is an image of something that once was but it is not real like the flower in your hand that has texture and perfume and living energy.

QUESTION 36 -When a spirit communicates who was blind when on the earthly plain do they have a problem in describing their form for identification, as they could not see their face, Answered by Sophia.
No because they send vibration, and a vibration is a vibration of their personality, their wave length, their vitality and this is then decoded by earthly brain and makes picture. They do know what they look like, they have inside their "head", a picture of themselves. They know how people look by feel, they feel others faces to get an idea of what others look like and feel body. They feel their own body so they have built a picture of themselves in their conscious reasoning, when they were on earth and perhaps those they were with said to them you have blonde hair, of they could feel curly hair. They may say you look like your sister, you have same shape of nose, or you have long fingers, there again they could feel long fingers. So because they had no vision, their other instincts are very acute and so they can form a mental picture of themselves, and this is what they send on their vibration to the one that is reaching out, and they decode the vibration. You perceive that they cannot see colour but colour has vibration and they know of colour, they know red is lively and bright like fire, they know that blue is cool and calm so they are one step ahead of you because they have this instinct already without relying on their vision. In one way it is easier for them to send a vibration because it is a vibration of sense rather than just one picture. You often remember a person at a certain stage in their existence, you perhaps remember them when you were at an age when everything was new and fresh and people made an impression on you and although you see this person over many years if you did not see them for a while the picture you would imagine of them would be the picture you recall when you were most vibrant yourself. You do not notice somebody gradually changing. If you recall your relatives who are no longer with you in the body how do you visualise them, as you last saw them or when you were young and vibrant yourself? When your senses were vibrant and you noticed things more. You become lazy as you mature in age. You do not notice, probably, a spot on the face or a mark on the skin or whatever, you just take for granted. A child will say to you 'why has that person got a funny leg?' or 'why has that person got an eyebrow one way and a different way the other side?' They are observant but you would probably just accept and not notice. Because at that stage you are learning and looking at everything it make a deeper penetration within you. Also, of course your society teaches you not to be impolite and notice things so much.

This is where you must be careful by not taking things from someone else's mind when they are remembering someone, you are not taking that picture from their mind rather than taking a decoding from spirit. It is good when you perceive a spirit that is not in someone's mind. This is why we try to bring you people who have to be thought about. You notice that when we do bring a spirit who is known to one of your sitters we try to bring something that the sitter is not aware of. It must not latch on to mind.

QUESTION 37 - Mafra responding to question regarding why it has been noticed that the medium sometimes uses phrases that are remembered from communicators particular way of saying things.
This is a trace left behind, we try not to do this we try to clear. You would probably notice that sometimes when there are two or three visitors one visitor comes and when the next one comes for the first little while they sound a little like the previous visitor because they leave an implant. You know that when we have left the medium says there is a feeling but gradually this goes. You must understand that also in your and her memory there are many dialects and phrases which you do not normally use. These are dormant but if these have been aroused they have been brought to the fore again. It is similar to you reading a book on your earth or watching a programme on your box in the corner of your room and it reminds you of something or an area perhaps that you visited. This makes your mind recall when these memories come to the fore. When you have a visitor who speaks in a dialect which has been locked away from perhaps a previous generation it stirs a memory. This is not that the memory is coming to the fore and overtaking spirit, that is not what I mean but it is arousing a memory. You all have memories deep inside which your are unaware of from your ancestors. When the country which you live in was more separated and more divided the way that language was spoken was different in different areas and you have traced your family histories you know that you come from various sources. Some of your people have stayed within the same area for many generations but you have learnt that your families have come from very wide aspects, so you must have within you very many memories of various kinds of accents and ways of mannerisms, instincts, habits and beliefs. You have very superstitious memories within you from pagan times which you do not know of but they are deep inside you. You see all these things merge with your modern world. You have a vast store house, each generation has a little more to add, your child has more than you because she has another generation. There is much untapped knowledge and instincts that are dormant.

You speak of your friend George, he as you know speaks in a mannerism from your City of London. The medium has ancestors from London, not that area of London but there is still memory links with that area and this stirs within. I try to explain, the memory the medium has within her memory bank is of another part of your city but those people in her lineage would have met other people from other parts of the city so there is a knowledge of other areas, not just the area where they resided. You were brought up in one area, regardless whether you moved to another area we will just concentrate on the area where you were a child and where you were a young adult. During the time you were in that area you were surrounded by others in your vicinity but also in your day to day life you met others from other areas a little further outside that area where you resided so that has gone into your memory. You have also meet people from a different country, or from a different part of your own country, and that memory would have gone inside your own memory. So you must imagine how much storage space that you must have. There are not many areas where you do not have knowledge of. You gain knowledge from the more you read, and with your new systems of communication, also your education, the entertainment facilities you have, bring you, all the time, more knowledge from other parts of the world. So there is a vast knowledge store to communicate with, within yourself.

Even your short journey to my homeland (Portugal), you may not recall what people said to you, or the conversations you heard around you that you did not understand, but they were absorbed, so there is a knowledge of them now. You would not have understood what the words were, but as you know you absorb another level of communication at the same time, so the thought process was being transferred. So the thought process of those that were talking around you a language you knew not of was being translated for you without you realising. If you heard that voice again or that word or inclination again you would say 'that sounds like when I was in Oporto' without understanding the word you would recall the dialect. You would not know what they were saying but you would be able to say where their homeland was. You do not understand a tiny part of your brain it is so vast, it holds so many layers and configurations, so much storage and it is a fallacy that you are taught when you go to spirit this is no more, what would be the purpose of all this being left behind ?, there would be no purpose so you must take with you your knowledge.

So is it possible for spirit to bring this knowledge back? This depends on the amount of experience. I am able to bring a certain amount with me but not all because it would not be compatible with the medium's brain. I would be able to recall events and tell you but not draw it from the medium's brain. Before you visited Oporto I described to you where I resided, this was knowledge I was imparting in word form from my knowledge. I could not draw from within the medium because she had not been there. This was the information I was bringing to you but because I was speaking to you and you knew not of the area I could only tell you a small part, I could not go into great details because it would have been of no importance. We try to narrow down what we bring to an essence so it homes in on the point. *After we have been to your country another time will there be more information you can give us regarding the area?* Maybe yes, maybe no, because it is not the country that I lived in. Some of course will be the same, some will have changed as everything changes from one day to next. Even the language is not the same, you would say it is as you say your language is the same but if you recall what your language was when your writer Shakespeare was writing it is not the same language as you speak in your tongue today. You understand other countries are the same including my country. You see the language was different in different areas, the villages spoke their own tongue, as in your country your villages spoke their own tongue. When communication was more difficult people did not move so much and the various settlements, whatever you wish to call them, villages whatever had their own way of communicating. If they visited the next they probably would not understand each other. You have a phrase you use in your country, 'the King's English' or perhaps it is the Queen's English' now which was the language used by the men of trade and your politicians and your diplomats but this, of course is the language of your country today. A few generations ago not everybody spoke your King's English. In your land today you have many cultures and tongues also. It is like my country things are always changing. It is good to rely on a different level of communication other than the tongue, there are no barriers with that.

The word you would use 'multilingual' it is above language. Your animals have no problem with this they communicate on a different level. *Is this like music?* You talk of music but in your country and my country we also have common words which goes back to the ancient languages, the Latin and the Greek and in your professions these words can be used in various countries and understood by your professional men because it is a universal language, for example the medical profession. If you think of spirit wave lengths on this level you can understand how it covers all languages.

QUESTION 38 - John Lyon speaking further on words spoken by Brother John relating to the ability to reflect on life's experiences. He was asked whether this state of reflection was similar to the natural sleep state.

When you are at sleep your subconscious is working. Your subconscious is going through your actions during your daytime and your memory bank. Your sleep is in cycles you have degrees of depth of sleep while you are at sleep, you have sleep patterns so your mind is not in the tranquil state, it is changing. Your mind is active in various degrees of activeness. If you studied you would know that in some stages of your sleep there is movement with your eyes even though your eyelids are closed. Your mind is working and sleep is a way of relaxing, also it is a way of your subconscious reasoning the events that have taken place and storing these events in the appropriate memory banks. You relive certain events so as to make logic of what has occurred and this is when you have dreams. You are reliving events and they are portrayed in dreams to make sense of what you have experienced. If your subconscious cannot made sense of what you have experienced you have this dream again, perhaps in a different form but recurring in a different location or with different people within your dream until your subconscious makes sense of this event. You see you are not quiet, you are not looking within, you are exploring your brain is working.

When you withdraw, as your Brother John has explained to you, you go into a form of meditation how deep is entirely up to yourself but you have been taught how to meditate. The important factor for meditation is to close down your sensory factors within your body, your senses. This is the reason you have been taught to tell parts of your body to sleep. You lose all sense within your electrodes which bring sensation to your brain, you put your physical body in a sleep state. Also, you put your mind in a sleep state. You are then free to delve within in a peaceful situation not as a dream where you are searching and trying to make sense, you just withdraw within yourself, to your inner self and draw from your inner self without reasoning, with the thought process, just go within and let your conscious reasoning fall until you are feeling very, very peaceful. You are not concerned with what is happening outside your body, you are not concerned if there is a noise outside, you are not concerned if your body has an irritation, you are not concerned with it you cannot feel it. You have shut your body down, you are not concerned with what other people may be saying to you or if there is a bright light or anything that could distract you, a noise, you would not hear you are really shut to the world you are within yourself.

At this stage you can draw from the wisdom which is already within you. This is why you need really to be somewhere peaceful, it is not good to do with when you are with others, perhaps if you were travelling you would want to do this but it would not be good because it would not be the right environment. It would be good to do it when you are somewhere comfortable preferably your home or somewhere where you are content and happy. If you wish to wander and sit somewhere under a tree or a green field, somewhere where you cannot be disturbed, somewhere where there are no others who will disturb you. Perhaps if we are talking of your world when your weather is at a better state than at the moment you may wish to sit in your garden and absorb the energy from your garden or if your climate does not permit perhaps in a room in your home where you are comfortable.

It is good to reflect every so often to make certain in your mind as to which direction you are taking. You have gained much insight in the short while you have been sitting. You have endeavoured to find your course and, as you have said yourself you are attracted by education, this is good. Whereas at first you did not know why you were having these experiences you have now ascertained that education is playing an important role and once you accepted this it was reinforced by spirit and you opened the doors. You had much confirmation from spirit that education was in their plan also but this was withheld from you until you made the affirmative yourself that education was of importance to you. Spirit did not force this on you. You became aware of the training team that is here is spirit working with your team but you see, we do not lead we guide. You have to discover for yourself the path it is not our prerogative, it is in your learning to discover for yourself. You need to learn yourself, the plan is already written but you have to define the path yourself.

There are many who visit from the world of spirit who are educated alongside you. It is impossible for me to describe the education system. It is intangible to describe the parallel paths that are taking place with spirit and yourselves. There is the spirit path and the mortal path of education but they are overlapping and inter linking without you realising and you are each learning from each other and those in spirit who are teaching you both at the same time but on different vibrations. It is something your human brain cannot understand or comprehend. It transcends many levels and it has a continuous effect. It does not mean that while you learn here and when your time with spirit ends for this session it is shut down, the learning process is continuous. All that has been learned is continued, it is passed down. What you learn as a mortal is within you and is used by you when you have contact with others. What is learned by spirit is continually passed to other vibrations and sent out on the vibration to many others that are stretching out and seeking for knowledge.

You see, when there is learning in spirit it is absorption of knowledge and this knowledge cannot stay in one context. As you know we communicate with each other in spirit by vibration. If a spirit vibration has accumulated knowledge from education it glows, it makes that one brighter, That one has suddenly understood something that it may have been seeking for a very long while but it has now resolved the query that it has been seeking, perhaps for lifetimes. As that one absorbs this the energy of that one grows. Now there are many others in spirit who are also seeking for this answer and their vibration links with the one who has the learning, so this learning is then shared with the others who have reached the stage in their evolution when they are ready for this answer. Only when they are ready are they able to link with this vibration. There are many more that are still seeking but have not reached the level in their evolution when they are ready for the answer so they do not make contact. Those who's destiny it is, they have gone that one step further and are ready, can absorb this energy. You see this education is continuous. These ones that have now reached the stage when they are ready for the information are able to link in and absorb it. They in turn absorb the information and there again they are then able to pass it on to another level of spirit who are just at that point ready to accept and so on, and so on. It is continuous. It is not like my schoolroom where boys would come and learn the lesson and then shut their desk and shut their books and go home and forget their lesson until the next day. It is not as such, it is continuous. It would be comparable to my schoolroom and the schoolroom being full and the boys learning their lesson and shutting their desk and going home. As soon as they have left the classroom the classroom is full again with another collection of boys who were waiting outside and were ready for their lesson. They in turn would leave and there would be another queue of boys waiting to come in. This is how I can best explain it so you will understand. The boys would not be ready to receive all at the same time. So those boys who were there originally were ready for the lesson, the next group of boys were only half way up the hill, they hadn't reached the gate, and the next class were down the bottom of the hill but by the time the second class had finished they had reached the gate so it was their time to learn. It is not advantageous for everybody to learn until they are ready, it is a waste of energy because the lessons are not absorbed. It is partly stored waiting for a later time but no knowledge is wasted it is there but is best if it is given at the right point.

    You see when you have an earthly group who sit at the same time although the group is in harmony it does not mean that they are each at the same stage of leaning so it is not possible to give the lesson at the right time for everybody. This does happen where it is stored but it is not lost, it is stored and at a later time it will be revived and updated. I try to bring you information that is of use at the time and not to be too repetitive. I have to reinforce what has been said before without being repetitive.

    John Lyon discusses family connections then goes on to talk about destiny - What is of more interest is the future and education. The past is of interest but do not let it take up too much of your energy. I understand you wish to secure the link for your own satisfaction but fore soothe, you know there is a link and you have my word the link is there. It is not the link I intended, it is not as I wished but these things occur, this is destined how it was to happen. There has been good come from it education has continued and there is still much education taking place. None of us can foresee what the world will be in time to come, I had a vision and my vision was ahead of my time, I know, it was good for a while but I could not envisage the future any more that you can envisage what will happen two hundred year's hence in your world. You can only make plans for the foreseeable future and you have to leave the rest in the hands of destiny, the power that is there. There is a plan for not only your world but the universe and this a plan which is above all of us and whatever we say, whatever we think, however we live our lives, this cannot be altered. We are cogs in a wheel. Fore soothe, I say this and you must remember that you just play your part and do the best you can, do not reproach for anything that has not occurred. We are, as individuals, very small specks in destiny's will but having said that we are all very important in all our way. Not just I say this because I have a name which is important but anyone who has lived, breathed, aspired and walked a path is important in their own right. However humble their path has been they have been part of creation for a reason. Fore soothe, remember this. It is a kaleidoscope of vibration. One cannot live without the other, you rely on each other's energy for existence.

  I reproached you (Paul) for looking backwards. It is good to look backwards because you learn of yourself. It enables you to understand the genealogy which is inside you which makes you what you are. That you have inherent within you diverse backgrounds and these diverse backgrounds make you comprehend the lives of others whether they be of noble birth or low birth. Your world today has not the divisions of previous generations. Those that have interbred with those from the nobility have much to give your world with knowledge and learning but because within their inherent experiences they do not have the experience of those that have worked and toiled for their living in a different section of your society they find this makes life difficult for them to comprehend, the other side of the coin. You are at an advantage where you have in your genealogy diverse backgrounds. This enables you to look at others and understand their way of thinking. You can look a king in the eye and you can look the humblest peasant in the eye because in your ancestry you have had contact with both on an even level. Whereas many have not had this experience and they find it difficult to communicate with either a high rank or low rank. There should be neither because this is only an overcoat we wear while we are here. Within we are spirit and spirit is the same regardless of what overcoat we wear while we have a body. This overcoat does put restrictions on us while we have it. Man has to conform to the surroundings life has bestowed on him.

QUESTION 39 - Felice (Felicity) this was the first time that this spirit has communicated (March 1997). She spoke part in French part in English. We have included this in our records as it is interesting to learn how spirit are educated and made aware of their abilities when they learn alongside ourselves.

Bonjour - I come to listen. I listen to your John, he has much knowledge. He teach well. He teach in our vibration. He comes to teach you but also he teach spirit when you are not here. He make plan, he has plan, he teach one lesson and has plan for next lesson. Take one class first then goes on to next class. It is not the same in spirit we can learn different, he can teach many levels at one time. We take different energy from lesson depending on what we seek. He teach me to talk to you. I learn how to learn now. I have no desire myself to teach. This is making me aware of myself. I talk of myself, I learn of why I learn. I have no body, I am spirit I learn of spirit and opportunities open to me. He is man of organisation, when we are in spirit it is important that we are aware of progression and he teaches us that there is a path forward for us in spirit and we take steps on path. As we take steps on path opportunities arise and we have to make plan as to our pathway, he is helping me to put my steps on pathway. By talking to you I am confirming with myself what is happening. I have to make sense of what is happening to tell you, so I am talking through because in spirit we have no talk, so as I talk through it is making positive statement. I know now I am on pathway forward but as yet no decision as to which route to take but I now know I am able to learn not stay at one place. There is opportunity for me to go forward and learn. I will come and talk again and will tell you a little more when I know myself what I will do. My name is Felice (Felicity).

QUESTION 40 - John Lyon giving us more of his wisdom. Sitters were questioning why a blue colour had been perceived earlier in the room.

Spirit was using energy that was built up in your room. You do not perceive how much energy there is around you. The room is alive with energy and spirit was using this energy twofold. One, was a very important function and that was to send out healing. This energy was amassed, it cannot stay in one place it has to be dispersed. When you amass energy together for a purpose as you have, you have asked for healing in your prayers you have asked for healing, and that is the opening of the door. This was the first step, you then sat and joined together with this intent and the energies came together and we were able to send out healing to where it is most needed.

The other factor, which too is important, but perhaps you do not consider to be as important as healing is the build up of energy for spirit to show themselves. Now when I say show themselves you imagine you are going to see a person standing in front of you. I do not mean this at this stage of course. The intention is that you will be aware of spirit around you in the form of perhaps, a shape, a light, a colour. If you look around the room and open yourself to the room gradually you will be able to perceive different energy vibrations that are around you. When you look and expect to see a form as your form you are actually putting up a barrier to open yourself to spirit. You are putting a thought in your mind that is how spirit will look when you see it but in the early stages this is not so. You will be aware of spirit around you by other means. As you know, we had a long discussion, not myself but others, last week of spirit of when you are in spirit if you have a body or if you do not have a body, this was explained and I do not want to repeat again because it will be going over ground which we covered last week. As was said to you, you are an essence, you are a spark of energy, you are a vibration but if you wish to have a spirit body you can have a spirit body. What you could perceive initially would be the spark of energy, the vibration. So when you look around your room and you perceive perhaps a light or a cloud, I do not want to put ideas into your head because you will perhaps each see spirit in a different way, as you open yourself to the room. It is good that you sit in darkness because your senses are able to perceive these energies, whereas if there was light it would not be so easy for you at first. As you look around the room and you perceive these signs, I use the word signs rather than put an idea into your head, you are actually perceiving spirit. This is spirit you are perceiving because this is how we show ourselves. There are many, many visitors here with you. As you become more aware of spirit you will be able to decode these signs you are seeing and perhaps you will be able to perceive what that one looked like when they had a body. You will decode the essence into a spirit body, you are some steps from that yet but at first be content that you are seeing signs of spirit around you. There are many, many with you tonight. If all the energies that are in this room had a body there would be no space, they would be outside the door.

It is difficult for myself to explain a different dimension. This is our existence, we are not many miles away from you but we are with you but in another dimension. Because of the magnitude of spirit energies there are if they all had space as you have space in a confined dimension as you live within we would have a vast problem. Our dimension does not have the limitations of your dimension it is infinite. It is as if you step through a door into a vast abyss of space and there are no restrictions, there are no limitations. There is no distance whereas on your earth plain if you are in one location and you wish to travel to another location it would take you a matter of time depending on how far that location is but in spirit there is no distance. If Jack, you wished to talk to your daughter and there was no such thing as a telephone it would take you a while to reach your daughter but if I wished to speak to my daughter regardless she is in this infinite spirit world, that you call us, I can communicate instantly, we merge instantly. We can be in more than one place at one time. I could be with you here my friend and I could be with your daughter at the same time because I would travel in my dimension not your dimension. Do not worry too deeply that you cannot understand because you human brain in not meant to understand. You do understand because you knew of this before you came to your world so do not be afraid that you cannot understand spirit because you already know of spirit. It is just that a curtain has come across those memories because they are of no use to you in your world today. You are here to live today and once you are in spirit your knowledge is there, you have not lost it.

John now continues with thoughts on meditation. It is good to sit and relax and meditate and to recharge because you have been told this is something you must do. You must sit and relax and go into yourself and find the peace and silence within to restore your energy. We do not wish you to vegetate in this state, we want you to also be alive, mobile and perceptive to what is going on around you but obviously in your own time. You have your quiet moments where you meditate and go within we do not want you to drift so you are in this state permanently because there is much work for you to do. Once you are working we can find much use for your thoughts. Your thoughts will then be alive and vibrant and we find much use for them. When your warmer days come and you are working in your garden, when you are absorbed in a pastime which you are enjoying this is often as good as meditating because you are literally going within yourself. Your body is functioning you are animate, you are moving but your mind is relaxed. Of course, there are the extremes when you become over zealous, perhaps when you are rushing to finish a task at a certain time. When you are usually involved in a pastime you are usually doing this as a recreation to relax and your mind in is a mode where you are half aware of what you are doing and half going within yourself and here is good way of, not meditating but, going within. You are shutting yourself off from the outside world, you are absorbed with what you are working on at that time whether it is absorbed in your garden, your painting, your needlework, in your craft work whatever.

Perhaps it is writing, you are writing words you do not know you are writing because they are coming to you from within yourself. You must try this, sit quiet - not sit quiet and hold a pencil or pen and think I am going to sit and write, I am going to write words which come from spirit, this is not the way to commence. You are putting ideas into your mind. The time will come when you feel you wish to sit and write. You will not necessarily think on this as if you are writing with spirit, you may think I will just sit and write a short note to somebody, or I will just sit and write a note of what I have done today, or I might just sit and write a list of whatever I have to do, whatever, you may wish to write a record of something. You will be writing without thinking what you are writing and the words flow, this is writing from within not with intent. There are many ways in which you can link with spirit without realising you are linking with spirit. You do not sit with an intent, you sit and drift into this situation and this is good because your mind is relaxed. When you sit with intent you are putting ideas into your mind, you sit and know it can happen, you are aware these things can happen but you are not demanding they happen, they happen naturally. Some of you have mentioned that you sit and talk to people and words come which will help them without your prior knowledge. This is another way of linking with spirit.

It is so natural. Spirit communication should be natural, it shouldn't be a show, it shouldn't be a performance, it should be as natural as breathing. It should be part of your everyday existence and it is but you often do not realise that you are literally hand in hand with spirit, it is very natural. It is not something which you have to sit at universities to learn the skill. It is something you know when you first come to earth. Children are with spirit without realising they are with spirit and as they grow in the material world they grow further away because they are taught it is strange to do things with spirit, it is not something that is discussed. It is so natural you do not know what you are doing. There are many in your world who actually link with spirit and are receiving advice, communication from spirit and passing this on to others and they do not realise, they are not aware. Many of your writers and those who give counsel and advice, those who write music and words do not realise how they work with spirit. If you dared to tell them they would be most indignant that these were not their thoughts and ideas. Do you often perceive when you read in the newspapers of your day or through communication through your radio wavelengths you hear the same story but it is coming from different directions. You may hear a piece of music that is very popular at this time but then you have another piece of music that is very similar and when you hear that you think that reminds me of something I heard yesterday, or there might be words put to it that sound familiar. You wonder why there is so many at the same time sounding similar. This is often, not always, because those who are talented enough to write these words or write this music are picking these vibrations up from the atmosphere around them and each are decoding this vibration in a different way but there is still a theme running through. This is why you have trends, you have fashions with your world it runs in trends and fashions. One year something is very topical, the next year something else is very topical whether it is music, literature, clothing, colours, design. This is because there is a time for everything and the energy and the vibration is released to earth for a reason and those designers of whatever purpose home in on this energy at this time and each portrays it in a slightly different manner. That particular year in your time that is fashionable for a reason. Perhaps your world needs a certain colour at that time so your fashion designers all seem to pick the same colour without realising because they keep their design secret, do they not? Often when they release their designs to the world you see many similarities. As you know colour and music vibrations are very similar, you may have a year when the melodies are very similar. In fact, there have been many instances in your world when your song writers and your musicians have complained that others have taken their work, this again is what is happening. Those who are talented in this field are picking the energies up and using them in their way but others thought it was their idea.

Everything is on a vibration and there is time for everything. There are periods of existence which are ordained to be and at certain times in the history of mankind events are steered in a certain direction for a certain reason. There is a vast plan which is far beyond most of us that comes from the higher realms for your world and for other worlds but you have enough to worry about with your world without worrying about other worlds. There is a plan for existence and if you look back through history you can see how the plan has unravelled and way into your future there are plans also which are already in existence because our time is in the future already. The future, past and present are as one.

QUESTION 41 - *Sophia answers question regarding subconscious and mind energy.*

It is good you ask questions on mind it makes your mind stretch, this is how you grow. Your minds are linking with each other do you realise? When you sit here you are not only talking to each other but even when you sit and do not speak you are still having communication with each other in your mind field. You answer each other's questions. Your subconscious is your mind which is attached to your physical mind, your subconscious makes sense of what happens to you during your daytime in your physical brain but I am talking about your higher mind field, mind energy that is better, your mind energy. You communicate with each other on a more spiritual level. You must not practice this with intent it is a natural function, if you think too much of this you bring in your conscious reasoning and you do not want to do this as it is a different level of communication. Although I have told you of this because it is good to know do not think too deeply on it because you will bring in your mindful reasoning and you do not wish to do this. It is better for your progress if you just let it happen naturally. You have sat for a while together, you are now linking good. You can do this when you are not in this room, you do not realise but you can because you are brothers and sisters. Not only do you link with those from spirit but you can link with each other.

Some teach that you need to contact one of your spirit helpers who would then contact one of your friends on earth but when you are close as you are, because you have sat together for a while this is not needed you can stretch your own energy to reach your brothers and sisters, as you can your human family because you are close. If you are involved in healing you can stretch out to your patients with your mind energy. You do this when you practice absent healing, you link. I am not telling you anything you do not know as you know of this already. It is something which is a very natural occurrence but as it is not a physical occurrence, it is something that does not enter your physical brain, you do not think too deeply of it.

I come to assist with mental thought this is why I am explaining to you the way you communicate on a different level, this is the field I chose to work within. I thought I would just come to say this to you but not to make you think too deeply of it, just so you are aware. Do not be concerned that because you can communicate with each other anything that is in your mind that is closed just to you will not be revealed to others. This is not the case there is a communication yes, but anything that you do not want to reveal to others, others cannot touch. You have this ability to communicate with each other. Although this may be new information to you for your physical brain it is not new information for your spirit, you have known of this from time infinite. Your spirit thought is in control without you realising so we do not have to educate you how to use this ability it is natural and as with your physical brain, your physical brain in control of your physical thoughts and your physical thoughts are put into words which make conversation with those whom you speak to on your earth. There are things in your physical brain which perhaps you would not tell others on earth so you would not put these into words so others would not hear these thoughts. It is the same with your spiritual mind, your spiritual mind is in control of your spiritual thoughts so those thoughts which you wish to communicate to others are communicated. Those which you wish to keep to yourself are not open to others. You are in control of your whole being your human being and your spiritual being. You are not used as a puppet, you are in control of your entire being both physically, mentally and spiritually.

Perhaps, some person on your earth has a physical illness where they are no longer in control of their body due to a disease or accident this does not affect their spiritual being, your spirit is still in control. It cannot be damaged, it cannot be harmed because it is not part of your human body, it is outside of your human body. I do not mean it is physically outside, I mean it is not part of your human body. Spirit has to be in control of spirit and whatever happens to your human body it cannot harm your spirit body or your spirit thought process.

Sophia was then asked 'Is the soul within the spirit or is the spirit within the soul?' These are names you give in your language to describe spirit or soul. What do you envisage with soul? What do you envisage with spirit? Your words whatever language, whatever tongue you speak you have to use a language and this language whatever makes so many confusions because you are trying to describe something that is intangible. You cannot say this is a 'coat', this is 'shoe', this is a 'glove', it is something you cannot visualise. It is something your various religions have taught you that you have and you try in your mind to visualise. As you come to earth you bring with you an infinite spark from spirit which is 'you'. Also you inherit from your ancestors another spark of the infinite which has carried on through the generations, a spark which has a life force, a creative force. With this you mingle your spirit life force from spirit. So you have what you call a soul which is your true self. Then this 'self' is encompassed with a human body, a human overcoat but also it is encompassed with a spirit essence, overcoat, whatever you wish to call it, which functions alongside your human thought power. You have your human brain which worries, frets and handles all your thought processes that your human body has to cope with. As well as this you have your spirit thought process which is part of you but also is above you because it is infinite, it does not stay behind when your body is no more. It encases what you are, what you have been and what you will be. This is going very deep and I do not want to say too much to confuse because as I am talking I am trying to use words within a human brain. I am using words from a human brain, to use a human voice, which will be listened to by human ears but at the same time I am also communicating on a different level and this is going directly to your spirit mind and this will be understood a lot clearer than that which is being spoken through the human frame.

Sophia was then asked a question by a sitter regarding what he perceived to be an 'etheric body'. Yes, you have what you perceive to be an etheric body. Let me take you on a journey - you are in your body now sitting in your chair and if the light in this room was on your friends would be able to look at you and would see your human body. They would not be able to see your spirit, they would not be able to see what you call an etheric body, they would just see your human body because they have human eyes. When you leave your human body behind when it is of no use to you anymore, you go home to spirit, your spirit essence goes with you. All that you have brought with you into your human body, all the experiences you have had during this existence, all your memories go with you to spirit. If you visualise a bright light leaving your body, this is the best way I can explain for any of you to understand. If you envisage a bright light leaving a dark shell behind, because you are leaving behind darkness in comparison to where you are going, it is bright, it is vibrant. Your body you have left behind is of no function any more, there is no life so it is dark compared to your spirit which is bright. This leaves your body and enters what you call 'spirit world' another existence, another dimension but not thousands of miles away on a far planet, just another dimension, just pull a curtain and you are there. Now this bright light which is your spirit enters your spirit world. Depending on who you are and what knowledge you have when you leave your earthly body you enter your spirit vibration at that level. If you are at a level where you and your understanding believe you will go into a atmosphere of peace, sleep this is what will happen to you. If you believe you are going home to spirit and you will see your friends and relations, this is what will happen to you. If you believe you will wake up in a garden surrounded by flowers, this is what will happen to you. This is how you leave your earthly body, this is the earthly thoughts you have and your earthly thoughts form a pattern. When you are in spirit you will meet those whom you know are there waiting for you and you will see them as you recall them to be except they will be a lot brighter, a lot more vibrant than you remember because they are spirit, they do not have the worries of earth and the concerns of earth to darken them.

When you have been in spirit a while you may wish to continue seeing them as bodies, as spirit people in a spirit bodies but according to your progress you may wish to dispense with body because you are spirit, they are spirit and you will look to communicate on a different wavelength, a different dimension and you will decode their essence as a light, a colour, a vibration but if you wish to perceive them as they were on earth you still can. They will have what you called an etheric body but that etheric body need not be there all the time. It can be there if you wish but if you do not wish you can just still know they are there, know their existence, recognise them for what they are, their thought, their energy, their love. You get a faint likeness of this on your earth, only very faint, when you are talking you have what you say a telephone. You pick your telephone up and you dial a number, perhaps you dial your daughter's number, you hear your daughter's voice and you can if you wish visualise your daughter, you can see your daughter in your mind what your daughter looks like. If you wish to be very inventive you can try and visualise what she is wearing that day, what colour she is wearing but if perhaps it was a quick phone call and you just wanted to talk to her very quickly you would just be communicating with your mind level there would be no picture. This is a very faint way of me trying to explain to you what spirit communication is like. You don't need the body but if you wish to have the body you can have it. You have an etheric body and no one can take that away from you it is there but if you do not wish to use it, it is not necessary. (06.04.97)

QUESTION 42 - The Vicar of Malmsbury telling us about spirit progression

There are many who share the truth that I preached at one time and although it is a truth which has deep foundation there are many more avenues open to those who wish to progress. There are many in our world that have not the vision to see beyond their earthly limitations. When they come to spirit there is so much more open to them and I endeavour to assist in this duty. I, myself have travelled the path so I understand their dilemmas and anxieties. It is to be of credit that those carry their faith so strongly because the faith is of importance but what can not be envisaged is that this faith also encompasses so many other beliefs also. Other religions of your world each having their own separate name, their own separate creeds and restrictions, also avenues for advancement. What is not realised is that so many of these religions are the same. We all strive for the same end. We just give that end a different name but we all travel the same path. It does matter that we have faith, we cannot say it does not, because this gives us strength of mind, of character and of spirit (the trinity). Without a faith many souls would be wandering and have no belief whatsoever. So it is important that there is a faith whatever the name. This assists during the earthly life and it also assists when the time comes to leave the body because they have belief that there is eternal life and this is of great importance for the transition to spirit. They are not frightened, they know there is eternal life but once in spirit it is time to shed the narrowness of the various religions and unite with others for the general belief of a divine power, whatever name that has been given.

There are many beliefs that the hierarchy of the next life is similar to the hierarchy of the earthly life where a soul has to be of a calibre to be able to ascend to great heights of progress. The class system which you have on the earth is of no importance in spirit. Those of humble birth are equal to those of the highest rank and it is not their positions or the influence of their peers which influences their progress in spirit. It is light within their spirit, their desire to progress, their love for one another. The love for giving of themselves for no return, not to give that you put yourself above others because you are benevolent, you give for the love for others. In spirit this continues, of course we do not have monetary funds to give but we give of ourselves, of our spirit. We give not for our own advancement, we give because we are wishing to see others enlightened but by doing this we are advancing ourselves. This is not the reason for this work, if we undertook this work for this reason we would not progress. There needs to be a genuine desire to assist our fellows and when they advance we are happy for them and when they falter we are there to assist and give them the strength and encouragement that is needed, not to discourage. Criticism is an earthly quality it is not of spirit. There are many who come through yours sittings who we are able to help.

We must all strive for a universal truth to shed aside the differences that confine. When one enters spirit there is much of earth that has been brought with that one. It is not a different existence where you change your character and your outlook. You bring with you what you have believed during your earthly existence and it is not for us to criticise and say this is not right. It is for that one to acclimatise themselves and to seek and then we can help and assist. They see the light of spirit around them, they become acclimatised to the different dimension and the different thought process, the different intermingling of vibrations. This opens up channels where they can stretch and seek but if they shut themselves from these vibrations they are suspended in their beliefs from earth and there is nothing we can do. They are not suffering, there is no hardship for them they are just happy in the belief they have brought with them and many continue this existence for some while. Eventually, slowly, through their surroundings they realise there is more to their existence than what they have believed so far. When this thought is sent out on their vibration we are able to filter through to them on this vibration and gently guide but you must not think that these one are suffering because of this, they are content in their belief. There is no progress for them, they are inanimate, they are in a vacuum.

You may ask why don't their families in spirit guide them and lead them but perhaps they have been brought up in the same religion as their families and their family are still locked in this situation also. So until there is a breakthrough whole communities can stay in this confine. (22.04.97)

QUESTION 43 - E-om-ba (assisted by Mafra) answering question, when spirit speaks through body of medium do they hear words spoken by sitters through physical ears or by another means?

It is going through ears but not physical ears, it is going straight into mind. You have to make sound it is not good you thinking words, because we are using human body. If we were not using human body you would not need to use voice but because we are using human body you have to make sound which makes vibration. The vibration is picked up from the medium. It comes through ears but also I am one step ahead, so I know what is coming but to get reaction through body it has to go through human process. I know what is coming but you have to speak words so that it can be absorbed in brain and brain can give response. If we were not using body that would not be necessary. Also, it is good because when there are several in room there are many thoughts going round and perhaps, even when numbers are small there are many thoughts in brains but you need say those words yourself so that you knew which question is to the fore. You have to think through, by speaking you are thinking through question and while you say one word your brain in working out the next word. Your muddle of thoughts is being put into some system to form sentence. Your thoughts are going round and round you know you have to make sentence of these so your mind is putting those thoughts into a way that can be understood. This is channelling question through you out of your voice. That voice then enters the medium as a clear statement not a muddle. If it was muddled you would not know what question you were asking, we would not know which question we would have to reply to. Your brain is multifunctional your conscious reasoning is thinking of the question which is in your mind at that moment but behind that there are other questions which are going round and round which you are not aware of.

Your brain is working out questions for you to speak later. Your brain is absorbing something it has heard previous and trying to slot this into knowledge you already have. If this does not fit in knowledge you already have your brain throws this out because it cannot absorb it and through throwing it out you are then making question of it. You could not absorb it because you have not the background knowledge to absorb it, so you throw it out as question 'why do I do this?', 'why do you do that?', 'I do not understand'. Instead of saying 'I do not understand this', 'I do not understand that' you make sentence so you are clarifying your thought process also. You do not understand how your brain works. You are aware of perhaps two or three things which you are not certain of and were thinking 'I must ask question about that, which one shall I ask first?' Beyond those two or three questions there is other absorption going on in brain from other knowledge you have amassed. Where you have amassed knowledge and you cannot slot it in, shall I say file, it is thrown out and it stays there in-between until it is explained to you more clearly, then you can put it away in file where you can open file when you need it. If you did not know which file to put it in you would not be able to take it out again.

The human brain is very complicated, many things going on at once which you do not know of. It works hard without you telling it. This is where there are problems when there is illness because the brain does not function as quickly as it should and thoughts go to wrong area and causes confusion. When there is confusion that makes anxiety, that make tension and that makes matters a lot worse. If you do not understand it is best not to worry let it go, it will come back again. Sometimes it is not destined that you should understand. These items you do not understand are left in suspension, thrown to one side, if it is not intended it is time to understand. If you do not understand everything do not be concerned. (22.04.97)

QUESTION 44 - Running Bear gives a deeper understanding of the way in which spirit communicates.

You sit in group, we are part of team. We work one way but other groups have their own team, they work their way, not one right, not one wrong but each work own way It is good to hear how others work. You realise then that you all strive for same end. What is right for one is not always right for other. You all walk path of light.

I understand there is confusion. You are confused as how one spirit visitor can talk through one medium and not another. There is a common link between those who come to talk with you who are on different level. You have those who are very close and are your mentors, these are assigned to you only, this does not mean you personally, your group. These will only come to your group and talk to your group, These at this moment in your earth life come through this medium and Mafra is in control. It is possible for those to talk through you (Paul) also because you are very close, same vibration and perhaps in time if others in your group become more advanced they will be able to do this also, but not at this moment in your time.

There are others who come to visit who are not mentors. They are visitors, helpers, friends, guides but not mentors, not so closely linked.

These can visit you and also visit other groups. Others can come from other groups to visit. Some of your group will not wish to go to other groups to visit, some will need to for own experience. It is not good for those learning to stay under one master, they need other masters, other experience. We have told you we are training teachers and teachers have to know how to work in all circumstances with all questions, all thoughts, all levels of understanding. They must travel to other areas to see how others work before they decide to choose their path. They will choose path of own, this may not be during your life time but maybe in times to come. Maybe in your life time but they will return to you also to greet you because they are friends and have made link and are happy for help they have been given by your friends.

When a visitor comes to your group they are under the control of Mafra. When one of your helpers/friends visit other groups they must be under the control of the leader of that group. They may not wish to talk in that group, they may wish to just sit and absorb energy vibration. We must allow others to come because they gain knowledge but we come later to give little bit more information. It is not that they give incorrect knowledge but they do not give the depth. (6/5/97)

QUESTION 45 - Sister Celeste explains how Running Bear teaches on different levels.

He was teaching on different level. There is teaching where you are talking direct and giving information but there is also teaching where you are discussing, this is different. This takes different energy level, it is as if you are talking of subject and someone interrupts and you are diverted from that subject to another subject. This is good in discussion group but this time he wanted to relay all the facts because if only half the facts were told it would not be the complete pattern of events. Discussion evenings are good because this enables them all to take part. It is good to talk direct from spirit but people do not have concentration to listen for a long while they lose where they are, their mind goes off in another direction. It is good when you have group that you have short questions and short answers and go on to another question and another answer. (6/5/97)

QUESTION 46 - A visitor from the high realms gives their wisdom linking with Sophia.

I come from a different dimension of spirit. there is great light but I am back in dark, it is a different vibration. There is much for everyone to learn. Our vibration is quick, I have to slow down because spirit vibration is quick. There is much to learn of spirit, very very wise things to learn. It is very good to learn but you will not understand them unless you have taken lessons before. So you must not jump lesson because you would be given knowledge and it would be no good. I will try and take you through stages but I first have to lean to talk to you but there is much for you to learn.

There has been many questions asked of other worlds, this is good because your world is only part of a vastness. You cannot learn of other dimensions until you have been to different levels of understanding. There is much to learn but we have to take it slowly. Your world is only a very small part of a vast, vast plan. Spirit is another dimension but there are many dimensions of spirit, many higher dimensions and these link with other parts of your vast universe but you do not understand what I say because you are not in that position yet to understand. It is good to stretch but slowly, slowly.

We are spirit, you are spirit and I am spirit, earth is only one existence which we leave behind. It is more important what is to come than what has gone. There is much energy in your world in which you exist. You have to learn of your energy in your world before you can learn of other parts of your universe. Much of your world you don't understand still and much of your own mind you don't understand. Unless you understand your own mind and your own world you do not stand much chance of understanding others. You exist in a physical level, you need your oxygen but also your spirit level needs it's own spirit oxygen to exist, it's own life force. This is special for your minds from your world, this life force, this life energy is for your world only not for other parts of your universe. That is for future talk. There is a problem when there is a clash of energies.

I will come again and try and lead you slowly but it is best you understand about your circumstances before you jump ahead to others because it would cause too much confusion in your brain and that would cause problems with your reasoning. This is where you have many problems with people on your earth when they delve into other things. There is no evolution, there are missing chapters so this causes disturbance in brain. This is why sometimes when you ask questions you are not given answers. It is not that whoever is answering does not know, they are not disclosing information because it would not be right.

Your world is timed in years, it is many of these years since I was in your vibration. I have used Sophia as a link as her work is involved on thought vibrations. I do not recognise anything of your earth conditions. (22.04.97)

QUESTION 47 - Kimyano speaking of colour vibration.
I like colours, bright colours. It would be good if you understood colour, colour opens the door for you because colour is vibration, we are a vibration so we link with colour. It is just a step for us. Once you understand colour vibration you will find it a lot easier to open door to link with spirit. In your meditation you travel to your garden or perhaps another location, think of the colour in that place. If you sit on the grass or on the beach look at the sunshine, the sun is gold, the sky is blue, the ground is green or yellow depending on where you sit, the rocks, stones or pebbles are different colours. Different coloured birds, butterflies, animals. and absorb the colour and vibration.

Colour is very important because it is us, we are vibration but you are colour also. You are colour in your energy, in your thoughts. You send thoughts, thoughts are energy, thoughts are vibration which turn to colour as they leave you and go off wherever. You must think of sending out good colour not dull colour. The more love sent the more vibrant your colour, the more positive your thought the brighter the colour. You send healing with love, that is good, you send knowing that healing is going so that is good, that makes colour brighter. It is knowing that makes it easier for us to help. If you visualise the one you are sending healing to, visualise their face and surround their face with colour that helps. If you want to go to the part of the body where healing is needed, visualise that part of body and put colour around there and send it. It is like key it opens door. We do not like dark colours. It is good to have a dark colour but you must have a bright colour with it, that is good. All colour has energy, even greys, but if you put bright colour with the dark colour you have more energy because you have contrast. It takes one vibration from the other and makes stronger energy. The bright colour bounces off the dark colour so the energy becomes more vibrant. In your fashions you see patterns, perhaps if you had curtain and your curtain was all one colour. Perhaps it is red, very good red very bright, but if you put red on a black background it would become brighter because it would bounce off of the dark colour. Black is no good on it's own but helps to assists other colour to reflect energy.

It is good when you consider the soft tones and you merge them together, not what you call your primary colours, your more pastels colours which are merged from other colours. Similar colours, perhaps you have pink, mauve and blue and they merge together because they are compatible because they have the same colours in them. This is like people, like attracts like. People who have the same interests, the same beliefs, the same energy within them merge together and are compatible as your colours which have the same energy within them. One assists the other. It is the same with your animals, you have your animals in the wild and you have your pets. In other countries you have animals which live in same area sharing the same colour. Those which share same colour are safe but if you have one which contrasts there is a problem because it stands out and others can see. (22/4/97)

QUESTION 48 - E-om-ba Talking about the springtime.
It time of awakening for your land and this makes energy, earth gives off energy. It is vibrant, everything is new and energy comes from earth. Your animals and birds they feel energy, they are close to nature. They are more active, they feel vibration, they are closer to nature. It is time of rebirth. As your plant life and foliage awake from sleep they give off vibration. During your cold time they are waiting, there is life still but life is submerged, cannot be free. When warmth and sun filter through this begins awakening and gradually more awakens. It is like chain, more awakens and more and more energy. It is good time for those who need healing because energy is good. Your earth is awakening and energy is moving quickly. The vibration is quick so when healing is needed response is quick. It is good time for mending. If you have cut on body, hand, whatever your body will mend quick. So it also good time for healing because your body is responding so when energy is given to body for healing purposes your body will react quickly and accept. Sometimes when healing is given it takes a while of your time for body to respond because body is very depleted. Your body is depleted after winter but as earth gives off energy so you absorb energy and body also awakens and vibration in body is quickened. Your reactions are quicker.

Sometimes this time of year you are vibrant but you are so vibrant you have to be quietened, so you sometimes feel tired. This is because your body has absorbed energy and is reacting too fast and you over react, you want to be here, you want to be there and you are becoming acclimatised to vibration. Eventually you will find level of vibration which is good for you. You revitalise but there is a period of adjustment because everything is lively and if you absorb energy too quickly you burn out quickly. You do not have to rush so much. Because you feel vibration you want to be here, you want to be there, you want to be everywhere and your body is tired after your time of winter when you had not so much light and you had to fight various coughs, colds and illnesses. Although it is good to see sun and feel vibration enjoy vibration, enjoy your colours, enjoy the surge of energy that is around you but enjoy and relax with it. Do not become too vibrant because you will not feel the benefit as you go farther into your year.

There is much healing at this time of year, all new greens, blues and yellows give off energy also, the energy from your ground. (27.04.97)

QUESTION 49 - Mafra explaining that spirit persons communicating still have their own ideas and use their experiences to explain their understanding. He now responds to question which was in a sitter's mind 'If someone had conflicting views to Mafra would Mafra tell you their views?'
You see I am here as messenger and it depends on what views. If it is something very personal, my own (Mafra's) views do not come into this, I am just messenger from one to another. If it was something spiritual that would be very different. That one would not be communicating with me because our vibrations would be different. So we would not have this to overcome. Although we vary in ideas, you see E-om-ba comes from a different background to myself and his views when on earth in his last existence were different from mine in my last existence. Because we come to talk to you in a body we take on our last identity because we have to take on an identity to come through a body. At heart E-om-ba and myself are same but our experiences were different. E-om-ba lived a lot more with nature than myself so he understands the vibrations of nature a lot more than I would in my last existence but at heart the truth we bring is the same. We just came a different road to that truth. We would not give conflicting truths. This is how we progress, we progress on that vibration. So those whom we contact who are on higher realms are still on same vibration but are more evolved but we would stay on same vibration and take that route.

Your experience on earth is different from ours so perhaps you can teach us something. Now this is a surprise to you because we teach of spirit but you are in contact with the spirit of others whom you travel with on your path of life. So you bring to your meeting here ideas that you have perhaps taken on from those whom you have walked with on your earthly existence. We are trying to help earth so we need to know what questions are being asked, what worries you have, what anxieties you have. By having this contact with you we are in contact with others on earth and we are able to help where it is needed. We learn from you, you learn from us. It is no good us coming to help if we talk of times gone by which are of no use to you, we need to help you in the life you are treading now. There has to be a continual advancement if we are going to walk hand in hand. It is similar on your earth when an elderly relative sees a young child in their family perhaps only at Christmas and no other time during the year and tries to talk to that child, they do not know what to say or how to start because there is no link between them, they have not walked everyday with that one. If we try and talk to you and have had no contact with you in your world we would not be talking same language, I do not mean your tongue language I mean your spiritual language. Also it is good for us to experience what you experience because we are not always serious, we wish to know what you do, we wish to be part of your learning but also part of your fun. If you have new things to take your attention we wish to experience this also.

You note that I understood you to say that when E-om-ba talked to you, you were surprised that he was a happy man, you thought he would be serious. You see he comes as his last vibration on earth but he is spirit so what you are perceiving is not the body he last had but his real self.

It is sometimes difficult when your visitors come and they have to slow down their communication because the vibration in spirit is very fast and they try to talk and they are saying their last word before their first word because earthly communication is very slow compared to the speed of our communication. Earth vibration is slower and denser. If they have not been in body for a long while they also have to experience body before they can even communicate.

Mafra was asked to give guidance on how to develop awareness of colour vibration. - You absorb the energy vibration this is how we communicate in spirit we absorb the energy vibration and then decode whatever vibration it is. This is similar to the colour because vibration is colour, colour is vibration. With your colours that you have it is good not to worry about name for colour because it is like name for person, it is just a tag, just an identity. What really matter is the vibration of your person, so with colour ignore name of colour first of all. First of all have your colours, look at your colours in the light not in dark and absorb the colour, I would say drink in colour. Feel the vibration from the colour with your senses, your touch and your eyes. Absorb the colour and become used to the colour and when you see that colour you feel that energy, then put that colour down, pick up another colour, clear your hands rub your hands, clear one energy from your hands, look, feel the energy from this new colour, forget about previous. Do this for each colour and then discuss with each other what energy feels like for which colour. Have colour in front of you, do not give it a name and put that colour on table, say 'I feel so and so with that colour' and see how you compare. Then when you become more accustom you can then give colour name. This is not a thing to hurry, if you wish you could just do one colour a week, there is no hurry you have long while to learn so there is no need to rush and try to confine yourself to time which you have on earth. We have no time so be like us, enjoy the experience, get to know each colour in turn and the energy and the vibration of each colour. The more thorough you are the deeper it penetrates and you will understand colours, it will grow. You will be able to close your eyes and see colour and feel the vibration of colour but we are going a few steps ahead. The exercise is not to learn colours because this is something you do as a child at school, you learn what colour is which, a house has a red roof and a green door. We are not teaching you colours, we are teaching you vibration and energy so name does not matter. If this does not come quickly do not worry take it slowly. (27.04.97)

QUESTION 50 - Golden Ray (Visitor from higher realm) gave this name as the nearest interpretation of her vibration. She gives wisdom.
You do not realise how much goes from your group out to where it is needed. Much energy is created and your spirit helpers are able to take to where the need is greatest. There is no boundary to where, there is no limitations to how far love can stretch because it is a sincere wish that you wish to help other creation. Your love is able to go on the path of light to many areas where help is needed. Many places in your world that are troubled. All humanity, children or adults, or the animal kingdom, to those of the realms which are not of earth who are in darkness your love is able to penetrate.

You may wonder why your love is needed because there is so much already in spirit but you are also spirit. You have body but your home is spirit so what you are actually doing, you are uniting again with your spirit energy which was yours before you came to your earth and you are able on this vibration to send pure love to where this is needed. You are not sending it as a human form you are sending it as a spirit form. You are here to experience your world that you live in but you are spirit. For a moment of your earth time, your spirit which is within is taking precedence and you are using this spirit, as you used it before you had body, to assist where love is needed. So you see we are not using your human body, you are uniting with us, you are joining us as a spirit to send love.

This is a question often asked why do those in body need to send love when there is so many in spirit who can do this, but you are spirit also so you are joining with your spirit family and assisting your spirit family in their work. Because you have earthly body you are making contact with those on earth who are in need. Those are brought to your attention who are travelling path with you so you have a direct link which is of assistance when you are asked to send love. You are joining with your spirit family and sending this love, you are not sending this love on your own. There is no divide from spirit, you are part of family although you wear human body you are still part of the spirit family and this link is not severed. While you are in your human reasoning your knowledge of spirit family is no more because you need to live your earthly existence and you cannot be part of two vibrations when you are involved in your material world. Your spirit is within but is part of you it is subdued but when you lay aside your worries and anxieties of your human world there is reversal. Your human side is quiescent and your spirit part of yourself comes to the fore and you are able then to link with your spirit family and be part of them because the link is never severed.

If you take an example of your earthly life, you have family, you may have many members to a family and some members of that family may travel away from their home and while they are away from home they live a different life, a different existence. They have to sever some of their links with their family, there may be thoughts to the family but their attention has to be on the life they are leading in the different part of your world. When that task or whatever is finished they can come back to family and it is as before. They are still part of family but they bring back with them new thoughts, new ideas, new experiences so this is the same as you and your spirit family. The link is never severed you are always part of them but you draw away from them when you have your human contacts but there is always that link and you are as one when it is needed. This is why they draw close, it is not so much they drawing close as you draw close to them. You are taught by your churches that spirit draws near to you. it not so much they drawing near as you shutting down your mundane world and drawing near them. There is not a spirit world and human world it is just another dimension, there is no difference you are part of family but your awareness of spirit family is quietened, is subdued while you have to live your human existence. It is not them drawing close it is you linking back with them.

I must stress it is so important that you live in your world you must not live in spirit world because you are not of spirit world in this existence. This is when there are problems when too much of your time in your journey on earth is taken out of your journey to return to spirit. Because you are spirit and all those whom you encounter in your world are spirit wearing human clothing you are able to link with them. You see now why some whom you encounter you feel content with and some you do not feel quite so content with. You see it is your spirit trying to find it's own level, it's own vibration and compatible vibrations. When you meet someone, you meet them you look at them with your human eyes and you talk to them with your human voice, you exchange your words but above all this your spirit part of you is linking and your spirit knows immediately whether they are on same vibration as yourself. There is sometimes a thought coming into your mind, you are not at ease with that one. This is your other upper level of consciousness linking together but you may meet that one at another time in your existence and then you feel more compatible, this is because you have both walked a bit further along your road and you are perhaps at different levels of vibration. (13.05.97)

QUESTION 51 - Question to Mafra asking whether it is a problem if a sitter touches the medium whilst in trance.

There is no problem as long as we are prepared. It depends on who is here, I am able to adjust. If you touched me accidentally there would not be a problem because I am able to adjust but some who have not had so much experience of coming to a body and when they are new to body, coming for first or second time, they were only just becoming aware of the condition of the body. Your sense in your body is something different than what we experience in our world, our vibration is very quick so everything is magnified, a slight touch is much greater. As we become accustom to being in the body we are accustomed to the vibration of the body and we slow our vibration down to accommodate your human condition but those who come for the first or second visit still come on a very quick vibration and have not lowered themselves to the human level. So their senses are quicker than your senses and they respond quicker to your human vibration. If there was noise it would seem louder to them than it would to you. Sometimes when you have noise outside your room you do not hear but those who are in this body do hear and for a moment they may not talk to you or they may hesitate. You see it is becoming accustomed to the human condition again. We would not allow anything untoward to happen because I am here to protect. If there was a condition that there was someone here for first or second visit and something untoward happened in your physical condition and that one was not able to cope I would step in immediately. I would not leave that one to cope, for reason your one and our one, they both have to be protected. (13.5.97)

QUESTION 52 - E-om-ba was asked question, when someone moves from a home where there were a lot of links with people who are now in spirit, what happens to the spirit vibrations linked to the building and the person who is moving from that building? Do they need to be welcomed to the new environment?

There is no need to welcome, it is good to welcome but no need because where you go they go but if you wish to place picture, flowers or whatever to say 'welcome' that is good, it will be appreciated. They will be there for you. They attach to building because of vibration in the building not the bricks of building, it is the vibration of the building, the vibration of what has happened and what is happening in the building. As you leave the building you take with you memories, you take with you emotion, love, sadness, all you have experienced. You take with you memories of your children when they were small, memories of your children when they had grown this is all part of memories of house you do not leave those memories behind, you take them with you, these are part of you. Also, they are part of those who are close to you, so where these memories are they are. They would visit the building but they may visit building because of interest because we have interest in what was ours when we had body and for a while we will visit if there is a reason but if there is no reason for us to return we would not go.

I would not wish to go back to my home, no, not now, no. I have my home with me, I bring it with me as it was in my memory. I can build that in my memory. I could have it here as it was. You, my friends, if you wish to live in house you had when you were children you could build that in your mind and that would be there. That house would now be altered in your physical world, they change colour, they change door, they change window but you would have it as it was, they cannot take that away. Each of you have your own memory of your experiences as you walked through your world. Some you wish to not remember and you put to back of your mind because for reason you do not want to remember but it is still there, something will occur and that memory will come to fore. You would put it back again and bring forward memory you prefer to keep. Nothing is gone because it is part of you, it has made you, you but there is much to look forward to in future we must not talk of looking back. We must look to future, we and you, because we have future also. Our future is with us now but we progress.

A SUPPLEMENTARY QUESTION WAS ASKED - Do you look forward to your future, your progression? - We have our path of destiny as you have your path of destiny. When you come home to spirit you must not think 'I home, I put my feet up'. No, we have much work ready for you. You plan and you walk path if you wish. If you wish to stay in one phase you will stay in one phase. Many do not wish to progress or may stay for long while and then decide there is something different they want to try. You see, we have future but it is not as your future because you measure your future in days, weeks, years. We do not have time, we have hopes, ambitions, we strive to learn but not in time. We know our path, you do not always know your path it is clouded for you, you think you know then something will stop and you will have to change path. This is because you are in a material world. In spirit it is different, we choose path and we travel path, so we know future but we are not at future because we have to learn as you have to learn.

This is difficult for me to say. I try to give example, that would be better. When someone comes home to spirit they are greeted by loved ones, after time of adjustment the one that comes to spirit finds their path where they have left path to come to earth. They are on path, then there is much love with helpers and members of group, because they are all part of a group family in spirit. They then may wish to gain more knowledge, perhaps they decide they want to become teacher, this is just an example, so they then travel path to learn to become a teacher. This is different from when they were on earth because in spirit you know you will become a teacher, on your earth path this depends on whether you pass this exam, that exam, whether something stops you, you have not enough money but in spirit you wish to do something you can achieve. So your future is there already but you still have to go through learning process. This is why we bring ones to you to learn because you learn so much in spirit with those very close to you, those who walk path with you but also those from higher realms who can help but we sometimes need to bring those who are learning back to earthly condition to experience a condition on earth. This enables them to understand better the conditions they have to work with. (11/5/97)

QUESTION 53 - *Kimyano was asked if the sitters concentrate with colour vibrations how can it assist spirit communication?*
It provides energy for us to send your love to those in need. You see, the more energy you create, it provides momentum. You start with healing colour which is good because it send healing to those in need on the colour vibration but what you send also returns in other cycle. You are always making more energy and this energy then makes different energy, first it is healing energy, healing is sent throughout your evening but also other energy is created. Healing energy is very similar to energy needed to move your table, it is not the same but similar. It is a lively vibration. You start off with healing then energy is divided into energy for healing and energy for use with table. Because you are opening your minds we are able to link with your minds and come closer so you are perceiving spirit easier. You may not realise this but you are all of you, we are that much closer to all of you because you have opened mind more intently with a desire. You have desired to send love and there is nothing greater than love. Your mind is open on love vibration, so spirit is able to come very, very close and as you are learning to perceive spirit more and more you will be able to communicate with us, pick up our vibrations more and more, and sense us with you. It is good for you and good for us because we are a team, we work together so we can link.

You must remember that there is nothing greater than love. There are different kinds of love, there is love for love's sake, love for duty, love for man for lady or lady for man. There is love from the heart which doesn't wish for reward, a desire to help, that is greatest of all love. Sometimes you give love because you feel you should give love, that is good but not as good as genuine sincere love to help. Many, many kinds of love. You see the word 'love' what does it mean? It means so many things, your words do not describe. You say 'love' but love means so many kinds of love. It is just a small word but a word which has so many meanings. It is a word which is used many times in your world, in your communications that you read and on your pictures that you watch but it means so many different things. It can be changed to mean what people want it to mean. This is an example of what vibration is and what vibration is turned into when you try to give it a name. That is just one word and there are so many words in your language which all have different meaning and different levels. You take word 'friend' that can mean so many different things. Language is very difficult, it was the same with my language we had the same problem. All countries have problems explaining what they mean in their heart.

When you talk to your fellow men and ladies, whom you walk with, you do not always want to tell them what you have in your heart so you make word to fit. It is not so in spirit, we send vibration and we communicate on vibration, there is no pretence. There is no reason for pretence because we do not need to pretend, we learn from each others of our desires, our wishes, our hopes, our energy, we share. We share with others, there is no this is your's, this is mine, we share. In your earth body you have to build a shell around yourself to protect because there are so many other vibrations that can hurt you, both physically and spiritually. So as you go through life you build a shell around and you pretend to be someone other than you are because you are frightened of being hurt. You have been hurt in past and you are frightened this experience will come again so you build a shell. This is not so in spirit because we are on different levels, those whom we are with are all our level and we would not wish to hurt each other. As we descend to other levels we have cloak of protection. As you sit you ask for cloak of protection, so you link with the level which is compatible with your level. It is important that you do this because you do not wish to be harmed by other influences not of your level.

Kimyano was then asked by a sitter who had been told there were seven levels in spirit, was this correct? - There are many, each level is divided into other levels. Seven is a magic number, magic is what you have made, what man has made. Many things are divided into seven and as your ancestors have built your civilisation the number seven has had meanings in all religions and before religions as you know them, when there was time what you would call magic. It was not magic it was spirit, there was natural worship, natural communication with spirit which now has been lost through civilisation. The number seven has come through many generations and has evolved with you. As you have evolved this number seven has come with you. Seven is a number which is a sign of spirituality.

When your earth was young and there was many forms of natural worship the number seven took an effect in this worship so there became superstition that seven was to be respected and looked up to. As this is in your mind all through your generations seven has been created by your civilisation as something special. So, you today in your world, through all your ancestors going back to when time began have created seven as something important. To your civilisation it is important. As you know when you come to spirit you bring with you your thoughts and your experiences so when you come to spirit you still expect seven to be special. So when someone from spirit returns to earth to tell of spirit life they try to explain to you something which is very special, something which is very precious so they say seven, because seven has been created by many generations as being something special. In spirit there are many levels of progress, advancement, I do not know the top because I am nowhere near the top, it goes on infinite. Seven is a number which is good to look to because it is as far as you can visualise. If we said 107 you would have difficulty but 7 is far enough away for you to aspire to but too close for you to think 'I am nearly there'. As you go a level there are seven more. I am nowhere near 7 x 7, To answer your questions, yes there are seven levels, but there are seven more, and seven more and those sevens are divided into seven more. (11/5/97).

There are other numbers which have devised as not being good numbers, and others which have been associated with bad things. These have come through generations and generations and you have created them in your mind, I say you but I also because I also trod path.

QUESTION 54 - Hanns talking about healing experimentation using combinations of vibrations and his work in this field.

I still work with experiments but this time not with chemicals but with vibrations, mix what will go together, work out best way to work. Not vibration for communication. Vibrations for attacking infection, healing process. Our vibration when we are asked to assist, we have to formulate a system which attacks disease but it is not the same for each person. Each person is different so the vibration has to be altered to adjust to each level of vibration. Your doctor gives the same medicine to each patient for same illness, it is no good for us to do this. We have to find vibration for each person different, so this is where we experiment. Sometimes we have to work with body that does not want to recover. If body does not want to recover it is not easy for us to work so we have to adjust to attack other part of body. I will try to explain a little clearer. You have body of a person who has a illness, for example they have a sore on their leg which will not heal, we construct formula of vibration which would heal leg but the more we heal the leg the worse the leg becomes. So we know the formula is not working. We have to look for the reason why the formula is not working, the reason is inside the person does not want the leg to heal, they still want the leg to be bad. There may be many reasons, they may want the attention, maybe not wanting to return to work, maybe unhappy. We have to then find the reason why the leg is not getting better, then we send a different formula of vibration to the reason in psyche why they do not want to recover. We must heal that part first, then when that part is healed we then go back to the leg and make the leg better. Then leg will heal.

It is not just a case of healing bad part of body we have to heal what has caused bad part of body. Your doctors do not do this, they treat symptom not disease. This is why so many times disease is treated but another disease comes because there is imbalance in the body. That one cannot cope for a reason so we have to find why they cannot cope. Quite often reason is there is no love, they need love. So we send much love to make that one happy then the vibration is lifted and the vibration responds to our healing. You see, I still experiment and when it does not work I continue until it does work. Hanns is not beaten.

This is a lesson for you, when you send healing thoughts, first send a lot of love to surround that one, encircle with love. Then direct healing to part which is bad. Love first so it uplifts then treat the part which is bad. Treat whole body with love, gentle love but when attack disease then it is a different vibration not love. The vibration to rid disease, tell disease 'out of body, not wanted'. A more determined vibration 'the body does not want you - go'. Do not send love to bad part because you will make disease grow, you say 'out, do not want, go'. Draw it away from body, go but do not keep it yourself let it go. You do not want it. Then close with love again. This depends of course on the problem, this system is of no use if there is a broken bone or similar. That would need a different formula, that needs to help knit the bones together, to mend. You have to be careful where you direct thoughts as to the reason for the problem. This is why I say every treatment is different, every disease, every person different. If you build love for that one they can treat their own illness, they are nearly there to rid themselves. (20/05/97)

QUESTION 55 - John Lyon explaining how we link with our spirit family.

There was a visitor came who spoke from a higher level of existence, this one has been through many levels of spirit since they had an earth body and they came and talked. I will try and endeavour to put into words what was communicated although my existence in spirit has not been so long my progression is far less than theirs. I will try and portray a little of what they said.

When you communicate with spirit you sit in a human body and you perceive that spirit has come to join in with your little group as if you had opened the door of your room and you greeted them and welcomed them in. If we look at this in a different perspective. You are in fact a human body sitting in this material world, in a material room. Your human body is made of skin, bone, flesh, organs, whatever. Nevertheless, because of the knowledge you have amassed in your searching and seeking through your time with spirit you have become aware that within your human existence there is also your spirit existence. Your spirit existence was spirit before it took on the human body you have at this moment of your time. That spirit existence has been in existence through many experiences of your earth life, various earth lives and through much progress in the spirit realms. Each time your spirit leaves spirit to take on a body it comes to experience the life it is to live and returns home to a spirit family. You are part of a spirit family.

Take your mind back to when you were part of a family with brothers and sisters in a home with a mother and a father. As the family grew, one by one the brothers and sisters left home and went their own ways. There were times, perhaps, when they did not communicate with their family for various reasons but they were still part of that family. Occasionally they would come back to that family, maybe at a time of celebration or maybe even a time of sadness. They would come back and be part of that family. If you compare that with your spirit existence, you have left your spirit family to take part in your earthly life but you know you will go back to your spirit family. While you are here in this room communicating with spirit you still have your human body but you have thrown aside all your physical worries, all your physical cares and by doing this you have released the spirit that is within you. So that spirit is able to link with those from your spirit family. It is not so much your spirit family coming to greet you, you have gone home to them for a short while. Even though you are in your human body you are united because there is not one world and another world, it is together, it is just a separate dimension.

It is another way of looking, instead of looking at a mirror and seeing your reflection you are looking through the mirror and seeing what is behind the mirror. You ask are they still here listening to you? You are part of that family, that group and all those who talk to you and communicate to you and come and visit you may not be part of your family but they are on the same level, the same vibration. As you have your earthly family with the mother, father and children, you also have your uncles and your aunts with their families, this is similar you have the same vibration but different families.

A sitter then asked a question regarding dreams. There are various reason for dreams. You have your subconscious which when you enter the world of sleep your subconscious tries to make sense of what has occurred in your physical world during your day. Perhaps, not this day, it may be a day gone past. If your subconscious does not make sense of your experiences of one particular day your subconscious will return to that situation again and again until it does make sense in other periods of your sleep. Dreams are very much linked to your subconscious.

Having said that you do have other dreams which are different, you can describe them as being more vibrant, more real, a different dimension. These are linked to experiences in the dimension which you call spirit, where you link strongly with those from the realms of spirit, you are one with them again. There are two reasons for dreams, one is a purely physical reason it is your subconscious making sense of all the problems and upheavals you have experienced, also the nice things the pleasures. Also, there is the other dream state. These dreams you often remember a long while afterwards and they are very vivid and usually pleasant memories where colours are vibrant and the experience is a happy one. These are quite often linked to experiences with your spirit friends. Also, there is another reason, you sometimes travel from your body to be with someone in your world who is in need of perhaps, healing or comfort, or perhaps just a memory link and you could be with them while you are asleep. You may come back and have a memory of that one and you think it is a dream but it is a dream but you were actually with them exchanging on a thought vibration some occurrence. You might have relived something which you did with them in the past. This is the exchange of memory. You can be very busy travelling to many places and still stay in your bed. You should not come back exhausted, if you do this is wrong. (18.05.97)

QUESTION 56 - Sister Celeste answering a question on how important it is to open up correctly when communicating with spirit and asking for 'Cloak of Protection ' to be put around sitters and medium This followed an article in the newspaper regarding a person who had experienced rather strange communication resulting in traumatic results.

The one involved has opened themselves to a level which is not good and once there is this link it is very difficult to separate what you call an attachment. It can be withdrawn but this needs help from those that are higher evolved. When this occurs that one is shutting themselves away from higher levels who could assist, we only visit where we are invited. It is not for us to intrude where we are not welcome. There are two reasons: one is we must not interfere with another's destiny and another reason is we have to protect ourselves. There are those in our realms who's work is to assist with such problems and this is specialised work, they have to learn how to cope and how to protect themselves. It is not for any existence in our spirit realms to go to that circumstance, it is only for those who are skilled because once we touch these ones who are on a lower level of evolution we have to be careful not to bring this back with us. There is not evil as you would envisage with your stories that you hear, it is just a lower level of evolution. As we have evolved, we have evolved for a reason not just for our own satisfaction, we have evolved for our progress but also for our destiny and for the work we are involved with. If we go backwards we are causing problems for all those whom we are striving to assist, we cannot perform our duty on our own level. It is a specialised, dedicated work to assist with these lower levels of evolution and those who choose to take this work must be very strong.

Those of us who do not do this work we have evolved on another level and our work involves us being calm, placid, sympathetic but we must not be strong in that way, we must be gentle. This is the vibration we work on. Those who work on the other level are high evolved spirits, they are not spirits who are lower than us they may be higher but they are on a different vibration, a stronger vibration. We would not be compatible, we would not be strong to help and assist. We would only hinder the work, we assist with our prayer as we have been trained when we had body, we had been trained to send prayer where it is needed, so this is how we can assist. We send out our love and our strength to those who are working in this field, we ask for strength for them. They in turn are made stronger with not only our prayers (vibration) but other vibrations which enable them to help those who are in this situation. If it is an earthly condition they also need an earthly link not a spirit link on its own, there has to be an earthly link to make the connection. There are not many that are dedicated enough in the earth world, and strong enough. There are many that are aware of spirit and would like to help but sympathy is not enough, this is dangerous. So many can be pulled to this level through their wish to help but not with the understanding that is needed. They cannot detach themselves. Often these are sympathetic people and they wish to help and assist but they are pulled into this whirlpool of emotion and many find they cannot disentangle themselves. It can happen quite innocently without realising.

This is why your priests and your fathers are against what they say is dabbling with the occult because of such consequences. They have in their experience been involved in occurrences which are not good and unfortunately, this through generations of your Christianity has grown to a total disassociation with connection with spirit because of the experience they have had. When this occurs it has been the ordained ministers of the church that have been sent for to assist, so you can understand their opposition to contact with spirit because they have only seen the side that has involved themselves. They have seen at first hand the manifest problems that have occurred and the damage it has done not only to the physical body of the one who is involved but also to the spirit of the one within Also, the damage it has done to many others who are in the area concerned, those who wish to assist have been pulled in through love and ignorance of not knowing how to protect themselves. Although, there is misunderstanding between the church of Christendom and other religions you can see how this has occurred.

Unfortunately many people take their contact with spirit as a adventure, a means of excitement. They do not know what they are embarking on. This should be done with reverence and sincerity, seeking for truth not for pastime pleasure. You are aware that when the earth life is no more and the spirit returns to spirit they go with their own level of progress they do not suddenly become higher in the evolutionary scale. So if someone goes to spirit in torment with many problems with not good ideals this goes with them. Then they are not happy in their new surrounding and they try to find a way of returning to earth to influence those who are there, to try and fulfil what they have not succeeded in accomplishing. They do not realise there is progress open in another direction, they just want to continue what they were involved in before. They cannot do this in the spirit world because there is no room for such occurrences so their only way is to return and this is where these weak souls who, perhaps mean good are led astray and are linked with those who wish to influence them.

Going back to your original question, once this has occurred there is never time to give up hope, there is always an opportunity if only that one can be surrounded with the right influences.

You can understand why your clergy are opposed to communing with spirit only through themselves because they have seen through many generations how not good can come. They do appreciate that good can come from communion because they hold communion in their own services and they hold healing but this is why they ordain it is only through their own church and through those who are ordained. You, yourself, who have experienced communication with spirit and have had evidence of how close spirit is and the influence spirit can have as a link with the human world. If you witnessed someone on a different level meddling with spirit without knowing, you like your clergy, would be opposed and would advocate that they only came through those who are trained to deal with these circumstances. Unfortunately it is like a magnet these ones draw sympathy and those who are sympathetic are very gullible and they feed on such vibrations. The church has it's rituals, it has it's pomp, it has it's ceremony which if you are not used to this, you would think it is just for the sake of show, just for the sake of egos but you can understand a little now how your church has evolved. It has evolved to protect itself. It has evolved to make those who worship aware that there is an order, there is a continuum of progress but it has to be controlled through channels. There has to be respect, there has to be reverence. This is why those who wear the cloak of priesthood have to be revered. It has grown out of proportion to the original intention but this is why through the years it has evolved because there is no respect by many on your earth today for any kind of authority and this is where your church has failed, it has taken itself a step too far.

Those from the realms of spirit who are assisting are backed by an army (a body) of vibrations from other levels of spirit who are providing the strength for those. We are sending our prayers, we are sending our love, although we cannot help directly we are providing the backup, the strength that is needed. This is why ones like myself who have had many years of experience on earth of praying for others, we are able in this existence to help. (27.05.97)

QUESTION 57 - Running Bear introduces his squaw.

I have brought companion with me, I gave her chance to sit here for a while. It is Squaw, my squaw. You see we are companions we make companion for life, we no change, we are companion. She called 'Moonbeam'.Running Bear was asked if Moonbeam would talk to us, his reply was 'you wait see '.Subsequently a member of our group visited a meeting with a psychic artist in attendance and was given a picture of an Indian squaw (she was not aware at that time of the above communication). The next time we were all together again she was told that Moonbeam would work with in her healing work and it was confirmed that the picture was of Moonbeam. (27.05.97)

QUESTION 58 - Running Bear continues with comments regarding Question 56

Your sister spoke of reverence in your churches. This is so but also we have reverence for our elders, it just a way of explaining. No matter if it is your church or other religion there must be reverence, there must be respect. We did not have high priest like your church but we did have our own ritual, own ceremony, we prayed to White Spirit. We linked with ancestors, we prayed to Mother Earth. Your other friend E-om-ba, he prayed through ancestors not the same as Running Bear. We involved ancestors but we prayed to White Spirit and Mother Earth. Whatever way there has to be respect and there has to be levels, you have to acknowledge there is something higher than yourself. Man has evolved and considers himself to be very clever but he is not so clever if he does not realise there is a higher level of existence, not as clever as he thinks. He has evolved and has found many easier ways of living so he thinks there is an easier way of gaining respect but it is not easy. There are problems if he takes shorter road. There are many in other realms of spirit whom we are respectful of, many higher levels and they respect us, as we respect you.

On your earth today your life has become much easier because you are in control of your own life. Generations before you they did not have control of their own life, they were under control of those who supervised them, you say lord of the manor or employer. Now, everyone on your earth, not everyone because there are countries where things are still in traditional way, but in your western world everyone thinks they can control their own destiny. They do not understand destiny is something much more involved than they realise. They have great awakening when they come home to us. There are no short cuts. (27.05.97)

QUESTION 59 - *Mafra explains the vibration in the land which has been created by those who have loved in that land. First he talks about his homeland of Portugal.*

It is an ancient land, many have trod paths in that land, there is much energy vibration from ground. Those who have lived and earned living from the land, they have worked on soil and taken from soil and have returned to soil. So the energy is there. It is not just those who walk on ground it is those who work in ground and provide a circle of events involving the ground. Many have gone from the shores of that land to far places, to new worlds, much exploration. Many have come to the shores from other lands so there are many vibrations in that country.

Each homeland has its own vibration, it's own energy. Your homeland has a certain energy which is there from those who have lived generations gone past and also those who have joined your community in recent years. It has changed, it has evolved. So have other homelands. You have to have an energy but this energy is added to by those who live on that land. It makes the energy of that homeland what it is.

You go to lands where there are vast open spaces and you feel a different vibration because the land has not been utilised. There is a pure vibration, it has not been changed by conditions. Whatever has occurred in a land is there for generations to come. It is added to by new vibrations but beneath that is the energy from before. This is what has attracted those who have come. Those who come and are not compatible will not stay. (27.05.97)

QUESTION 60 - Running Bear talking about natural worship.
This time of your earth year (Spring), in your part of Mother Earth is a time of awakening, it is a time of much vitality. Your earth is awakening from sleep, and there is much growth, you have land that is prosperous, I do not mean prosperous with wealth, I mean with abundance of earth produce. You are fortunate that your land provides for your needs and you have seasons, in your land, at this time of year when there is new growth your land gives off much energy. As creation awakens there is a rise in activity in soil there is a rise of activity in plant life in trees. The sap rises and this flows through all that you call nature, you are surrounded by nature, natural conditions, you cannot help being part of nature, Your animals sense energy, they are more lively at this time of the year, You say that animals are more lively because there are more hours of daylight, yes this is part of reason, but your animals either of home or field, forest, they are close to nature, they live by nature. Not so much those you have in the home but those that live in wild, live from their sense of survival. They sense and feel energy from nature. You know that your birds come and go according to the seasons of the year. They prosper and multiply according to seasons of the year. This is all part of the vibration of nature, there bodies are attuned to the energies of your earth. You too as children of nature also absorb these energies, but because you have travelled many paths away from natural law and surrounded yourself with material conditions your sense of nature is not so acute as those of your animal kingdom. Never the less, within you There is still your instinct, however much you cloud this instinct with material possessions and thoughts, you still have this within you. You too absorb the energy of new life, this is more vibrant when you are away from town and in countryside, but even so when you are surrounded by big buildings, you still absorb from trees. There is nowhere where there is not signs of new life if you look hard enough, in your cities, you have areas of new life. If there are areas where there is no new life, there is not a corner of your city that does not have a visit from your feathered friends, they bring their energy. You do not have to look to see, your body is absorbing, so as you absorb this new energy, this new vibration, you are making use of this new vibration, unaware of what is occurring, your body is recharging itself physi-

cally. You skin feels more vibrant, you notice your fingernails grow more, your hair grows more, so you see you are absorbing physically. As you absorb physically, you are also absorbing spiritually, and your body is in balance. If your physical body is vibrant you spiritual body is vibrant, you have to have balance, so this is a time to go forward, to use this energy to become more aware of spirit. Make good use of this time to step forward. Do you wish to ask question, do you understand? *So you are telling us that our psychic abilities can grow quicker at this time of the year.* Your psychic abilities grow quicker because you physical body is absorbing, and as your material body is working on a higher vibration so your spiritual body is conjoined it is balanced. *Is there anything we can do to speed things up?* You must not strive too hard, although I have come and explained to you, it is good that you know what is happening, what is occurring and why this is occurring, but it is not good to concentrate too hard. You then bring your conscious reasoning and that effects balance. You are finding path and whatever path you find comfortable, if you feel comfortable meditating, good, but if another does not feel comfortable they feel happier perhaps just walking in green area, and absorbing energy that is good for that one. Each finds own path. So you watch your creatures of your earth, and observe their habits, and you wonder then at their links with the vibrations with your Mother Earth. Your physical body needs to have rest, you cannot continually recharge, you have to have period of growth, then period of rest. This is also the same with spirit work, but although spirit rest, it must not be dormant, but prepare for next step forward with energy. Time to absorb, time to contemplate, on what you have absorbed, and to build, then time for another surge of energy and move on. You see Mother Nature, Mother Earth is part of your physical condition, because you are of this world, and you need your world's energy to stimulate you. As your physical body is stimulated this energy is also absorbed by spirit essence. If you had no material body you would not be of this world, and your energy would be different, you would not need to have rest and recharge, but you are not of that level at this moment of your existence, you are of earth, so you have to abide by earthly natural law. (03.05.97)

QUESTION 61 - Running Bear answers question regarding his tribe and their closeness to spirit.

You say 'are my people closer to spirit that your people'.Unfortunately my tribe are coming further away from spirit than when I walked the earth. When I walked the earth, earth was our temple we respected land, we took from land but we asked first if we could take and we replaced what we took. Now my tribe lives in buildings not so close to nature. They are now becoming aware of their tradition and are trying to recover the tradition of their ancestors but unfortunately there has been a gap of generations when the lure of the white man was followed. They wanted what white man had because it was new and exciting. They did not realise they were losing their tradition but like all things you value when you have no more. So now they are trying to look back on ancestors and regain what ancestors had. This is still dormant within them. As with you, you have instinct way back to primitive man. It is within them but it needs much awakening.

We respect white man, we are not as portrayed in your pictures, no. We respect, much harm was done to our tribe by your pictures. They paint bad picture of our tribes. I talk of our tribes, our tribes were all different we all had our own way of existence. There were hundreds of different tribes throughout land, each tribe had their own law, each had their own way of existing. There were tribes which were peaceful tribes, there were tribes that were not so peaceful. Before white man came to our land there was not peace as you would think. Many tribes fought with neighbour tribe so you cannot blame white man for all problems but in own community we were at peace, but there was always a problem of territory before white man came. As tribes grew in number, the number of people in tribe, the more was needed for that tribe's existence and in some areas there was much hardship because of natural weather conditions. So what was available was needed by many because much land was not cultivated just areas which we inhabited. Some tribes were not industrious, some would be happy to take from other tribes who had done work so there was not always peace between tribes. We respect white man, white man when he came had his own way, brought disease to our tribes because we did not know disease. White man brought disease and caused problems but also white man brought with him knowledge which we were happy to share, so we respect white man.

Do not believe all you see in your pictures. We would take in white man's children if they were left without parents and we would not kill for sake of killing. If we were attacked we would defend ourselves and if there was child without parents lost from family we would not harm that one we would take that one in and treat as our own. That is my tribe, there were other tribes who would act differently. As in your land you have different tribes, you call them families, some more warlike than others. It was the same with our race. Blessing be with you, respect Mother Earth and Mother Earth will respect you. (03.05.97)

QUESTION 62 - *George explaining how a tree can absorb energies and in return give out energies. This particular question related to the Tulip tree on the lawn at Stansted.*

This tree has been there for a long, long while but since it has been part of the college there has been a theory that goes round that it is special. People think it is special, they go out there and put there hands on it, they sit in a circle around it. The tree is alive, it lives, it absorbs energy so that all this energy that has been thrown at it has been absorbed by the tree and it is like anything else what you take you give out, what you send you get back. So, it might not have been special in the beginning but by people's positive thoughts it has made it so. If it has absorbed all this energy it gives out energy. People go there who are not very well and they get healing from it. (03.05.97)

QUESTION 63 - *George continues his visit by answering a question regarding why a spirit usually keeps to one trance medium rather than using a variety of mediums.*

We can't chop and change because we have to get used to a body. When we first come to a body that body is new to us, it takes us a while to know how to think and send messages from the brain to the mouth. We are in control of the body and we have to learn how to control. We become part of that body for the time we are in it but when we go, obviously, we have to leave it behind and shut everything down. When we go the medium will say to you 'they have left a feeling behind'. When we go we also take a feeling with us. Although the medium has a human body she has also got a spirit because she was spirit before she had a body. So when we go we take a bit of that spirit feeling with us and everybody's spirit feeling is different, like your earth body is different. If I went into another body I would find it different to this body. No one is the same because you are all individual, you all have your own memories and experiences what make you what you are. The more we come to a body the more we get used to that feeling, that one's essence vibration. Each time we come it is like putting a hand in a glove that has been worn many times, we get more used to that. If we chopped and changed with different bodies there would be danger that we would take a feeling from one body into that of another body. That would not be right. That would be against all natural law.

He was then asked that when the feeling is taken from the medium does that harm the medium in any way? It doesn't stay, she will sense the feeling of me perhaps after I have gone but it doesn't stay it soon goes. It stays in the memory. It is a decoding. To try and explain I will talk about communication through your table. When you get people come regularly on your table you begin to recognise who they are by the way the table moves and behaves so when they come again you recognise that vibration and you decode it as that one. That is the sort of thing I am trying to explain to you. Although, we don't keep that vibration we keep the memory of it. The next time we go into a body, not the same body we have still got the memory of what the feeling was like in the other body. It gets really complicated. It is not good to swap bodies. If there was a period of time for example, your years, between one of us being able to communicate that would be different but when there are mediums who are working in the same time zone that would be different. Both of those would be operating at the same time but if there is a gap, if the original medium went to spirit and I wanted to find someone else that would be different. That would be the end of that 'telephone line' and I would have to find another one. If a spirit visitor went from one medium to another medium and then back to the original medium that would be wrong, it would be against natural law. (03.05.97)

QUESTION 64 - Beda tells us how they learn in spirit.
There is always more to learn you never learn everything. We have not learnt everything we are still learning. You see, we learn the same as you. We learn in various levels. We are spirit, we have much knowledge from before but we are still learning because we have to learn with you. If we wish to communicate with you we have to understand what happens in your world and how you absorb information in your world. This is the way you absorb it when we give it to you. It would be no good us teaching you as if you were spirit because your brain in not trained to understand that way so we have to relearn what a human brain is like and how it is stimulated. This enables us to talk to you in ways that you understand. As your world alters we have to alter the way we approach you and teach you. If we were talking to people in your world fifty years ago they would be used to being taught in a different way to what you are today. Our method of teaching would have to be different. There was more sit back and believe what I tell you, now it is more prove what I tell you, prove that it is right. This is good because you must use your own reasoning to grow, we cannot tell you we can only lead you. You make your own decision as to which path you take and when is the time to make the decision to go one way or go other way, it is for you to decide not for us to tell you.

Certain things are laid down in your destiny that happen at times when they should happen but others are left to your decision. You get there in the end but which route you take is your decision. There are times for certain things to occur but not everything. There would be no point if your life was mapped out for you day by day before your arrived, you would not be walking that path it would already have been walked for you. (February 1997)

QUESTION 65 - *Running Bear giving words of wisdom concerning a fuller understanding of teachings and the importance of water.*
You have saying still water runs deep. There is much wisdom in teachings depending on how deep you look. Those who wish to look at surface good, those who wish to go deeper can find more. When you read teachings again you see what you didn't see at first. You only accept when you are ready. You understand more the more you learn. When you have had more experience on your path you read deeper. So I say still waters run deep.

Still waters will give you calm condition, no hurry, run smooth. When torrent, when flood the vibration is too fast you are not able to absorb. There is much flotsam, much passes without being grasped. It is good to have still waters, you can reflect in still waters. You can look in still water and see yourself so look at words given in calm and see your own meaning. See how this affects yourself. See your own experience.

When on earth we would look into still water and meditate. We would sit by still water, not rippling water, clear water and look at our image and we would go with our image and see much vision. We would see ancestors, we would see signs of wisdom. There is energy from water, much energy. This energy rises and you are as one, not submerged, just looking down at clear, pure water. We would have visions, see face of ancestor then face would clear, then we would have vision of what ancestor wishes to show us. If we needed assistance, help we would look and wait for sign. It was a way of concentration. You know of many ways of concentration in your world. Your Romany people have ball into which they look, it is a way of concentrating thoughts.

Water is very important, it is vital to existence. Without water you would not exist. You need water to survive, water to drink. There is water within your human body, without water your human body would not function. Your world is two thirds water. So you can see how important water is and what energy water gives, life force. Water has to be respected. You cannot be master, water is it's own master. You have to obey water. Those who live by water will have much knowledge of this, they respect water. Those who visit water do not understand and imagine water always calm and peaceful. Waters of your oceans are controlled by forces outside your world, your tides are controlled by the moon. There is much magnetism with water. Water rising from your hills in springs, where does this come from? Underground yes, but why? who knows where this begins, what force but you accept as normal but there is much majesty with water. There is too much waste of water, water is very precious. I share my lore with you, my respect for Mother Earth.

Water is part of Mother Earth but it is also part of greater force. Your wild animals understand water they know where to find water. Those in lands where water is scarce they know where to go to find water. They walk many miles to find water but they have instinct. They have instinct within them which is a magnetism towards water and this attracts the energy field. Animals will follow this energy until they find the water hole. You see this instinct is within all but man has lost his instinct. Water divining is a natural ability but over generations it has been lost, only preserved in a few. Anyone of you could do this but you need the ability to shut your modern world away. Your modern thoughts and ideas and be at one with nature to attune. Man survived many years with this ability. When you read history books of primitive man he survived. In your country also your primitive man's first settlements were by water, your towns that are now vast started as small communities by water holes. Now you cover water holes up, they are not important. You can cover water up so that you cannot see but energy is still there and will find it's own level. Your trees and plants know where there is water, their roots go in the direction of water. (24.06.97)

QUESTION 66 - *E-om-ba answers a question about the term we use God, Divine Spirit whatever, all different types of religions have some sort of concept of a higher power.*

There is a high over all supremacy which has no name. We are all vibration, we are all made from vibration. This is a very high vibration, frequency. It is over all, you cannot put picture because there is no picture. Man has given picture over years, different man, different country has given different name, different picture. Man is human but because he is human he has to associate with something to believe in. So a name and picture has been given to assist belief, to identify, to help understand. Your churches, your various religions have given name to educate the nations of the world that there is a higher being that is over all world. So people can understand they put in picture for them to understand but over the years this has developed into more and more detail, more and more story. All religions are story for those who are teaching people. They have brought fear into religion, not love. So people look at picture and fear, this is not what was intended There should be no fear.

How can supreme energy, light force, whatever, who creates so much love, so much life be feared? There are things that happen in your world which are not good but your religion blames this on evil but there is not a battle of good and evil as your religions teach. There is good and there is not so good, nothing entirely bad. This fear that has been created through many of your years has built and built vibration and this fear has created much unhappiness. You know with your thoughts, what you send returns. So if you send love this creates more love but if you fear you send not so good thoughts and this in turn creates not so good happenings in your world. Do not blame, I say 'God' because you have to give name, the supreme energy. A lot of this is created by thought, fear thought. If only there was love and no fear your world would be much happier. You talk of supreme over all energy over the world but why just your world? Why just your planet? Why when you are no more are you still part of this God? Do only those who believe in 'God', as your term God, survive this transition as your religion tells you? What do you think? There is so much more, your people of your world have been taught through fear only those little ones who have been given blessing are received in spirit because they are blessed through your Church! There are so many others who are not blessed what happens to them? This is fear. This causes much anguish in hearts of people and this anguish sends vibrations which causes not so good thoughts to form a reaction. This does a lot of harm. This does not only happen in your countries of west in your religions but in many other countries of your world in their religions.

Now you have people moving from one country to another and bringing their religions with them. There is much fear because in one country, I give no country name but in any one country where there are many religions each religion fear the other religion is stronger and this causes not good feeling between people of those religions. All through history of your world there has been trouble with one person in one religion and another person in another religion causing bad feeling. You see how much trouble has been caused through what you call religion. There is no true religion as your scribes and your church men, whoever, would have you believe. There is over all supreme energy or love.

A question was then asked by a sitter, ' When we have been through all our reincarnations and have become perfect do we blend with this supreme energy? I am not perfect. When I get to that point I will tell you. We are not perfect, we still learn. There are many on higher levels who we still wish to progress to. I try to give my thoughts. You are spirit, pure spirit and you are on level of spirit and you wish to progress. So you have path you wish to travel and you have choice, you travel in what you call spirit world or you take a human body and learn through that body. This you do several times but the choice is yours. There is not someone up there on a throne who says 'you go down to earth because you have been bad and you have to do many bad things and good things until I let you come home again'.That is not so. You choose your path and if you wish to stay where you are on that path you stay on that path. Many do this but after a while they find they are not fulfilled, they wish to stretch themselves, their energy. They return to earth and choose their path before they come to allow their spirit to grow so when spirit returns home it can go to another level of spirit vibration. This you can do many times but there are only so many lessons you can learn through body but when you decide you have had enough of body and you wish to progress to higher level which you are unable to reach when you had body you then go through vibrations of spirit.

This is like school, you do not have body in spirit world and sit at tables and look at blackboard. But you are linking with those that are more progressed than yourselves and you are sharing their energy, you are sharing their strength and their experiences, you are learning from them. You can learn on your own or you can join with your loved ones and learn together. When you return home you can stay a the level you are at until your loved ones join you if you wish or you can progress in spirit but still keep contact with those on earth, so when they come home to spirit you are there to help draw them up to your level if they are ready. Only if they are ready, you are not able to if they are not, it is not their destiny yet, it is open to yourselves to choose which way you go. You can only go forward if you are ready. I am still going forward, there are many more levels I could aspire to, so I do not know the answer to your question as to who is at top of ladder.

E-om-ba was then asked about his incarnations. I have had many incarnations. I come to you as E-om-ba because you are human and you need to know a personality so I come as my last body. I was others before but I have to give my name. When we meet in spirit I will not be E-om-ba, I will be a vibration. I will still be me, I will still have my energy. We can take on a spirit copy of our earth body if you wish or if we wish. This is often when people first come home to spirit they are not aware of vibration in spirit this is something you have to learn. So those that they know in spirit take on form that they had on earth so they are recognised and they can stay in this for a long while if that is their wish. The one that has come home may wish to progress. You know yourself you recognise people on your earth by their features but also you recognise them by their vibration without knowing. Sometimes you are aware that someone is in the room with you because you recognise their vibration. You turn your back not knowing who is standing behind you but you recognise their vibration, you turn round and you know who you are going to see. This is how I try to explain spirit vibration. A vibration is also an identity. I come as E-om-ba with E-om-ba's identity because this is what you associate with me. When you come home to spirit you will see me as E-om-ba until you become familiarised with my vibration because my vibration in spirit is a mixture of all my experiences and all my energies not just E-om-ba. You will have to be introduced to all of me. Aren't you lucky!

All of our experiences are there in all of us. We have times which we wish to remember and there are times which we do not wish to remember so the ones which we are happier with are the ones which come to the fore. We all have to go through bad times and experiences which we would not wish to boast about because this is how we learnt when we were on lower levels of progression The higher we have progressed the more we leave those conditions behind but we still can remember if we wish but we wish to put these behind.

It is difficult to find words to explain but there is no one God with a name. There are many higher levels of vibration than me and many more above and when I find who is at top I will let you know ! We have faith that there is a plan because there must be love which has come down over all. There must be a divine source of all.(29.06.97)

***QUESTION 67** - Question to Rosa regarding psychic artist's drawings of spirit friends who's identity was unknown these were produced over twenty years ago the sitter inquired whether these spirit helpers would still be with him now and can they still be identified?*

You will have to bring the pictures and ask because it is good if we feel the vibration from the picture. Once the image is on paper there is a vibration and we can feel vibration. You say are they still there? You say 'guides' but I prefer word 'companion' because guide means we guide you and make you do something We do not, we are companions, we walk with you by your side

There are many that walk with you. Some are ones which you have known before when you had body before and they walked with you in that body. Others are perhaps, more evolved spirits from higher level who are there with you assisting you on your path now. When you return home they will be there to welcome you and teach you when you go to spirit world. There are many who are with you; some are with you for a particular part of your existence, you are going through a part of your existence where their experience can help you so they walk with you along that path. When you have walked that part of your path their help has helped but you are now ready for a new experience so perhaps they stand back. I do not say they go away, I say stand back Then perhaps another companion will draw closer because they are of a closer link to you at that time.

I will give you an example, this medium whom I am using now has a companion who is a dancing girl (Beda). This entity, vibration who has given name as Beda, she was given to this lady a long while ago when she was a quite young girl (30 years ago). She talked through a medium like I talk through this one and she talked to your lady that is sitting here. She was quite friendly with this medium, her life changed, different things happened in her life, her life sometimes touched with spirit something it did not touch with spirit. There were many other distractions in her life. This one who has given name of 'Beda' just stood back and waited, she was there if needed because she had made close link. She was always close, if there was need she would help and assist. When the time came for closer link with spirit again she was back and introduced herself again. Now sometimes she comes and talks to you, sometimes she comes on table but not all the time, she lets others come. This is how we work, we are always about but those that are closely linked with the phase you are going through are closest to you. Perhaps, also, they help others not just you If you are in a phase when they do not need to be close to you they are helping someone else because you know we can be in more than one place at once They are always near so if you have need you have army behind you of all of us ! (29. 06.97)

QUESTION 68 - We often have visitors from the world of spirit who are brought to our sittings to re-experience being in the body and to assist in their progress. There visitors are not known to us but there seems to be some link with our experiences that they can have in common with us, just like a common interest brings strangers together. One of our visitors is Hannah and firstly there is a description of her followed by an explanation from one of our helpers as to the circumstances.

Hannah, comes to talk to us and to make herself known, she tells us that she was a lace maker but also taught young children (a Dame School), the children came to her with their penny, but if she knew the family could not afford the money she quietly sent the money home again. The children wore boots in the winter but came bare footed in the summer. The children learnt to do things with their hands and learnt by singing and chanting lessons. She lived near Princes Risborough where she walked to go to market but her home was under the cross (cut into the hillside, near Whiteleaf). She tells us of the good Queen who was a widow lady. She had heard of trains but never seen one. She is a very happy soul and enjoys her visits as she has no one else to talk to.

Queen Victoria became a widow in 1861 and passed in 1901. The railway came to Princes Risborough with the line to Aylesbury in 1863 This suggests that her time on earth was prior to 1862.

Rosa gives the following explanation. I know Hannah she was like me she had her own little house. She came because she saw light, you are friendly and she wanted to talk to someone. Not particularly to teach as some come to teach but as she has got no one to talk to she thought she would come and talk to you. Although she has been in our world (spirit home) for a longish while she is just waking to us and realising there is so much more to learn so she has come to learn. By talking to you she is learning too. She is not here to teach now but she may later when she decides what she wants to do. She speaks of when she had a home on earth so this is helping her to realise that was her home on earth but now she is in spirit and she is getting used to her different vibration. She has to talk through what her home was like on earth then go another step and have knowledge of what spirit opportunities there are, what path she wants to take and how much is open to her. It took a long while for her to realise where she was. She was quite a lonely soul she did not have many help her. When you go home to spirit there are many there to greet you. You are fortunate you are aware there are many in spirit to greet you, both those you knew on earth but also a lot of us not known to you when you were on earth. Some souls when they go home to spirit are not aware of this. Although there are those there waiting to say 'hello, welcome' they cannot make themselves known to that one, they are there but they cannot make themselves known. It was like that with this lady, Hannah. They are getting through to her now and they are gently bringing her to you, she is learning and they are showing her what opportunities there are for her if she wants to take them.

A sitter asked if she was in a sleep state or had just cut herself off to her new environment. She was like in a mist, a fog. She knew she did not have a body anymore but it was like she could not reach out to those who were there to say 'hello' to her. They were there because no harm came to her, they were there welcoming her but she was like in a fog. This is the best way for me to explain 'fog'. Gradually she came through fog and she saw your light, they bring her to you to help her talk through what she left behind to make her realise that it is left behind and she has now got so much more. This lady saw light and because your light was a compatible vibration, also she was linking with earth condition and you are near her earth condition physically. She still links with her earth condition, not to frighten those that live there she is not worrying them but she is still linking (06.07.97)

QUESTION 69 - E-om-ba responding to question regarding communication, the difference between trance communication and communication given via a medium on a platform to a church congregation.

When we talk, we talk through this medium because we take body. As we are using this one's vibration our vibration has to be similar although different level of progress. The vibration is the same but level of progression is different. You have in your electricity frequency which can be used for different things but same frequency. Some more powerful than other. This is like our frequency, we are at a different level of progress but the frequency is the same. Your frequency must be the same throughout your existence on earth but the more you walk your path, hopefully the more progress you make but your frequency is still the same frequency all the time, whether you are new to earth or old to earth. It is still the same frequency but more progress. This is why we have to be compatible.

Now, when your medium gives clairvoyance, clairvoyance does not take over her body so the link does not have to be the same. She has one in spirit who protects and this one is the link. This one brings her vibrations from others, different vibrations but is able to make those compatible by relaying. They may stand there and say to whoever is communicating 'tell me so and so....' but really that is told through their helper, their protector. The link is not so much with those who are in the physical body who they are talking with but it is with those in spirit who are sending the message. When someone comes to church the medium can give message to any vibration in the congregation but it is not the one in the congregation's energy they are linking with it is the one from spirit and that one from spirit is being filtered through the protector of the medium. It does not matter what the vibration is of the earth person, it is the spirit vibration which is more important. It is a different level of communication from trance mediumship. There is not the infringement on that medium as there is through trance medium. They are able to cut vibration easier and jump from one to another.

Their training is different also, you have been trained differently. This is why it is preferable that each medium works in their own way and tries not to do one and another method. Some of your mediums try all ways, they try trance, they try clairvoyance, they try reading cards, they try many things. It is good to try just one, you are best trained for one and not to mix. This is why your mediums sometimes have problems when they do not work well because their vibrations are confused. There companions are not knowing which vibration they wish to work on. Your physical mind shuts off from your world differently for trance to other mediumship. Your medium's mind is experienced in working one way but if you chop from one to other the mind gets confused. This is when mind gets disturbed and imagination and conscious reasoning come into play because of jump from one to other the physical mind is confused. It does not know what level to shut off at, then sometimes it is open to conscious reasoning and what you call imagination.

When your mediums stand on your platforms and give from spirit they give from spirit but also their own conscious reasoning is involved, this is not so with trance but if they jump from one to other they have to be careful their conscious reasoning is shutting down completely when in trance. It can sometimes not work properly and the medium's physical mind is influencing talk from trance. When a medium is on a platform and that medium is used to giving talk through trance, the medium on platform shuts down too much, that is not good when in public place. The need to have their reasoning powers with them in case of physical disturbance. They are not protected as you are in your own room. Things can happen in public areas and they should have their 'wits' about them. So you see it works both ways. It is best to stay on level of vibration which you choose to work or which spirit are happy to work with you, which you are comfortable with together.

E-om-ba was asked If this applied to healing You are talking of healing with full consciousness. No, this is different because you are not giving communication with spirit. You are receiving guidance but you are not relaying that to your patient. This is another occasion where there has to be a warning. When you have trance healing, this again is another category and there has to be much care with this. There again, they must not jump from one to other, the same as mediumship must not jump from one to another, healing must not jump from one to other.

You are saying 'why when we sit here and we sit for table and trumpet movement is that different?' Well you see, you finish with one form of spirit communication first, then shut one down before you go on to other form of mediumship. (13.07.97)

QUESTION 70 - E-om-ba talking about time.

Don't worry about time. So much of your time is wasted by you thinking about time. Do not waste your time thinking about time just enjoy each moment you have. Make the most of each moment you have. For you time is very precious because you have so much to do in your life span. This does not mean you come home to spirit tomorrow! If you lived 200 years it would not be long enough for everything you want to do, so time is very precious to you. You would still not have enough time. So, make the most of all the time you have. You must not push yourself too far, just worry about today not tomorrow. You will have tomorrow, don't worry! It will be there tomorrow when you open your eyes but don't worry about it yet. You make problems for yourself if you worry about what will happen later. You worry about something it may not happen! Think of all that time you waste and all that negative energy you create. That is harmful so do not worry. It is harmful to other people but more harmful to you because what you send out comes back to you. It is harmful to create negative thoughts because this makes negative responses to those you contact but also that comes back to you, so it is harmful to you. It stops you going ahead. (20.07.97)

QUESTION 71 - John Lyon giving his thoughts on how the high atmospheric pressure affects communication.
There is a stillness about the atmosphere, this is partly due to your atmospheric pressure which is around at this time because you are restricted to earth's vibrations. Of course, we have to penetrate these to talk to you. This does not affect us now, we have to become acclimatised to your climate. It affects the way you breathe, the oxygen in your air, so of course this intake of breath affects the flow of oxygen around the body which releases oxygen into your system and supplies your red blood corpuscles. This circulates your body and penetrates to each part of your body including your brain cells. The way you think, the way you breathe affects the way you use your body including your thought processes. Your thought processes affects the way of transmission of 'electric', senses. This is no problem to us we just acclimatise ourselves. (22.07.97)

QUESTION 72 - John Lyon responding to question 'words that we use which have particular meaning in the way we communicate, for example God bless you and other phrases used to express a devout feeling '.
As explained to you before words are a label, a tag, for a thought that is there before you find a word to describe the thought. When you have a very sincere thought, a devout thought, you have to find a word to describe the thought whichever language you speak, whichever denomination you worship if you do worship a particular religion. When it is something sincere and earnest coming from your heart, I do not mean your physical heart, I mean deep inside yourself, your spirit heart. You search for a word that has a deep penetrating meaning because you do not want to put this thought into something which is flippant, something which is a passing fad, a passing phrase, a transient word which has come into your language for a short while and is superseded by another word a few moments later. You search for a word which has deep penetration, a deep meaning, a word you have heard before used in sacred circumstances, a word which you have heard others use perhaps when talking of religion or you have heard when visiting places of religion or reading books on religion. To emphasise

the seriousness and sincerity of this thought you use a word which you are happy to use, that is not alien to you but also a word which you know others recognise also as having this sincere and devout emphasis. You perhaps use the words 'God bless you' because 'God' is a word which is understood wherever the English tongue is spoken. If you were in a foreign country you would use the word that came naturally to you for 'God'.We are talking of your English tongue, wherever the English language is spoken has a very deep and meaningful meaning. You wish to bestow a blessing on someone, a blessing is a sincere wish for that one, so in your sincere wish for that one you use the word 'blessing' and to show how deep that blessing is, how sincere and devout that blessing is, you use the word 'God' because there is no other higher word you can use more supreme than 'God'.It is a word which has been handed down through your language as far back in aeons of time since language has been recorded. It has been called a different word when you ancestors spoke Latin, French, Danish or whatever, or when your Druids ruled your land and spoke your original tongue but we are coming back to the modern idiom. For you modem idiom means twentieth century but for the history of your land the modern idiom is in the last 1,000 years, less perhaps depending on what part of the land you reside in. Whether it be in the heart of the city or whether it is in your border counties of Wales, your northern counties or your counties which are not far from the shore which faces France. I am trying to explain a word which goes back as long as your English language as you know it today has been spoken.

There are other words you are talking of also. Here again, your mind searches for a word which is acceptable to those whom you are addressing, a word which they can easily take as a word of truth and sincerity. If you were of a particular faith there are words which are more pertinent to that faith. Roman Catholicism has it's own words, a lot of these words are of Latin origin. These would be of no value to someone who did not worship that religion so they would only be used within that circle. Whereas, if you were of a lower faith, I do not mean lower in value, I mean lower in degree of worship, You do not have the high altar with your incense and your chants, this does not mean the worship is any less sincere in some cases it is more sincere. You have a different language so you would not quote the high faluting language of Catholicism, you would speak a more mundane language. If you were a Quaker, I am not being derogatory to Quakers because they are a very sincere people, but they only speak for a reason. Words are superfluous to them, they only speak when it is essential. Their services are conducted mainly in silence until a member feels an impression of which they wish to speak, they then arise and stand to their feet and they say what word has come to them. Those who listen know that this to them is a sincere word. Now, if someone from another faith heard that word they would shun that word and say it was sacrilegious because it has not got all the trimmings of a high religion but to those in that faith it is as sincere as the incantations of the high church.

It is a word which the one that speaks finds to express a sincere thought. It does not have to be the same word for every human soul, it is a word which is acceptable to them in their position in life whether humble or of rank. There is no derogatory thoughts by spirit that those of a humble faith are less sincere than those of a higher faith. This is not so, in some cases it is the other way about. It comes from the heart not from the lips, that is what is important.

I have just given you an example of 'God bless you' but you may think of other words. A word is just a label to express a thought. (22.07.97)

QUESTION 73 - George was asked how spirit helps those who have recently passed to spirit to be aware of their new circumstances.

When anyone goes to spirit, before they go, they have an idea in their mind as to what is going to happen. All through their lives they have ideas what is going to happen to them. This varies according to the person; some have no belief at all that anything is going to happen to them they just live their life and they think when they 'pop their clogs' and that's it. Others have varying ideas according to what they have been taught or what they believe, a lot of churches and religions teach them vary strict ideas about what happens to them and because they are so indoctrinated in their belief they are not allowed to think any other way. It is like the old horse who had blinkers on, they can only look ahead they can't look sideways.

So when they come home to spirit, the first dimension when they leave the body is very like your earth vibration. When the spirit comes to our world, the spirit knows where it is going because it has come from our world to start with, before it came to earth. Part of you knows you are going to survive in another dimension, but this part of you which knows this is surrounded by all the thoughts and all the influence it had when it was on earth. When it first come into the spirit dimension even though that spirit is wanting to be free and wanting to say 'hooray I have come home', it can't because it is weighed down with this heavy condition of your earth that it has brought with it. The earthly conditions tell them they can't be in heaven yet because they have got to go to purgatory first, or there is no life, because life on earth is finished and that is the end. You have to get rid of all these thoughts before your spirit can be free and join all those others who are waiting for you.

Our job is to gradually bring the light. I am explaining it as a light, it is really a vibration. The best way to explain is to call it light because a lot of people when they come to spirit and have come back to earth afterwards have told you stories of seeing a light. This is what our vibration is, it is light and we gradually bring this vibration through this mist, doldrums, murk, and gloom until they see this light and they follow this light. This light is a vibration. All this time there are those who are there to welcome this one home to spirit. Although they want to welcome this one they can't because that one can't break free but gradually they are able to come through all this gloom and say 'you are home, you are here do you recognise where you are?, this is where you came from, we are having a party you are home'.I have tried to put this in language so that you will understand.

George was asked whether those who thought they would sleep until "Gabrielle 's trumpet blows" is this what happens to them ? They do because that's what they have been taught. We have no such thing as time, you would think it takes hundreds of years but there is no such thing as time so it is not long. You might get someone who comes back to you and says 'this person is just making themselves known' but you would say 'good heavens, they went to spirit fifty years ago it has taken them a long while'.To them it is not, it was yesterday they were on earth and now they are in spirit.

He was then asked ' if someone from spirit links with a person on earth for the first time after a number of earth years, is the one in spirit able to comprehend all that has happened to the one on earth over the intervening years. When they first come back, what they do is they don't link with the person, they link with the person's vibration. So the vibration of the person on earth will be the same, just a little more mature, a bit more experienced. It would be a similar vibration. They are not linking with what the person has done in the last fifty years they are linking with the spirit within the body of that one. Gradually as they tune in with that one they are communicating on the higher level of communication that we have told you about. They will pick up all the things that have happened to them gradually but they don't want to swamp them at first but they have made their link and they are tuning in. I will give you an example; if you had a sister on earth and perhaps when you were 10 years old your sister moved away to America and you didn't see her for another fifty years. Then she would come over on holiday, you hadn't written to each other or talked on the telephone. You wouldn't tell her all in one go the things that had happened in those fifty years, you would tell her the important things. You would tell her of the important things that had happened to you during your life, then when you had been together a bit longer you would tell her some other bits and pieces which were not quite so important, and over perhaps the next year you might tell her all the bits of 'gossip', that are not so important. (27.07.97)

QUESTION 74 - Golden Ray explaining spirit vibrations and the limitations of human understanding
So much wisdom has come your way. You ask what more can we tell you. This is difficult for us. There is much we could impart but this would be given to you at a time when this knowledge is of no use. You are in a human body with a human brain, your thought process is a human thought process and you can understand on the human level. You require guidance for your life here on your earth. There is much that is envisaged for your work here on earth so we can assist you with this. When you ask us questions we are able to give you answers but you see, there is only so much we can give.

There is much wisdom of deeper knowledge, deeper progress in what you call spirit. There are often questions asked of what is the structure of spirit? How many layers, how many vibrations? What is the hierarchy? What is the purpose of spirit? Why do spirit return to earth? When you are in spirit what do you do, what do you learn, what is the point of learning? How can this affect others? What more can you learn that you haven't learnt already? So many questions which have been asked over aeons of time. What use is this knowledge to you when you have your earthly life to lead? There is time for these questions when you have set aside your earth body. There is a whole vicissitude of progress open but you do not start to plan now, you walk your path which is assisting you with your progress. You are gaining continuously through your earth life and what you are gaining through your experiences in your earth body, also your communications with spirit are assisting you on your path of progress and helping your knowledge grow. This knowledge will go with you when you have no body.

You are learning all the time because you are not just learning how to exist, how to survive on your earth, you are also learning how to communicate with others on your earth. How you can show them a light, how you can open their vision. I do not mean their vision so that they can see spirit people, I mean open their vision of progress so they ask questions and seek knowledge of their reason for existence. Also, those who are experiencing problems with their physical bodies your are able to open their thoughts that they are not just a physical body, they are a spirit within and that spirit within is all powerful. This knowledge of this spirit within can assist with their healing progress. There are those who are troubled because of loss of companions on their earthly path and here again you are able to assist when they ask, when they seek. People seeking are drawn to you, if not to you directly to the words you have written or your other members of your group who come across these souls.

The knowledge we are imparting is of use to you. It is intended to be of use to you while you have an earthly body, not only to you but to those whom you associate with. This is our purpose for coming, this is our purpose for walking with you and sharing our knowledge. It is to assist you and to assist others whom you associate with, to make your earthly existence more tolerably, more bearable. To show those whom you walk with that their earthly existence is not everything, there is much more to existence, much more to self than your flesh and your bones. There is much more in the spirit within, they are not just flesh and bones they are a living soul which lived before they had an earthly body and will live again after. This is what we are trying to achieve, this is your destiny, this is why you are treading this path. You have chosen this path and we are walking with you to assist you with this path.

Of course, in your quiet moments when others are not pulling on your attention for help your mind is able to wander and to ponder on things higher than the human realms. You stretch out and you gain from the knowledge which is deep within you and the words that have been spoken to you. You may ponder on your continued existence and what your continued existence is. This is good but it would be wrong for us to tell you too much because, as I have explained, our purpose is to assist you with your earthly life.

It is honourable that you ask questions of those who walk with you, your spirit companions because it is good to know of your spirit companions. It is good to know of their vibrations but because you are human to explain a vibration to you we have to give a physical example. This is why we are always asked what is your name? What part of our world did you live? What did you do when you had a body? This is of no use to us, to us we are vibration but you do not understand vibration. In the sense of your human conditions you think of a vibration as a vibration of your communication on your earth. Then we try to explain it is a natural vibration, then perhaps, you think of the vibrations of the wind in the trees or the water running, your oceans. It is difficult for us to explain a vibration, you do not understand while you have a physical body because you have a physical mind. To try and assist with your questions we try to give personalities to our vibrations.

There are going to be some who will be disappointed when they return to spirit because they are expecting to see a physical appearance of their spirit companions. As we have explained, when you go to spirit you will experience what you wish to experience. You will see a spirit replica of the picture we portray to you. You do not know what I look like and I am not going to give you a picture because I just come as a vibration but there are others who have given you a picture of themselves whether on paper or through psychic sight, or through sensory vibrations, or through this voice. When the inquirers come home to spirit they will see what they expect to see. As at first you are only a step away from your physical body it is a way of learning vibration. You will have to learn what a vibration is. It is a way of learning. When you accept that you do not need physical senses anymore you can take away all the fetters that bind you and tie you down, you will then be free. Free to explore so much in vibration, the energy is much quicker, the vibration is brighter and of a much different level, but of course, you have to become accustomed to this.

At first it is understandable that you wish to see a physical appearance. Although they are spirit companions you have put an identity to them, you wish to get to know them as a friend on your earth, you have to see them and visualise them. So often you do not see people on your earth, perhaps you only hear their voice but you imagine in your mind what they look like and quite often when you meet they look totally different. It is a vibration, you are linking with, their vibration, you are making your own picture. It is a small way of explaining what occurs.

We are happy to answer questions, do not stop questions coming. If questions come we deem are too far advanced for your human understanding or they come too early in your development you will not receive the answers. It is of no matter, we do not want to stop questions. It would be difficult for us to try and explain and then you do not understand correctly. This would bring the wrong information and once you have information you are fixed in this image, in the concept whether it is right or wrong. Because you have struggled to understand something which is very difficult for a human brain to understand you have probably contorted it into something different than it is. Before long this becomes a fact and this will be a hindrance to your development because you will have difficulty accepting the truth because you have already created this 'fact'.As you create a picture of a voice on your wave length on your earth and then you realise when you meet that one, that one's picture is nothing like the picture you envisaged you find this difficult. This would be similar to your thought process and the concepts you have built up you will have to relearn completely. This is not progress this is a step backwards.

I try to explain why we come but not to discourage questions because it shows there is a stretching out, a seeking and when the time is right the answer will be given but not until the time is right because we do not want someone to create something in their thought field which is not going to be of use to them later, or will be harmful later to their progress. (29.07.97)

QUESTION 75 - Running Bear talking about 'signs'.
I talk of signs. There are many signs of your world which you know how to read. We followed signs, mother earth signs. You also have this instinct within you. You know of your seasons by the signs of your birds, animals, trees. You have forgotten many of your sensory perceptions of signs. You listen for noise of tree as to change of weather, this was of great importance to your land at one time when many people lived close to nature and their livelihood depended on the surrounding area. When they farmed ground they read signs of change in your weather so they would know how to tend their flock or harvest their fields. They had to be one step ahead of your weather conditions, so your animals and crops were protected before oncoming of storm or heavy deluge. On other side of conditions when weather was very dry, arid your animals and crops had to be protected also. This is a natural process that is within man. It has been used for many years, many generations. It is still there. You use these senses without knowing you are using these senses. You do not use them for the same reason, you have no need as your life does not depend on earth conditions as your ancestors earth conditions. Your livelihood is earned in a different way and you survive by other means. Your food you buy in packets, boxes not from ground but this does not mean these senses are not still in use. You are perceiving these signs and not realising you are perceiving them because you are not perceiving them for a reason. This is an example of how you read signs.

Once you start to question you then start confusion. You must rely on base instinct. Once you say how do I sense change in vibration of weather? you are bringing your conscious reasoning and you are creating a disturbance, whereas your instinct reads on it's own without your direction and supplies you with this information without you realising. I have given you example of sign. A material example of sign, I have used mother earth as an example so this is understood. I have tried to explain perception of sign.

There are many other signs which you read without you realising you are reading. You all have natural ability deep within you of reading signs of spirit of which you are not aware. Many struggle to develop contact with spirit, the more effort they put into their investigation the more conscious reasoning they are putting in, the more they are causing problems because this is a natural instinct that is born within you. Your children have natural instinct. Many times you hear of children who have a spirit friend. If this is not questioned and the child is content but if this is questioned and suspicion or concern is shown this causes a breakdown in communication. This causes fear and fear is negative. When a child comes to earth and takes a body they have this instinct ability to contact spirit why does this instinct not continue through their life? My friends, it does but you are not aware. As you are not aware your human body is perceiving signs of your mother earth, so your spirit body is communicating with your spirit companions and you are not aware.

Once you start pondering on this you are then causing a disturbance in the vibration because you are putting conscious reasoning into this. I come to tell you this but perhaps it is not good that I do because I am making you think and by making you think this could cause the very disturbance I am warning of. What I say is, do not try too hard, do not think too hard of seeing signs from spirit. Do not analyse everything you perceive. Let it become as natural as your breath in your body. You may have, through many years, been communing with spirit but this has not been perhaps, obvious to you but because it has not touched your conscious reasoning you have not been aware. If it touches your conscious reasoning you then have the ability to contort, to alter, to change because you are putting your own thoughts with spirit thoughts.

My friends, there are signs all around. Signs of your earth life, signs from spirit and you are very capable of reading these signs. You do read these signs but it is not for me to say watch for this sign, watch for that sign because each person sees signs in a different way. You may be aware when spirit is close, you may feel a difference in the atmosphere around, this is a sign. I use the word 'sign' because the word sign signifies a word of your language and it is something which is used much. You have signs on your roads, you have signs in your writing, you have signs in your mathematics, you live by signs. This is a word which is understood. You are surrounded by signs without being aware and you have learnt to interpret signs which is feeding your spirit progress. How many times have you avoided a circumstance and you have not known why, something has been averted which could have caused a problem, you have read sign without knowing you have read sign.

I will talk of physical condition, perhaps there is something on your path which would make you fall, you have not seen this something but something has made you change direction to avoid. This is a physical condition but also I talk of your other path your path through life. Perhaps you have come close to something which is not too good so you change direction. This is not coincidence, you read signs so you changed direction. You will not acknowledge you changed direction intentionally, you say it is something which has occurred but my friends, you read signs.

I would emphasise not to concentrate too much on how to read signs because it is very natural and once you start to analyse you are causing confusion because you are stopping natural process. When you breathe it is natural you do not think how to breathe but if you began to think of breathing continuously, not just a few deep breaths for your exercise, but if you thought every minute of the day of how to breathe you would cause much confusion. (05.08.97).

QUESTION 76 - George answering question 'How difficult or easy is it for spirit communicators to learn to communicate.

They are all different. You get those who are like myself who have 'the gift of the gab'.We don't find it a problem. You get those who you think when they go to spirit would be very advanced and very good because they have learnt a lot through their earthly life. Perhaps they have been very religious and they have had very deep thoughts, they think they have got it all worked out and they know what is going on. It may not be religious through your churches, it may be religious through just reading and meditating but what they don't realise is all this thinking and all the delving they do is very good, they learn but they are not sharing what they are learning.

They are keeping it to themselves. If you keep things to yourself it is not good. When they come to spirit they have to learn how to communicate again. This is why we bring some of them back to you so they can learn to communicate.

When you go to spirit you don't change, you are just the same 'you' as you were on earth. You go with all your same thoughts and all your ideas, and all your memories. You don't become an 'angel' and suddenly find yourself on another plain. When you first come you bring with you all your thoughts and ideas, sometimes this restricts you from growing because you are cluttered up with these ideas, so you can't sort yourself out. There again, they have a job to communicate and we have to give them a hand.

Some find it easy to communicate in different ways. You know I come and talk to you but the other grandfather (Albert) he finds it difficult to talk. That doesn't mean he is not here communicating, you know when he is with you. There are different kinds of communication. I am talking to you and others come and make their presence known in other ways, but on top of all this, we are communicating on another level as well. We are communicating on a thought level.

When someone goes to spirit because they haven't got a body any more it doesn't mean you can't communicate with them any more. You have got this other level of communication going on all the time which you don't know about. You are sometimes communicating a long while on this level before you become aware that you are linking with your spirit friends. There are all these people in your world that are communicating and not knowing it, you are not the only ones. It is only when you become involved and understand a little more about spirit communications that you can accept communication is happening in this way. You begin to realise what is happening. You communicate with each other on earth without knowing it. When you go into a room you feel attracted to some people and not others, this is similar. You may call it a sense, a vibration, telepathy, you give it all sorts of names but what is a name? It is just a label you are giving it. It is communication, there again, communication is another name. You are communing with those from the other world without realising. (10.08.97)

QUESTION 77 - John Lyon explaining the recovery process for people who pass to spirit and need rehabilitation.
In the other dimension which you call 'Spirit World' there are what you term halls, spirit hospital perhaps is a better way of describing it for you to understand, where there is vast energy concentrated on those who have returned to their home in spirit. Some have been through an ordeal before they have come home, their physical body has perhaps suffered much, or perhaps their mind has suffered much, or they have come home suddenly and are not aware of where they are. Whatever the reason, there are many reasons, they are for a while in this recovery environment, they are here and are bathed in love. Very gently their spirit is released from the trauma or the conditions they have brought with them and gradually the spirit is free, because the spirit is with you now it is within your physical body. It is not something you find when you go home. It is encased in your physical body and your physical conditions, so when you leave your physical world you leave your physical body behind you, of course, to dispose of in whatever way, but you bring conditions with you. These have to be taken gradually so your spirit is free, It is a gradual severing of these anxieties. It has to be done gently because you do not want to cause too much disturbance. It all depends also on how enlightened your spirit is. If it is a spirit which has returned home several times before the spirit knows what is happening but if it is, a young soul that hasn't been to your earth many times it has to discover the new environment and discover the process of leaving the earthly body.

There are spirit friends who have chosen to be involved in this type of work. They work as healers and take over when those healers who have been helping on earth ask for spirit help for the transition of the patient. Earthly healers have to accept that although they can ease the path of the patient there comes a time when they have to say farewell to the physical body of the patient and this is when the spirit healers take over. When the healer says farewell they bid them 'God's speed' and ask for help for their transition. (17.08.97)

QUESTION 78 - Ruth Fruin in discussion about Spirit Names, that are often given to babies during naming services held by Spiritualist Churches or Lyceums.

The name given comes from spirit and in various ways is communicated to the person who is taking the service. Nandad (Albert Fruin), who often took these services while on earth, sometimes was given the name a few days before, at other times he would be impressed during the actual naming service. Others receive the inspiration in different ways, it all depends on their particular method of communicating with Spirit. The Spirit Name describes the spirit vibration the baby brings from their spirit home, and is pure and untainted by this physical world of yours. The name attempts to describe within the limitations of your language the actual vibration. It's not just a name for this lifetime, it's a name forever. (17.08.97)

QUESTION 79 - Running Bear answering questions on physical movement and noises activated by spirit during sittings.

We experiment, we know you like confirmation that we are here, so we try with using vibrations as we can use energy. We have to find level you are tuned with, because this is physical sound, and you hear with physical ear. So we have to find level that causes stimulus. We are spirit, we do not have a body, but we try to move solid object, so you see this makes a breakdown in structure of object, to enable use to do this. We do not have a hand to come and do the moving, so we have to use your energy and our energy combined, to make movement of your solid object. This is what is desired we could bring spirit sound, but that would be different, different energy and then you would hear with psychic ear, whereas now you are hearing with physical ear but the sound has to be increased to level your ear would react to. You are not like your animals who have wide scope of hearing. Your hearing is limited so it is not good for us to make frequency which your ear does not react to. There was also movement in your room with sounds on the floor. There again we are finding level which you can react to. We have to make movement of energy to make sound on your floor, wall or whatever. (19.08.97)

QUESTION 80 - *Running Bear responding to question as to why some spirit communicators are more compatible than others and problems relating to family connections with the medium.*

I will talk first of medium's family. The level which the medium is taken to is not very deep, it is trance but she is still aware of what occurs. Memory is not there because there is no thought process, she knows what word is being said now but because that word has not gone through her thought process she will not recall until there is a reminder. When one from her family comes she hears, this would make emotion.

The other reason is the one who is communicating they are touching the medium's body and within her body you say DNA, there are links with that one who is talking. They are linking with the DNA that has come from themselves. This has to be done very carefully because there is much in that DNA which is dormant. You have DNA from all your ancestors but only a very small part is active. There has to be care that dormant DNA is not awakened because those vibrations are not needed for her at that time. If there is a time in her life when there is need of part of that DNA it is aroused. You may observe in your life, in your child's life, in whoever's life you reach a certain point in your life and you need a skill for a reason. You did not know you had this skill but it is there, it hasn't been awaken. This is because there was DNA and that DNA was dormant but when time was right there was trigger from yourselves searching and this awakened DNA. This is how I find words to explain but it is more complicated than that it is more to do with your communication within your body from your brain fields, your electrodes but I am just giving easy language for your understanding. This is why relations have to be handled very carefully so as not to leave any trace behind which is not needed. If one came and aroused a DNA which may cause problems and this DNA was not shut down this would alter destiny.

So I have dealt with the medium's relations, I will talk of others now who come and talk. Maybe your relations or companions like myself. There are those who wish to communicate who have chosen their path to communicate. Maybe it is teaching, maybe it is protection, healing, so many reasons. They have worked for this goal, they have worked so they will be able to communicate. They have learned how to become compatible and how to find a compatible vibration but you have others who have no desire to communicate. If for some reason they come, they find this very difficult because they have not gone through the learning process. They will come with someone else assisting. Often you have Mafra who brings someone and he comes to ensure they come and go correctly, this is his way of teaching. There maybe someone who wishes to make their presence known but is unable to do so because of lack of experience, or perhaps it is not their desire to do this but for just one occasion they wish to come, just to say 'I am here I am all right, do not worry' but they may not come again. They have just come this one time to give this message.

Also, you have others who wish to come, but similar to your earthly vibrations, you are not compatible with every soul you share your life with. You walk your path of life some people you feel a stronger link with, some you meet and you automatically make bond with, some you may not see for many of your years but when you see them again it is as if there has been no time in between. This is because you have been together before, you have a bond between you, or perhaps if you have not been together before but in your DNA you have. You ancestors knew their ancestors so you have a common link. You have those who you are polite to but when you say goodbye, you say goodbye there is no wish to develop friendship further.

So you see when spirit comes this is the same there are those who are very compatible and those who are not so compatible. Quite often there is a problem if there is an incompatibility and communication is not possible. You may have one who has not had experience with that vibration they may have been before to a different vibration and feel 'I have spoken before so I can speak again' but when they come to the new vibration they realise it is not so compatible for many reasons. You all have your own personality, this is a vibration, this is an energy. You are all individuals, you all have your own free will this makes each one of you different and when you go home to spirit you are still indivdual. You go home to spirit family but you still have your individual spark which is within you. You are not as the animal kingdom which blends together, you are individuals. You work within your group in harmony but you are individual with your own memory, your own thoughts, your own ideas, your own free will and however much you are guided to a particular path if you decide 'no' that is your free will to say 'no'. Eventually you come round another way to that path but you are all different so when you go home to spirit you are still all different.

If one is meant to come for a very particular reason and it is not easy we would take the medium very deep so that the spirit communicator can come and override this one's own vibrations. It is possible for someone to come who is not compatible but if they need to come for a particular reason, not just for fun but for reason, they will be allowed to come but the medium's doorkeeper is the one who cares. The doorkeeper would take the medium very deep so there is an easy take-over. (19.08.97)

QUESTION 81 - *Running Bear talking about change of seasons and their effect and compares this with our spiritual progress.*

You have seasons in your part of world, there is spring time and harvest time, autumn. There is great change of energy of your earth in these two seasons. There is awakening in your spring much lively vibrations, in your harvest time you have shutting down preparing for your winter. Your Mother Earth is shutting down vibrations, closing vibrations, but also preparing for another year. So with the end of this year of fruition when your leaves fall from your trees and your daylight hours become shorter, your animals take to their warm places for comfort there is a quietening of energies, a stilling of vibration. With this stilling of vibrations there is preparation for new birth so the energy is subdued but not entirely shut. As leaves fall from tree the branches are preparing themselves for new life so the vibrations of your earth are two fold; shutting down and also preparation, this creates a variance of vibration. When there is colder weather this preparation will be ceased until awakening in your springtime but at this moment you have preparation for new birth. Your atmosphere, your vibrations of your earth are two fold.

Next will come calm quiet time so you must use your energies as you perceive. You do not realise you perceive, but you are perceiving these energies. You are perceiving the calming effect of end of vibrant period but you are also perceiving the preparation for new birth of Mother Nature. These are two energies you are perceiving. You can utilise these energies. With your shutting down you can use this time to reflect on progress made, give thanks for progress, it is good to acknowledge progress as you acknowledge fruits of your earth it is also good to acknowledge fruits of your labours, both physical and spiritual. Look back, take account of your path, what has occurred good and not so good, we do not say negative we say good and not so good. Path has to have stumbling blocks this is way of progress, you learn from stumbling blocks. If path is clear you do not have to strive to overcome so this is the way. As you reflect also reflect on those who walk with you both your earthly companions and your spirit companions. Acknowledge their existence, give thanks for their friendship and comradeship. When your time of reflections comes to conclusion you then prepare yourself for next step forward. You have phase on your earth when there is quiet, no life. This is also with progress you have to have time of taking into account and pause before new growth (16.09.97)

QUESTION 82 - *Hannah telling us more about herself and her work in spirit. (see question 68).*

'I have brought you something, I have brought my dog to see you he is laying by my feet.' It was perceived by a sitter as being a brown dog with white patches. 'His name is Patch, he is with me. He will be good, he will just lie quiet, he is a good dog. He is putting his nose on my knee, good boy.'

Hannah was asked what her work is in spirit.

'I give you a clue, you have to find out. I have brought my dog with me so what do you think I do?'

Do you have a link with the animals in spirit?

'I look after those ones who have no one to look after them. I will try and explain, when they go home to spirit they go to a group soul but sometimes there is someone in the spirit world who wants their companion so I try to find their companion for them.'

This must be quite a difficult job.

'No, because you do not understand our vibrations.'

When somebody has a pet is there an association between the one who loves that pet and the actual pet?

'There is a link. They cannot have our vibration'

For example if you are talking about cats, there are wild cats, there are farm cats and there are pets. There are animals who run wild and there are those who are pampered and of whom a great fuss is made. Is there a difference in that vibration?

'You have companions, you have Friends who have human bodies some are companions, some are friends. It is the same some have closer links than others. Of course, your pets today, you use word pampered. Our pets they worked, they did not sit on velvet cushions, of course some did when they were owned by people who had a lot of money and they were bored and wanted a play thing. Our animals lived with us and shared our life, shared our existence with us. No need to take them for a walk they took themselves for a walk. Our cats would hunt, of course we would give them food also. They would not have food as your cats have food, they would have what we had ourselves, left from our plates. Sometimes we would give them a treat if we had some spare but they would hunt. Your way of having food is different, we would have different food from you. Your food comes in packets, we would go to a butcher or he come to us, or whatever, sometimes we had food from farm or friends and there would be part of the animal we would not eat but we could give that to our animals. You do not have this now. My friend, Patch, he would have a proper bone. He would have whatever I could find for him. He was a good boy, he would look after me. He is not a tiny dog, he is not a big dog, he is in between. No special make, just dog. He came from farm. When he had bad paw I would make it better I did not take him to doctor as you take your pets to doctor. He would go and cut his paw so I would make it better.' (16.09.97)

QUESTION 83 - *Running Bear responding to question regarding the animals kingdom in the spirit realms.*

This is vast subject, where do you wish me to begin? I try to explain animals that spend their life with humans because this is the level you understand. Animals were all once you say 'wild', this is not wild this is their natural habitat. They fend for themselves, they take care of themselves, they are animals of pack. When the animal becomes ill, sick, weak the pack turn on that one. Your human brain says this is cruel but this is way of nature, only the strongest can survive. If all the pack were drawn down to the level of one who was weak the pack would not survive so this is nature's way of filtering. You say this is cruel but animals have different perception than yourselves, they have feelings, yes, but not human feeling. They are pack animals but within themselves they are also solitary. Your wild animals have sense, when they know their time has come they take themselves away from pack because they know they are no longer part of pack. This is a sense, not a feeling as you have, they do not sense and reason as you have sense and reason, they live on instinct for survival. They care for one another, yes, but for good of all. There are varying degrees of love depending on size of brain of animal. There are animals which are very like human kingdom and their brain has been evolved to think more sensitive than other animals who walk on four legs but there is still distance between these animals and the human kingdom

I try to explain when these animals go home to spirit they go to a group soul, they are not individual as you are. You go home to your home family in spirit you merge your vibration but are still individual, you still have your own memory and your own thoughts, own experience which you share with others but you also keep your own vibration as well. This is not so with animals, animals go to group soul

Now I leave animals of field and forest and come to animals who share their lives with humans. Over many generations this species have shared life with humans, their instincts are still animal but they have come away from survival. Many of your animals would not be able to survive on their own instinct so there is a step away from animals of field and forest. These are still animals of group soul but through their life on earth their instincts have become on similar vibration to human, whereas they can understand human thought. They know much more than you know of surroundings, they know much more of danger than you, they can feel sense of change of vibration in circumstance, in weather, in what is going to occur much more than humans. They do not reason as you reason but there is one likeness, you communicate on vibration and they communicate on vibration. As they have lived with humans for many years, many generations of years, there is aptitude to read human's mind. They do not understand your words because they do not speak as you but they know your thoughts because of this communication between human and animal kingdom. As you communicate on vibration level they decode your thoughts. They do not decode your thoughts into words, they do not decode you thinking 'I am going to feed my animal' they are decoding that you are going to take food from container, whatever, and place where animal feeds. This is what they decode but still their senses are different from yours. Their hearing senses, their smell, their natural instincts are much more acute than human's.When they go home to spirit they go home to group but when human goes home to spirit they go to group but are still individual.

Now, when a human in spirit thinks of the animal they shared their human existence with there is a possibility that the animal can leave the group and come to be a companion to that one in spirit. Sometimes people have an animal companion because it is the thing to do. There is not love for animal they just have the animal because it seems a good idea at the time. In spirit only if there is deep love for the animal companion can that animal accompany that one. Ultimately that spirit animal must go back to their group because that is it's home. It is still part of group. It can come from group and spend time with that one who shared their human existence. It is a companion for that one, it is something which they shared love with and they can still share love with, but as that one progresses in spirit gradually they grow apart and the animal goes back to group soul, but for a time they can walk with that one. Animals give much love and this is of great use one to other.

There is another thing I must explain When animal goes home to spirit and human is left on earth, when that human sends love to animal that animal can sense and can return to the one on earth as a spirit essence so the one on earth, if gifted with sight they can perceive that animal companion. If they are not gifted with sight perhaps one who is will say to them you have an animal with you and they will describe because they are decoding the essence, the vibration. They are not seeing animal they are decoding the vibration.

We still talk of animal which has gone home to spirit and human on earth. The human on earth may spend many more years on earth but still miss their spirit companion, because it is a spirit companion now. Perhaps in time that human will take another pet from small pet not full grown pet, infant pet and that one could have soul of the previous pet so that could come back into the body of the new pet. Sometimes you may meet an animal in your world and that one is drawn to you, and you wonder why this one keeps coming to you, it may not be your animal but this one keeps coming and you wonder why, this is because you have shared existence before. That one has come back. They do not spend long while in this group in spirit, they keep returning unless there is one in spirit who wishes to share their spirit existence with them, then they stay. If the animal goes home to spirit it quickly returns into body of another animal, of similar animal. You would not have one species jump into other species. You would not have fish come back as bear.

Purpose of animal is different depending on existence on earth Those who you share your life their purpose is love, companionship but of course, those of field and forest this is different they have duty to each other. They have duty of survival, to the pack. Also, they have duty to the existence of your earth because those of field and forest have effect on the surroundings where they exist.

We walked very close to the animal kingdom, we lived with animal kingdom, not as you live with animal kingdom but we were able to perceive animal kingdom because we used our instincts, which you have but are now lost deep within you. We lived with these so we were able to share our existence. We could sense danger when animals were near, we were able to sense this so we were able to protect ourselves. This is instinct which man has no more, except in areas where there is still close contact with surroundings of earth not mankind. There has been over many thousands of years this contact with man sharing life with animal kingdom. You now share life with animal kingdom because you now have what you call pets. Man has shared the world with animal kingdom for aeons of time and they have learned to live together. There are those who live in forest and jungle who learn to respect their brothers and sisters of animal kingdom. Then there were those who came and abused this system and destroyed for the sake of destroying and this caused disturbance in animal kingdom. This made an imbalance in animal kingdom and the animal kingdom became more ferocious because of this. This was self protection. The animal kingdom always was ferocious because they had to kill to live, when frightened they would fight back but for many aeons of time there was mutual respect between animal and human kingdom but I talk of many moons ago. Man has destroyed this balance now and there is separation between animal kingdom and human kingdom through fear and greed. (21.09.97)

QUESTION 84 - E-om-ba talks about healing bringing peace in peoples ' lives.

This is a very big subject, you cannot heal the whole world. You perceive now because of information you have had given you, there is much trouble all over your world so your heart goes out to those all over the world. This is not very good because the area is much too wide you cannot heal the whole world. Do not forget the whole world, do not turn away and say 'I can do no good'. You must accept that you cannot heal the whole world so start with yourself. Look within yourself, look where you are not happy. When you are not happy you cause a vibration which is not happy, imbalance. Heal yourself first, look within. Know yourself, learn of yourself, learn why you think as you think. Then when you begin to know yourself love yourself. Look at yourself, look at your body. Look at your hands, your fingers, your toes, your face, observe everything you do, think how marvellous your body is. You can touch, sense, feel, put hand down, pick up object. You can take food prepared with hand, put in mouth, tongue and teeth chew food, from then food is absorbed through body. Your body, without your help, knows how to digest food, knows how to take from food what is needed for your body. Think how marvellous your body is. Oh yes, you have aches and pains but what are aches and pains? They are signs telling you there are a problem. This again is good, because if you did not know of a problem you would do more harm to your body. Learn how good body is, love your body. When you have learned to love your body look within at the spirit within, how bright spirit within shines, how much knowledge you have within you.

When you have balance of spirit good in you, you can then start to look out of your body to those near you who are in need. Because your body is in harmony you are able to see these people who need healing with a different light. You are then able to share your love, teach them to love themselves, teach them to look within. Yes, they have problems, maybe they have problems with physical body, maybe problems with anxiety, or tension, or distress but teach them to love themselves. Only to worry for today, not to worry for tomorrow because this makes problems grow. When you are able to help those around you, you are then able to teach them to help those who they meet, their family, their friends. So they in turn help others, so you end up healing the whole world but you cannot start with the whole world, you must start from 'you'.

This is a little way of answering a big question. Love yourself, do not feel it is wrong to love yourself because that is putting up a barrier. It is good to love yourself, appreciate your human body. Appreciate if your human body is this perfect, even with it's aches and pains and problems think how much more perfect your spirit body is.

E-om-ba was then asked about imperfection, action in the past which we now regret. If you had not had these experiences in the past you would not be 'you', you would be somebody else. This is part of 'you', you have to love yourself as you are. You cannot look at a picture of somebody else and say I love that person not me, because that is not you. That other person may have other things which you do not know of. No one is perfect. We all have things in past experiences which we regret. It is because we have come through these experiences and learnt from them, we are stronger and our spirit has grown. No one is perfect, we have all done things that if we were to live our lives again we would not do but we have gone through that experience for a reason.

You are in your human body, in your human body you have human traits that have been handed down to you from your ancestors. For example, some people may have a temper, this is often something which is inherited, it often runs in a family. Perhaps you chose to come to this body with an inherited temper because you wanted to grow and learn more through becoming more patient. Also, you are in a human body, a human body is weak, it tires. When it tires your patience is low so you often choose the easy way rather than the way you think you should go. You are human you cannot go around with a smile on your face and halo around your head all the time. Those who you meet, those who you share your path with, they are human also. We have spoken to you of vibrations, some who you walk path with and you are happy with, another there is something in their vibration which does not mingle with your vibration. This make a disturbance and when you have this disturbance it is very easy not to be close, you tend to step aside and shun. Whereas, perhaps you will give a helping hand to one, to another perhaps you would say 'you help yourself'. This is because you have a different vibration, not only human but your spirit vibration may be different. At this stage of both your existence you are not compatible, perhaps that one has to walk a little more on path, perhaps you have to walk a little more on path before you become compatible. Perhaps not in this lifetime, perhaps when you go home to spirit you will not be on same vibration level as that one. One may be higher, one may be lower, not good not bad just different. When you walk earth your spirit within you senses this and that one's spirit within senses also, so you find it difficult to make companionship. If you have two people, one you have better vibration with, that one you will help and the other one you will say 'that is the way you walk therefore, I will not walk with you'.

You are here to learn lessons, you are here to grow. Not lessons like in your school but you are here to grow and learn. This is part of your learning. We also still learn. There are many things put in path to make you stumble but you become stronger when you pick yourself up. This starts with individuals but can also become problems with nations. (29.09.97)

QUESTION 85 - *Mafra answering question regarding a previous trance spirit communication when certain words did not record on the tape recorder.*

I will try and explain a little bit about what happened before because your friends will be very puzzled. (this communication was not in our full circle) There was one that has gone home to spirit recently and this one was friends of you all, he had no fear he knew he was going home and he was happy to go home. He wanted most of all, as you would when you go on journey, to send greeting to those who you had left behind and say I have made my journey I am happy, I am enjoying He wanted this but because he had not travelled that far he was not able to return himself but he was able to ask assistance of another vibration who was able to return to give his greetings for him. This one was one that was with him when he left your world and was the one that travelled with him to his new home and saw him safely through. Because your brother was a wise soul this one who travelled with him was of a high progression, he was a high vibration.

When he wanted to come back to give greetings he came and he gave greetings, he gave words of gratitude, thanks and things your brother wanted to be relayed to you. This was given as I am talking now, he was finding words and instructing voice to speak words, there was no thought as I speak now, there is no thought. I am putting a vibration which is finding word and the word is formed by messages being sent from brain to voice through vocal cords and tongue to make word but when this one first came, before these words were spoken, he came on very high vibration level. He made himself known by making sound direct through mouth without using vocal cords, so when the recording was made there was no vibration because your voice through your vocal cords is making a disturbance in the air. When you talk, when you speak, when you sing your vocal cords are making a noise and the noise is coming from your mouth and making a vibration, this vibration hits the receiver of your recorder and this makes impression on your tape. When this other method of communication was occurring there was no vibration, so there was not disturbance of the air and no vibration on your recorder to make impression on your tape.

This is similar to when voice comes from your trumpet that comes without vocal cords, direct from spirit. You have not experienced this yet on your trumpet but I say trumpet because you know what I am speaking of. This would not record unless we wished it to be recorded than we would make a vibration as a voice box. A spirit voice box can be manufactured by ectoplasm and then in this instance there would be vibration and this would be recordable. On some occasions this does not occur the voice comes direct through the trumpet without an ectoplasmic voice box, then this would not be able to be recorded because there would not be the disturbance in the air to make the impression on the recording.

Let me explain a little more, will you all put one hand in front of your mouth. Just a few inches away from your mouth not far. With your fingers facing your mouth, not the palm but the fingers. Now just say a few words and observe what hits your fingers. Do you observe the vibration, the disturbance of the air that your voice is creating? This is what I was trying to explain When you do not have the vocal cords in operation this does not occur. If you mouth a word without using your vocal cords, now observe what occurs on your fingers. Does this explain for you? I hope I was able to explain, it is very interesting is it not? You see we experiment with other ways of communicating there are so many. (29.09.97)

QUESTION 86 - Running Bear explaining spirit's ability to experiment and learn themselves about communication.

When we make noises, ring the bell or knock within the room your sitters know it is pure spirit without doubt as the ringing or noises are coming from areas where none of you have contact. We are working, like you we learn, we learn as you learn. We do not see the future, we strive as you strive we do not know all the answers. Just because we do not have an earthly body does not mean we know everything. We have to work as you have to work. You learn to work in harmony with each other, we learn to work in harmony with rest of group, mingle vibrations, merge vibrations in unison. We strive for this end but if we knew we were going to be successful we would sit back and say 'it is going to happen'.Like you we have to learn to work in harmony. You have personality on earth, there is personality also in spirit. We have to learn to be one level, one vibration Your world thinks it is so easy, once you have no body nothing is going to stop things happening but we do not know all the answers, we work also. We have much way to go up the ladder, we are not top of ladder yet. We strive for harmony, we strive for love, for peace, we strive for union of vibrations for goodness of energies so we can assist where help is needed.

Also, we learn to teach This is our aim to teach as many need to know answers. There are many ways of teaching, my friends. Many, many ways. You just think of classroom on your earth with teacher it is not so. Much learned souls share knowledge in different ways. We learn from those with more knowledge than ourselves but also we learn from each other on the same level. As you walk through your earth life you learn from each other, you learn from demonstration. You see what happens and you learn from what happens. You see what happens to others and you learn from that situation. Your greatest learning comes from your own experience. You cannot walk in your brother's shoes. You can walk along side to hold hand but you cannot walk in their shoes. Each soul is different, yes, we merge energy and vibration in harmony but each soul is different. No soul is same as next soul, even those born the same time are different. Each has their own spark within. You cannot walk others shoes for them. No one can walk your shoes for you. You have to walk your own path. You can watch and learn but to grow from learning you have to walk your own experience. Sometimes it is very difficult when you see someone close and you wish to assist, you wish you could walk their path for them but this is difficult lesson for you to learn. You have to stand back and watch, it is not easy.

It is not easy for us when we watch what occurs on your earth We wish we could share our knowledge, we can to some extent but that one has to walk their own path to experience for themselves. We can give strength, protection but we cannot walk the path for that one. I not talk of one person I just give an example. If you had an obstacle in your path we could support you, give you strength but we would not be able to walk that path for you. The closer you are to spirit the more we can surround you with our love and our strength to give you strength. If you do not accept spirit it is very difficult for spirit because they can see that one stumbling but they cannot get near to give strength This is a very difficult lesson for spirit to learn. This happens many times. Those in our world have those who they have left behind and those are perhaps grieving and because of this grief their loved ones cannot come near. This causes much clouding of vibrations, the spirit is not so bright as it wishes to be because it is concerned for those who are walking earth's path. This is path of progress for the one on earth and the one in spirit, both have to learn from this experience. It is an experience for both. As the one on earth grows in their knowledge the one in spirit grows also because as they come through this distressing time for them on earth they become stronger, their light becomes brighter, so the one in spirit who is close grows with them. They are happy to see them grow and come through experience, so their load is lightened also and they are able to become closer and give them strength. Gradually they learn to mingle vibrations so there is a two way learning. Even though the one on earth perhaps would not acknowledge the one in spirit, they do acknowledge with their higher level of communication. This does not perhaps penetrate to the conscious reasoning. Gradually the one in spirit can communicate with the higher energy level of the one on earth. This enables the one on earth to become more vibrant, more cheerful, not so distressed, not so depressed. Perhaps that one on earth does not realise why they are becoming less depressed because of this energy that is filtering through. The strength is being passed to them from their loved one in spirit, and because the loved one in spirit has been able to make this link they have learnt also, they have progressed also. As the link becomes stronger and more vibrant so they are both progressing.

Do not be distressed if you cannot assist all those who come your way. This is not a problem of you, it is not a problem of your earth, it is a problem of us all. We all encounter situations where we would love to assist but it is not the time to be able to do this. You have to learn first patience. Then you gradually, if it is destiny for that one to accept, you are able to merge energy and assist. If that one turns their back it is not a problem for you it is a problem for them. It is the same if you offer assistance before time is right, you create problem Wait for time for that one to seek, when that one seeks then is time to assist. If you offer too early you are making stumbling block for that one is not prepared. It is not their time. (01.10.97)

QUESTION 87 - John Lyon talking about spirit induced noises within the room during sitting.

I have been watching what has been occurring. There is much energy. There has been much happening which you have not perceived, there has been much movement around you. There have been many touches on shoulders and touches on arms and legs which you have not perceived. There has been much movement of energy. We experiment to find the level which is alive to your senses. We try to make sounds, some you perceive, some you do not perceive, no fault of your hearing it is adjustment of the vibrations to get the correct level of vibration for you to perceive. We are working my friends, we will cope.

A question was asked regarding the problems of tuning in with another group in another environment on special occasion. - This was to be expected, this was the first time you sat with this group. Many of them have sat together previously and they were more relaxed, you were conscious of being in a different surrounding with people who where not familiar with you. Whenever this occurs whatever the event, a social event or whatever, you are not easily relaxed you are a little apprehensive, that has to be expected. When there is movements and sounds and connections with spirit we have stressed so many times it is important to have harmony. Harmony is not something which occurs instantly it is something which has to be worked for. You have to lay aside all your thoughts of your own personality and mingle with the others in the group. This is difficult when you are meeting on an odd occasion. You are all individuals and you all have your own thoughts and ideas. To be part of a team whatever the team, whether it is a team for psychic reasons, a team for mundane earthly reasons, the longer the team are together the more experiences they share together the more they are able to mingle their energy together. You notice this in your places of work, when you have been through an industrious time when personalities have been put to one side and everyone works together to accomplish an end the team become stronger. Of course, you have personalities who do not always gel with the team and this is the same with whatever instance we speak of, whether it be spiritual or your mundane world. When this happens within a spiritual gathering sometimes the one who causes the problem is taken away for a particular reason and the group discovers that their progress has improved. The more you sit and the more you become aggrieved with that one the worse the condition becomes. Sometimes it is good to take a step back and to observe and look within yourself and look at the group and ask yourself are you going forward.

With this group I can say quite sincerely you are in complete harmony together, this is very good. Of course you are all individuals and you all have your own ideas, it would not be good for you all to be identical, no one in your world is identical. Each of you can bring your own thoughts and ideas and you have learnt to mingle these together in harmony. If one disagrees with another you have learnt to accept. If one has an interest in one particular facet and another has an interest in another facet, I will give an example. My friend (A) has an interest in art work, my sister (B) has an interest in healing, of course these mingle and they make you different in your outlook. Perhaps (A) perceives colours a lot differently to (B) because (B) thinks of colours as healing vibrations. (A) will think of colours he would use for his art work. So you perceive colours differently but you are able to merge in the group as a team and bring your own thoughts and ideas and share. You do not stand to one side and say 'I don't agree with what that one says' you accept that perhaps that one sees in a slightly different way but the end is together for harmony. This is a way of explaining it is not a way of criticising, it is a way of trying to explain. You each have your own experience from the past and you bring these together to the group. You have each come from a different family, even those who come from the same family, this occurs sometimes in other groups, within the family each one has experienced different events in their own life and different events have touched them and they have progressed through these events. So you have each brought something different to the team, it is good to merge your ideas, thoughts and vibrations. (05.10.97)

QUESTION 88 - John Lyon continues answering a question on the difference between the power of thought and spirit communication.

This is a wide subject. I will tackle the power of thought first. The power of thought covers everything within your world, everything within our world because thoughts are living vibrations. I will talk of your world. You are aware that thoughts are living vibrations and thoughts can have cause and effect. You are aware that when you send thoughts out of love to those who are in need, you have had vast evidence that these have been directed to ones you have desired healing for and there has been assistance. Maybe not a cure but that one has been given strength, upliftment, perhaps the degree of pain that has been suffered has been lessened, the depressions perhaps has been not so deep as would have been expected. So you have had proof that these thoughts are beneficial. You have sent thoughts to those who has passed from your world to our world and you have had messages back that they have been helped.

We have talked of the power of thought for love but there are also other thoughts. There are thoughts that cause disturbance, there are thoughts that cause anguish and anxiety, there are thoughts that cause confusion, so many thoughts. Some are intentional thoughts, some are thoughts that are just sent on the ether without any reason if you are anxious about somebody or something, your reaction is to worry. This is a human trait, it is part of your human emotion and you cannot help creating these thoughts. These thoughts, of course, are going out from your direction to wherever. Sometimes they go to a particular person, sometimes they are just pooled into a vast abyss. There is a great collection of these thoughts, these vibrations which go from all of you which are held in abeyance. You had an example of this very recently when one of your nobility went to the world of spirit, many of your population were sending out. They did not know where to send their love, where to send their anxiety, their grief, their anguish, they just needed to express this to relieve themselves of their tension. This was sent out into the atmosphere around, not particularly directed at any particular recipient This hung over and around your dimension for a while, some is still here, some has not been dispersed yet it is still around. Gradually these thoughts mingle with the atmosphere around your dimension and they are taken to various locations. If I say locations you perceive a place but this is not so. They have to be used, perhaps not immediately. Spirit at that time was working very closely with your dimension, our dimensions were very close and we were trying to neutralise these thoughts. We were trying to take away some the anxiety, some of the frustration because we knew this would rebound in your dimension because what is sent must return. There has been some rebound, there has been some recurrences already from these thoughts but spirit dimension has been very close.

You perceived, I believe, a great stillness, a great denseness of atmosphere at that time and this was heavy around your dimension and many in spirit were working. They had been prepared for this, we knew this occurrence was going to occur so we were ready. We were working to disperse this vibration and to some extent this has been successful but of course some of it has to rebound. Some of it has been used as a constructive energy. We were able to alter the vibration and use it to bring about an awakening to stir in people's thoughts questions, 'whys?', 'wherefores?', ' there must be other reasons for my existence than being here accumulating my worldly processions', 'why am I here?', ' what is the reason?', 'why do these things occur?'. So many questions. Spirit has been able to use this vibration to an effect to cause an awakening. As you say, in this moment of your time there are many events taking place which are drawing many of your earth people together because of these arousing of questions. They are seeking for something new, something that they cannot explain, something that is above what can be explained on your earth. You are very used to being quoted facts, figures, statistics and having a question answered precisely but this awakening is an answer to questions that cannot be answered. The population of your world is stretching that much further to realise there are these questions which are not answered. Because of this people are becoming more open, people are speaking more openly about these events. Before these were not spoken of because people were afraid of being classed an outsider, someone who was perhaps a little bit peculiar but now you find people in all walks of life discussing matters that they cannot explain and perhaps quoting someone they know who has had an experience and they can't explain that experience. This is just the beginning of a vast snowball which is growing.

Now, I have to go back to the original question. You asked about spirit communication. Spirit communication is not necessarily involved with thought because it is a natural condition. It is something which should occur naturally without thought. If you use thought you have to be very careful you are not using your reasoning power. If you are thinking 'I am going to ask a question', this is good because we ask you to ask questions. When a question is answered from spirit and you begin to analyse the answer you then have a problem of your conscious reasoning stepping in. When you perceive from spirit, I do not necessarily mean when a question is answered from a voice, I am speaking of when you ask a question in your mind of spirit and you expect spirit to provide an answer. The first impression you perceive is the impression which is purest, pure spirit communication. Once you perceive that and you try to decode it you are in danger of bringing in your conscious reasoning, once you start the process of thought because thought brings in experience you have had in the past and things you have read and heard. In that connection it is no good to think of thought. It is good just to observe your first reaction.

So you asked for thoughts on spirit communication, it is good if there are not thoughts on spirit communication you just leave yourself open to spirit. What you observe you question, of course you question this is a human trait and it is good you do. It is good perhaps if you just remember that first impression, perhaps if you can write it down and then think on afterwards but go back to your first impression.

It is a very deep subject there is so much more to discuss another time. (05.10.97)

QUESTION 89 - John Lyon continues by responding to a question regarding people who pass to spirit around the same time do they travel together or do they go to their respective families?

When one leaves your world they are taken, as you know it has been described to you as a tunnel of light. This is a good way of explaining because they are taken away from the earthly vibration, away from the darkness and heaviness of earth through into the light, to a much lighter and livelier vibration. This has much difference depending on the one who has gone home, the circumstances they have experienced, whether they are prepared. When a young one goes and they go suddenly, of course this is traumatic for those who are left behind and the one that has gone. They are often taken slowly and they are, I use the word awakened because that is a good way to explain. Their spirit is welcomed slowly into the spirit dimension because there has to be a time of healing, not of the human body but of the soul, the spirit because there is confusion. If the one who went home suddenly was taken too quickly and aroused too quickly they would have a problem accepting that they no longer had a body. This has occurred in some instances in your world, where those who have gone to spirit quickly cannot accept that they are in spirit. Some would have differing expectations of their new world. Some would be on different progression levels, some would be on compatible levels others not.

If they are on compatible levels, compatible vibrations. When they are fully aware of their situation they could then mingle their vibration, their energy but this would not be until they were at that time of awakening. In the first instance they would be surrounded with their loved ones, their helpers and their spirit family. Then they would be gradually led to whatever option they had chosen. (05.10.97)

QUESTION 90 - Beda talking about harmony within a group and table movement.

You must think as one, this is good. This is very helpful for movement of table. No one says 'the table is coming to me tonight so I will draw table to me'. They are just happy to see what happens. There must be no jealousy or desire for occurrence, someone special to talk or give message this would not be harmonious. If one has an objective this would override others so you need harmony. If one member of the group is depleted this does not matter because when you are in harmony you all work together and share the energy you have. If this was not so one would pull the others down but this will not happen if you are harmonious together. Instead of pulling down the group can assist the one who is depleted, as you know the more you give the more is created. Giving in an unselfish manner, the more you give unselfishly the more you create. If you give for your own satisfaction this is not the same.

The question was asked 'how can we ensure that the movement of the table is under spirit control?' - You can experiment. You try and lift, yes you can but the weight is different from when we are assisting you. If we assist you the weight is not there but if you lift it yourself you can feel a different sensation. You know enough now to know the difference between just energy and the energy of yourselves and spirit combined. It is a different vibration, you can decode. If one is over exuberant you will be aware when this occurs because you are able to feel the difference in energy vibration. If you feel this happening, stop - take your hands away and start again, clear and come back. You realise that when the table is moved very high this cannot be movement made by yourselves. Once we have the momentum movement begins, we are able to build higher movements. It is the initial starting that can be a problem. This is the same as your trumpet, once we manage to have it off the table it will be much easier, it is just the first few centimetres of height.

You are still part of earth and you have gravity, We have to neutralise the gravity so gravity does not pull back down. This is what occurs we are removing the pull of gravity. This is a substance of your earth. You are standing on the earth which is moving, earth is not flat, earth is round. You are standing at an angle on earth which is moving if you had no gravity you would spin off the earth so you need gravity. Everything on your earth is controlled by gravity. We work to neutralise your objects this enables them to be disassociated with the material substance of gravity, they can throw aside gravity. When they are at an angle away from solid ground we are able to lift and destroy the pull of gravity. (At this point Beda acknowledged that she was being given information from Hanns with his greater scientific knowledge).

Your thoughts are not controlled by gravity they can move around your world where they are directed. They are part of spirit dimension not earth dimension. They share your human body but they are part of a higher understanding that you posses, of a higher calibre. When you have thoughts that are gross, unkind, destructive these are of a material level they are of earth and they pull you down as gravity pulls you down. As your thoughts become lighter and more pure, more of love in your thoughts the higher vibration they become, they can 'fly' wherever. The thoughts that are not good are the ones that are destructive to those of that level. You cannot harm those of a higher level with these thoughts because these thoughts cannot rise to their level. They only attack those who are on that level. Those who are of a higher vibration can rise above these thoughts. This is why you ask for protection and we lift you to that level where these substances cannot harm you. I talk of earth thoughts but of course there are levels in our world too that are not so high. Those who come over to our world who are on a lower level of vibration do not automatically rise above, they are still that level so their thoughts can still cause problems to your world on earth. Those like yourselves who are searching if you do not lift yourself above you can be affected by those who are wishing to link with those on earth. You see this is why you ask for protection to be lifted above that level. (08.10.97)

QUESTION 91 - *E-om-ba responding to question 'do animals reincarnate?'*

When an animal in world takes on an existence a vibration comes from the group soul to enter that animal body. If you have an animal as a companion when their time on your earth comes to an end they go home to group soul, they stay in group soul. Your friend Hannah has told you what happens in spirit when someone in our world wants their companion. If the one on earth who had that animal companion is still on earth, then that one in spirit can be brought to that one on earth as visitor. They can be in the presence of their human companion. Sometimes you may notice that, perhaps, an animal is attached to you, an animal you meet on earth. Maybe you go to choose a new animal and one animal seems to come to you from group. Maybe, you are in your home and an animal from your area spends a lot of time in your area this could mean that this one was a companion to you before and they recognise your vibration and are attracted to you. You say, do they reincarnate this is my way of explaining. They can return to earth in the vicinity of the one who loved them. Maybe not as that one's companion but maybe in the area so they still have a link with their human companion.

E-om-ba was asked if an animal could return as a human in another incarnation. - This is not possible. Why would they want to return as a human, in some ways animals are much superior to humans. Animals love, animals do not have malice as humans have malice. When in a body they have instincts for survival which make them fierce but this is not malice this is survival. Animals do not lie they give trust so why would they wish to take step backwards into a spirit which is a different vibration? One is not superior to other. On your earth where there are humans and animals because the human walks on two legs and has command of the world humans consider themselves superior. We are not talking of a physical world we are talking of the spirit within. (12.10.97)

QUESTION 92 - Rosa talking about inner peace, being able to relax and shut out the outside world.

You are born to the life you have and you are part of that life. You dream of winning a lot of money and going to do this and not do that, it is good to dream it helps you to relax. It help you to take yourself into another world, dream world but you have to come back to this world. You must learn to take yourself away from your worries. I know this is very difficult but if you take yourself into imagination world for a little while, I do not mean live in a dream world you cannot do this. For a little while you can pretend you are in another world where you can create what you wish, you can create a garden, a big house, motor car, whatever. This is just releasing your tension. It is releasing you from your real world but you know you must come back. It is when you cannot come back that you have a problem. Some people in your world have problems with the way their brain functions, they live in this dream world all the time and this is not good. This is because there is a physical problem with their brain, it is a problem not caused by meditation, it is caused because their brain is not working as it should. It is as much a physical problem as breaking your leg is a physical problem. If you just dream for a short while, when you dream you know it is a dream this is a good way of relaxing.

You do not need to do this because you know how to withdraw completely, shut down from outside world. All of this group know how to shut down the outside world when you come into this room or when you sit in a quiet corner in your own home. You physically make yourself secure, you physically turn down anything that will disturb you, any noises that will disturb you are shut away. By making this effort you are closing down the outside world and releasing your tension from the outside world to go into your thoughts.

If you are talking to someone who has a problem because they have many stresses in their world you could say to them just for a short while imagine something different to take yourself away then come back. As long as they do not become so involved in this imagination they do not want to come back, you have to be very careful not to make it too much of a real world this imagination. I try to show you a way of shutting out without living in fantasy land. Sometimes when you lay in bed and you have problems sleeping, sometimes the more you think I am going to relax, I am going to sleep the harder it becomes. Perhaps that is the time to daydream, daydream yourself at seaside, daydream yourself walking in the country, daydream yourself sitting on a mountain, walking by river. In this daydream you are then relaxing, you are not saying 'I am relaxing I am going to sleep' you are occupying your mind with something different and then quite often you may fall asleep because you are relaxing. I just give you ideas. (12.10.97)

QUESTION 93 - Rosa continues by discussing spirit helpers who when on earth were nuns they described their work as 'a calling'. She then goes on to explain destiny.

These helpers say when you are dedicated to work for God you are called. She says she was called. Perhaps you have been called to do something. This is very interesting really. As you go through your life on earth and when you come to spirit also, you all have ideas what you wish to do but if it is not what you are meant to do you go round in a circle and come back and change ideas. You may say that you do not want to do that, you want to do something else, but spirit gets you back on that path in the end. If you have an ability to help in one particular way and you turn your back on that ability this means that you are turning your back on helping people. You are doing yourself no good by refusing to do this because you are not helping people who you could be helping. In the end you come back to that path and you take that path up. It is what is meant it is good. Once you accept this you blossom, your spirit grows, so that is good. We all do not like some of the things we have to do and we fight against them. It may be an experience you do not want to go through and you keep putting if off saying 'I am not going to do that'. You accept you have to do it, the fear of doing it is greater than actually doing it. Once you are on the road to do it you find it is not so bad. and you enjoy doing it or at least you do get satisfaction. You come for experience and if you do not want this experience you are doing your progression no good. I hope I give words that are helpful. (12.10.97)

QUESTION 94 - From time to time the subject comes up of what we term the Ouija board. Is this a good way to communicate or is it a very basic way - Running Bear gives his thoughts on this subject.

When you sit you communicate whichever way you choose. You

sit with intent in mind. You attract to yourselves what you wish, whatever your level of thoughts you attract that level back to yourself. You have learnt to ask for protection, you have learnt to ask for guidance but also within your heart you have sincere wish to link for purpose, for learning, for progression. You have learnt this over years, many have not had this advantage they know not how to communicate with spirit. They know not of desire to communicate on other level, they know not of knowledge that is open to them on other level, they just know it is possible to sit and contact another world who will answer their question. Some for amusement, some to seek answer to question. These ones are doing this because they know of no other way, they have heard of this practice. It matters not what instrument you use to communicate it is the thought from within, the desire from within that is of importance. If you would sit with what you call Ouija board you would not attract low vibration because you know of your routine but I do not think you would be happy because you are a step above, you have had experience of other ways. This way is very basic.

It seems that people with little knowledge are able to communicate using this method - It is as your pendulum. Your pendulum can be operated by your mind, so can table, so can so many other movements as you have discovered for yourselves from other experiences. The mind is very powerful. When those who sit with what you call Ouija board they want answer they can create answer for themselves or they may attract spirit but what kind of spirit? There are those in spirit who are of good vibration but they have not been trained in communication as we have been trained in communication. So if someone sat with this board they may have a relative in spirit world who wishes to contact them but this one knows not how to, there is no medium between to guide, no teacher. The one on earth is experimenting, the one in spirit is experimenting, both may be quite sincere in their desire to communicate with each but if they do not know the routine, the system, there are problems that other vibrations can come in. Those who are mischievous. This is why you ask for protection whenever you sit whichever way you communicate. This is where there are often problems because people do not realise what they are opening themselves to and of course those in our world also. They dearly wish to contact their ones on earth so when they see an opportunity they try and make contact, make link but when you sit in this way without asking for protection, without putting cloak of protection around you, mischievous influences can intertwine. There are those who do not sit for sincere reason they just sit for amusement and they are just opening doors for trouble.

We have explained that when you go home to spirit you are the same vibration as you leave so there are many in our world who are not advanced, who are not seeking for progression, many who would dearly love to return to earth to finish what they left off and seek opportunity to do this. When they had earth body they may have been confused, may have been disturbed in their thoughts, may have not known love so could not show love, they could only return what was given them. When they come to spirit they are in this state also and those more advanced souls have not been able to reach them because of their desire to come back to earth to finish or carry on. They may not even realise they are in spirit so when there is an opportunity they step forward to return to earth again and link with someone who is opening themselves to spirit. This is a great danger. This is why your men of the cloth of your churches do not favour spirit communion outside of their church because they have had to handle such affairs and they have seen the danger.

As you know there are many levels of conscious reasoning and many levels of spirit communication. Once one has had a problem it takes a lot of work for spirit to disentangle the problem. There are many who are in spirit world who seek to do this work. They return and try to solve such problems. This is work which has to be taken carefully and has to be highly skilled. Spirits who undertake this work have to be highly evolved spirits so that no danger can harm them. They must be above that level so that they are not drawn into that level. When one is training for this work one is not allowed to undertake this work on their own, they train as a group with a higher level soul who is very experienced. Those who are training accompany that one, merge with that one's vibration to learn how to handle such a situation. A spirit would not be allowed to return on their own to do this work, they have to have a team with them, a highly evolved team because it is so easy to be drawn. When one has accompanied the team for a while that one is allowed to try themselves to undertake this work, but behind them is a team standing to step in if necessary. There is much work of this calibre be undertaken.

We would commune with spirit when we were on earth, it was natural for us. As you grew within your tribe you were introduced by your elders. First as child you would sit and watch, then as you reached maturity you would be initiated into ceremonies and you would take part in ceremonies with the wise ones. It was natural progression, the communion with your spirit ancestors. You were trained but this is not the same with your land. There are many young ones, and not so young ones who are seeking but do not know the way to go. They experiment because they are aware from within that there is another dimension, also they know from without because there is so much bombarding them of supernatural and they want to experiment. There is not training, they experiment with their colleagues, their friends because it is an adventure. There is not the family traditions that we had in our tribe and you had once in your country. Your young ones are encouraged to be independent, they do not want to be part of family group, what the family does is not for them they want something new, something different. This is sometimes the reason because when they have grown they have been bombarded with knowledge from elders and they can see flaws in this knowledge that has been handed to them and they want something different. Their views have not been listened to, they are frightened of speaking because they have been told to be silent and do as they are told. They are told 'this is what is being done, this is what always has been done' but when a soul in body becomes a certain age it needs to stretch and find for itself. This part of the upsurge of energy within that one, the body is maturing and there is a sudden spurt of energy, there is an awakening of hormones and endocrine and this makes that one very confused in their thoughts, their ideals and they are searching for something new and experimenting.

This is not new this has happened through aeons of your time but because there is so many things to experiment with in your world now it is much more noticeable. When there were smaller communities there was still rebellion but it was easier to keep this in check in a smaller community than in vast cities. The denser your population there more ideas there are going round and round in the atmosphere. The more vibrations there are to absorb and your young ones absorb because it is the age for them to absorb because they are stretching, they are wanting, they are seeking. They are absorbing all these energies there are around them and this is how they react.

There is not the necessity for survival as there was in our tribe. In the tribe we struggled to exist because of our way of life. As young ones matured they did not rebel so much because they were part of tribe, they all had their own responsibility to the tribe to keep the tribe surviving. When senior elder men of tribe went from tribe to hunt to provide food those younger ones took on responsibility to look after squaws and children. They had responsibility placed on them at young age and this helped them mature. In your country not that many aeons ago it was similar when your families were not cushioned by those who looked after them the elder brothers, sisters in family would look after their younger brothers and sisters. You life spans were not that great there were elder relatives to care for because perhaps, one of the partners would have gone to spirit and the other be left so the children's responsibility would be to look after elders. Now the young ones are free to experiment and do what they will.

Some of the things I have said today I have said before, I apologise, but it is good to repeat because this gives a different view of same story. (14.10.97)

QUESTION 95 - *Running Bear assisted by others gives an explanation as to how the use of a pendulum can be used to provide communication.*

You wish me to speak of pendulum. Pendulum is object which you use to provide you with answers, this object which is inanimate on it's own. If you lay pendulum on table, on floor, wherever it stays, it will not move. If you hang pendulum from hook it will not move unless, of course, there is movement of air. But when you hold pendulum in fingers you expect movement. It becomes extension of your psyche. When you first take possession of pendulum you must make this your pendulum, you must hold pendulum, stroke pendulum, finger pendulum, talk to pendulum so you become one with vibration. You become used to vibration and substance the pendulum is consisting of. Then you ask question with pendulum held very still. You must hold so cord comes over finger. You have no control over movement, you must not be able to move at will, you must hold in such way as pendulum is hanging loose and you cannot force with movement of finger.

You ask question, now what happens when you ask question? You expect pendulum to move one way or other to give you yes or no. Before you ask question you must say of your pendulum 'show me yes' 'show me no' so you know yourself when answer comes if it is negative or positive. No good copying others because each of you will work in your own way. One will work 'yes' one movement, the next person may have different movement for 'yes'. You must become aware of how pendulum works for you and it must be you who asks the question. No good you holding pendulum and someone else asking question because the pendulum must answer you for your vibration. You ask question and pendulum will move one way for 'yes', one way for 'no' and you have your answer.

How does this work? You ask question within your higher level of reasoning not your conscious reasoning. You are aware of answer to this question, this answer may have been communicated to you from spirit or it may be an answer you already know but it has not reached your conscious reasoning. This reply manifests itself in the sensitivity in your brain. As you know, your brain sends messages through your nervous system to all parts of your body, if you wish to eat your hands pick food from wherever and put to mouth. This is because your brain is sending messages to your hands to do this but when you have the pendulum this does not operate in the same way. It does not move your arm and fingers to make pendulum move. It sends message through your impulses in your involuntary nervous system. This is a system which you cannot operate yourself as the voluntary nervous system which you use for everyday functions. The involuntary nervous system is the system which controls movement without you being aware. It is occurring all the time within your body, your organs in your body are moving without you being able to tell them. You may be asleep but your body still functions, your food is being digested, your organs are moving and digesting food, your heart is pumping, your arteries are carrying blood around your body and your veins are pumping this blood up through the valves back to your heart, your lungs are expanding and relaxing without your instruction. This is your involuntary nervous system. All these occurrences are happening this way.

When you receive this answer via the pendulum there is a relay through this system through your brain down through your neck, through your shoulder, down through your upper arm, through your elbow, to your lower arm, down through your hands to the very tips of your fingers where you are holding this instrument you call pendulum. Without your being aware this pendulum begins to move. This is because there is a very tiny movement from your fingertips that you are not aware of which operates the movement of this pendulum and this give you the answer you are seeking.

So my friend, if you think on what is occurring, your pendulum is moving because of the instruction that has come from your higher sensitivity reasoning. It is manifesting itself as an actual movement but if you consider this you do not need pendulum because the answer is coming from within and you are just manifesting the movement. Because you are human you are not confident in your thoughts, if you see proof of a movement this is better than relying on thoughts. This is why you use pendulum, it is just prop. Once you have used pendulum for a while you can dispose of pendulum because you have opened the doorway to this higher sensitivity and you are able to perceive these answers yourself.

Having explained what occurs I must also put word of warning because there are many who are over exuberant unintentionally. You have been trained through many years of contact with spirit to appreciate thoughts and how you decode thoughts. There are those who have not had this opportunity and they say 'Ah pendulum that looks a good idea I will try this'. They pick pendulum, they ask questions 'am I going to win lot of money'? Of course they want answer to be 'yes' so they can make answer 'yes'. This is back to what has been explained before, it is your thoughts within. If your thoughts within are sincere, of a high awareness you attract what your thoughts are. If you wish to just play, if you just wish to have this for amusement, you have it for amusement but do not be surprised if the answer you get does not come true. The higher your thoughts, the more sincere your thoughts within your heart the purer your communication. We used similar things, not pendulum but similar items to read signs. In our tribe we would contact ancestors and ask ancestors advice for what was coming, harvest, problems within tribe, whether we should move, whatever. We would go into seclusion with wise ones and we would read signs with stones and other instruments so I understand how this works but I have problem finding words of your tongue to explain.

Running Bear then continues by explaining the workings of the human body and how it is affected by evolution.

Your body is very clever you do not realise how involved the workings of your body are. You do not understand until you have problem then you realise it is not working as it should. You just take for granted. This is as it should be because you cannot think all the time of what is occurring within body you are on earth to live life and you have many thoughts on how to live life without having to think about what happens within body, leave body to look after itself. As long as you feed body and keep body in good health as far as you can you are doing your responsibility to your body. Your body will work on it's own. There are those who abuse body that is another question but as long as you live within reasonable conditions and do not over stretch or over tire or exhaust, over react you are happy to leave body to look after itself. Of course, body is made of matter, substance and as all things of matter there is deterioration but this is part of being human.

Many problems now can be solved through your medical men, we of course treated in different way but we lived different lifestyle at different time on your earth. You have to live in the era you are existing in, and live that way. You cannot become detached from the era you are in. You have to not refuse the treatments that are offered to you because they are of your age. It is no good saying 'I want to go back to treatments that were on this earth 200 years ago' because your earth has moved on. You may not say it has progressed but you are living in this time span now of this age, so your body is of this age. Your body has evolved, your body is not the same as it would have been if you lived 200 years ago. It was different because the work that was done was different, the living conditions were different. Someone of that era would not survive in your world today, as someone from your era would have difficulty surviving in life as it was 200 years ago. It is evolution, just for one example, you notice your children each generation they grow in height from previous generation. This is just one example of evolution, there are many other in human bodies you do not see. Fighting disease, your bodies now are very sensitive to disease because you have come to rely on the medications of your day. You have been introduced to medicines which treat infection but this was not available years ago and many did not survive only the strongest. Those who did survive were very strong because their bodies fought infection but now today you have all these wonderful things which cure you but still you have more problems. This is life, you are here to have problems. The human body will never be perfect because it is human. Once there is a cure for one thing something else will occur because this is all part of being human. We did not have that problem. (26.10.97)

QUESTION 96 - Hanns then came to ask if we would like any further explanation regarding pendulums. The question was asked 'There are two things spoken of, the answers already in our brain and the answers being prompted by spirit. Therefore, somebody who has not been trained as a medium can they use this process of using a pendulum to develop their mediumship?'

Of course, but they must be able to shut down conscious reasoning. This is the danger when someone very eager who has not sat and trained they are taking from their conscious reasoning not from their higher level of reasoning. You say this with pendulum but this is the same with any form of spirit communication or mediumship. This can come from two levels, pure mediumship will come from the higher sensitivity level but there are some who have not fully understood their purpose and have not trained to shut down their conscious reasoning. When they give, as they think from spirit, it is not always from spirit it is from conscious reasoning or they are interpreting not giving pure spirit communication. They are absorbing spirit communication but because they have not shut down conscious reasoning they are putting their own interpretation and own experiences to spirit's communication. This is not only pendulum, it is any kind of communication. Because you have learned to sit and shut out external influences you have trained yourselves to shut down your conscious reasoning. Many sit and go into meditation but after short while there are ideas and thoughts coming in from what they have experienced themselves, what they did today, what they did yesterday, what somebody said to them, what they read, what they saw because they have not shut down properly. This is why we say to you leave everything outside that door. Whatever worry you have, leave pick it up when you go out forget while you are here. You have to be strict with yourself.

It is difficult when you have concern because you bring concern into room to ask for help for that one but once you have asked for help think what you have done. You have said to spirit 'this one (give name) needs help for (give problem). Trust spirit, you have asked spirit to help that one's problem, you have given name and condition to spirit for their help, leave that one with spirit now, let them help, you forget the patient. Do not worry about the patient while you are in this room he is being taken care of by spirit and being protected by spirit. You forget about the problem, trust spirit to deal with the problem, shut yourself down, don't worry about the problem. This is what you must do. Because you are kind people you worry but once you have asked spirit trust them and shut down, you are here for another reason now. (26.10.97)

QUESTION 97 - The following question was sent to us requesting an observation that in the questioners experience of spirit communication there seemed to be a general reluctance of communicators to talk about money and questioned if it was a "taboo" subject. We only know the questioner by correspondence and as far as we know we have not met the person "face to face". The question was answered by Mafra, firstly he took the typed letter and was able to pick up the writer's vibration then link with the writer and the writers spirit helpers, to ensure that he had understood the real meaning of the question.

You know that when you cast your bread on waters it returns manifold, there is no need to be concerned. You all wish to have sufficient to survive, we all did on our time on earth but if your time on earth has taught you anything it has taught you that you are given sufficient for your needs. There are those who would argue and say 'no there is not sufficient for our needs what about those who have no home, have no roof, no food'. Yes, my friend there are those but there are reasons. In your mundane world there is enough food for all, there are none who should be hungry even in your lands where there is famine and drought there are neighbouring lands who have abundance. Your mankind is greedy, you must share, you must look to each other and share. This is not a talk to be benevolent, this is the system of your earth, your world, of the people who rule your countries. There are many with very big hearts who would wish to give all they have to those who they see pictures of who are starving. These are to be praised but by doing this they are solving no problem. The little they can spare is meagre in comparison to what is needed. It is doing good and that one is blessed for their individual work but this is not what the aim is. The aim is to have a world where those who rule your world, your governments, are able to manage their countries and the people they have control over and provide all with sufficient for their needs. Not some with abundance and some with nothing. Where there are genuine needs, I say genuine because sometime in countries where there are problems there are those who have and those who have not, if those who have could share a little with those who have not much would be different.

There are those who are of a different level of vibration who are despised by others, perhaps because of their traditions, their backgrounds, the way of their life, but within each one of you there is spirit. You each wear an overcoat of a human body, you have come to that overcoat of a human body for a reason. Perhaps those who come to this overcoat of a human body where there is so much suffering are learning much more than those who have a much more comfortable existence. I am not talking of money, I am talking of material substances, food, comforts, but there are reasons for this division. Unfortunately your world has evolved in one way but in another it has taken a step backwards. There are those who wish to progress and those who do not wish to progress and we talk of this on spiritual level and human mundane level. You cannot understand why you have those with and those without sufficient of your earth money. There are those who spend their existence on your earth concerned with money and those who spend their existence in your world not concerned at all with money. Often those who do not have much in their purse will give generously to others but those who have vast amounts of money locked away will not open their coffers for others at all. This is a concept, a way of thinking, a way of existence. Sometimes it is caused by fear sometime it is greed.

Why be concerned of money because you know whatever happens there will be sufficient for your needs. I have come back round the circle from where I started. Again you say, 'yes, but my need many not be the same as the person next door needs, my aspirations may be higher I may want a better standard of existence, I may not be happy with two meals a day I may want three meals a day'. This goes on and on and on. The more you worry over these conditions the more you are shutting out spirit because all your energy is consumed in worrying about existence. You are not shutting yourself away from your world of existence to commune with spirit. The more you are concerned about money the more problems it causes. It is a concern I understand especially where there are conditions where you have to find money to pay for your bills, for your heating to keep warm and for your cooking, for your livelihood if you have people who have a low income and are concerned that they will not have enough to pay a bill this causes much anxiety. This is causing tension and tension can cause many problems, health problems, many, many problems. Because you are in a human body you are very concerned with this. If only you could take a step back and look at yourself and think 'what am I worrying about this is of no importance to the much greater, vast existence that is open to me, this short life span on this earth is so small compared to what is open to me beyond this world'. Because you are in this human body you are locked in this cage of concern.

This is why spirit shuts down when money is spoken of because it is trapping the human soul, the human being in this cage where there is anxiety, there is concern, where they cannot see further than their four walls. They cannot see beyond, much more is open to them if only they could lift themselves above this vibration, there is so, so much more open, so much more progression, advancement, learning but they are not free to take this path because they are trapped in this cage of concern. So when money is spoken of spirit shuts away because through many of your centuries, your years of existence there has always been problems with money. Even before you had money as a substance, as a coinage, you bartered and you were concerned you did not have sufficient of these goods to barter for your neighbours goods. It is not money it is this anxiety that you are not going to survive but of course if you look at history you do survive. My friend, if you don't what happens? Of course you look around you at those who are close to you and you wish to give them as much of the world's goods as you can, you wish also to make your life as comfortable as you can but if you compare your existence with that of a generation before you are living in luxury. Are you any happier? You concern yourself with money, they concerned themselves with money and their ancestors before them concerned themselves with money. This will go on because money is what your world is about. Just look beyond money and it's worries. (28.10.97)

QUESTION 98 - *John Lyon talking about the oncoming Christmas season. Responding to the query 'What happens with all the extra energy levels which are being sent out from our world at the time we call Christmas?'*

The human race are often very narrow in its concept. You celebrate Christmas but there are many denominations and many other beliefs, creeds. You have spirit visitors who speak to you who are not Christians, I was a Christian myself. You have E-om-ba, your brother Running Bear they are not of the same calling yet you have many of the Christian faith. There is a link with your vibration and your believing and your understanding which attracts a similar vibration but also this goes deeper than this belief, you have other vibrations also.

Unfortunately your time of celebration is very small, your time of preparation is very great and your time of preparation involves much frustration, much worry, much anxiety. This is not always as would have been wished for the festival of Christ. This festival is not a religious festival any more. It is for a few, for a short while there is love but this is soon forgotten but for a short while there is this upsurge of energy coming out from your world to others who are perhaps not so fortunate. This feeling of love is not particularly monopolised by the Christian faith, many other people who celebrate at your Christmas are not Christian but because your Country celebrates at this time of year others who have no faith perhaps still celebrate because it is a time of coming together of families. A time of exchanging messages, greetings to ones you have not seen or heard of for a long while. It is not particularly a Christian festival in this sense because the cards and greetings you send are not particularly of a religious value, they are a greeting to say 'hello it is the time of year when I remember you'. Some of you send cards with a religious message and a religious pictures which denotes what the festival is about but this is a very small percentage of the greetings cards which are sent. Although the religious part of the festival is now celebrated by quite a small percentage of your population there is a lot of love generated at this time for others regardless of faith.

A few years ago those of your Country who celebrated Christmas celebrated it as a religious festival. There were big celebrations in those homes that had more, those that did not have so much celebrated in a much smaller way but there was not the holiday sensation that you have now, work continued. Time was spared for attendance at the churches but other than that there was not the great festival which goes on for the period you celebrate now. This is tradition, this tradition has evolved and has become very commercialised. This you say is bad, it is in the respect that your population does not revere a higher source, does not recognise there is a supreme energy. I will not say the word God because there are many gods which you worship in your world now.

What you are celebrating now at Christmas is a time of holiday, a time of respite from your labours, a time of exuberance but also this brings with it many trappings. It brings with it much worry, much frustration, much anguish because there are many in your world who have not as much in their pocket as they would desire. I am not saying there is much poverty because there are those who do not have as much as they wish but they have enough to survive, but there are those who still wish for more. They wish to be able to give to their loved ones more than they can afford, because of this they create many problems and tensions, there is much expectations that cannot be fulfilled. This is causing many problems. There will come a time in your world when you will have to stand back and take note and analyse what is occurring because with all the extras that you have now there is not the happiness, money cannot buy you happiness. Your tables are full with food, your childrens' stocking are overflowing with presents, your trees are glittering with gold and silver, this is figuratively speaking of course, but there is not the contentment and happiness in your homes as perhaps a few years ago there was with an apple or an orange, or a small gift.

Your world must stand back and ask itself why, and your world will realise this is part of the new awakening that is occurring. Your world is now looking for another reason for your being here other than just accumulating wealth. You are thinking there must be a reason behind all this, we have all this but we are still not content so why are we here? This is part of this new awakening.

So going back to the question what happens with all the extra energy levels which are being sent out from your world at the time you call Christmas. Yes, spirit does utilise this but also there are other vibrations which are being sent out also. There are many who are unhappy, who are lonely at this time because they feel they are not part of what is going on, they feel they are being left out and this brings unhappiness. There are those who feel they have not sufficient funds to take part and they feel they are not giving their loved ones what they wish to give them because they have not sufficient funds. There are those who work very hard in the preparation for this event, materially, in your shops, restaurants, in your manufacturing industries, in your transport, they are working so hard they do not have time to relax and to enjoy themselves, to take part in the peace which Christmas is supposed to denote. There is the advantage of the love which goes out but also spirit work hard to replace the unevenness of the vibrations. There is much tension and anxiety and this causes illness, you know tension causes illness, and much healing is required at this time.

As you approach your Christmas period do not get involved in so much anxiety. It is very easy for us to say this to you because we are not on your earth at your time. You are surrounded for such a long period, because your Christmas preparations start so early in your year you are forever being reminded of Christmas, you are being reminded of all the trappings of Christmas, not of the spiritual reason for Christmas. Try to step back from this, try to just think of what Christmas is, it is a time, whatever your religion, when you think of something which is higher than the material. If you are a Christian you acknowledge that it is a Christian festival when you celebrate the birth of Christ and the whole story of the Nativity and what this means. If you do not follow the Christian religion this does not mean you cannot enjoy the Christmas festival because there are many in your Country today who do not follow the Christian religion but can enjoy the festival because they can look to a higher level vibration. They can look to the story of peace on earth and love for one another, they can enjoy the time they have with their loved ones.

Try to keep your Christmas as simple as possible, the harder you work the more you wish to gather round you, the further you are coming away from the true meaning of Christmas which is peace and love to each other. This should be for your whole world whatever their religion because you know all faiths lead to the one Godhead. Your various religions just give it a different name, you identify different prophets, different leaders, different saviours, redeemers whatever you wish to call these icons you worship. I am not saying it is wrong to worship a particular religion rather than another religion because to have faith is something which is above mortal reasoning is good. It helps you realise there is a higher being, a higher wisdom, a higher energy and your world that you know is not so important, that there is infinity. Also, you must, in your world look to each other and try and bring the peace of Christmas into every day of your year not just the one day. (02.11.97)

QUESTION 99 - George answering question about spirit communicating through a medium in church always conveying the health condition they passed with.

When they come back they come with a memory, their memory is when they were last in a body and they come back with that condition because that is their last memory. I will explain what happens when we come to talk to you, after we have been coming a little while you will notice the way we behave and talk is not the same as our first visit. When we first come back to earth we remember when we had a body and we think we have still got the same body, we try and do the same thing. After a while we get used to borrowing a body, so we are getting used to using the medium's body.

You are asking about when a spirit comes to a medium in a church to pass on a message to a loved one. They link with the medium, they give the medium their vibration and they come on a memory link. They remember the last time they were on earth and they bring that condition with them. If the medium is properly developed they should be able to go beyond that stage, not link with the memory but link with the essence. There are a lot of other things that would help to identify them. A medium should be able to cut through this and say to the spirit person 'you haven't got that condition any more, you are spirit you are here to prove to this one that you are still alive so give that one something that they will remember, not your health condition because you don't want that it is gone.' There are a lot of other things they could give as evidence, they could give the number of their house, the clothes they wore, their birthday, the car they drove or the road they lived in. It doesn't have to be the condition that caused sadness. The one who is sitting there will remember that loved one with the illness and that is not doing the one who is sitting there any good. Instead of remembering the spirit person as they were well and happy they are remembering them as they were when they were ill. That is not good.

It is not for me to tell a medium how to work because I am not a medium, I wouldn't have been able to do their job but if I was sitting in a church and a medium came to me with somebody who I had loved who had gone to spirit I would want them to tell me that person was here well and happy. Also perhaps some evidence to prove, because I would question I would need proof. What colour coat did they wear? Did they wear a hat? Did they wear glasses? Where did they work? Where did they go to school? Tell me something else to prove rather than tell me something that would make me sad.

It is partly the one who is coming back because they are bringing the condition but it is a memory link. They have touched the earth vibration again, last time they touched this vibration they had a pain here or they had a pain there.

George was then asked 'I can understand when someone returns the first time they would bring this health condition but surely next time they should be able to progress from that condition' George responded - Yes, but it could be a different medium. It is the way the medium decodes that vibration and that vibration has got that memory. It is how the medium is trained, some mediums are trained different from others. Some mediums get on platforms before they are ready. You can't say to them it is bad because they are doing it for love, they think 'if I can get up and help somebody I will. There is not enough people doing this job so I will do my bit to help the churches'. The churches have not got sufficient financial resources and they need someone to come on their platforms so the mediums are doing it for good reasons. They do not realise that if they only waited a bit longer they would be that much better. They are not doing themselves or anyone else a favour. I do not know what the solution is. I can only think it is better training. Also, some of the people in your congregations want to hear it. They say 'It can't be uncle Fred because uncle Fred died of a heart attack and he hasn't told me that so it can't be him. You tell me he wore a bowler hat and had a red carnation in his buttonhole but not what he died of so it still can't be him.' People have come to expect this type of communication so that is what they get, they will not accept anything else. It is unfortunate.

It is difficult in a church because you have so many other vibrations all cutting in. You get someone who died with a bad chest, if you are lucky and you have got ten people in your congregation, nine of them will say to themselves 'yes that must be Fred, or Tom, or Charlie,' or another name and they are all grabbing this message because they all knew people who died with a bad chest.

It is not easy you know, it is easy for us to criticise, very easy, but it is not easy when you are doing it. The mediums have the pressure of people demanding something from them. You just think of it, you have got these people sitting in a congregation, all saying 'I want a message'. You have got all these people sitting there waiting for a message from Fred, Tom, their mother or whoever. Then you have all the people from spirit saying 'There is my little Freddie in the audience, I want to go and talk to him' and the poor medium is in the middle. How is he/she going to sort them all out? Then they have the person sitting next to them on the platform saying you have only got so long to give the messages get as many out as you can. It is not easy. It is easy for George to say they are doing it wrong but I wouldn't like their job. (02.11.97)

QUESTION 100 - *E-om-ba talks about the way his tribe chanted to enable communication with ancestors to take place.*
We chanted for vibration, we chanted when we worshipped, we chanted for ancestors, we chanted for coming together of tribe, we chanted for meditation. We would go into meditation altogether, we would go hm hm hm hm.... Can you imagine this all the group making this noise the same time and this energy (he then demonstrated a very long chant), all tribe doing this. This was how we meditated, we would go into trance, we would put ourselves into trance this way, linking with ancestors. You do not do this, you have not been taught to do this so there is no need but this was our way. You have other way, perhaps you give prayer, you sing hymns, you link thoughts, everyone worships in different way. Our way was handed down through the tribe. You have people who try and write this down but it is no good. We were taught from little ones to big ones, this was our way.

There was different tone for different reason. We knew without thinking which vibration to use. There would be a big group sitting around, no words but we would all link in the same vibration and all chant the same pitch, the same time, the same note, the same duration and would all stop together. This would not be planned we would know. You are surprised as to how this happened. You go into your schools with your small children, you watch they do same. They start to sing together, no one tells them. You go into classroom, no teacher just little ones amusing themselves, they start to sing together at the same time, same song. You have this ability within to link with each other but as you grow from little to big you lose it because you learn how to use your senses in different ways so you do not use instinct. You learn to talk, to write, many other ways of communication. You wait to be told, you decide you are going to tell someone, you lose harmony. When you come to earth you have this ability, you have instinct within, natural instinct but as you go through earth life this takes back seat because you become more of your world and use your world's systems. This is something which comes with you when you take body, this instinct.

I see question, part instinct from within genetically because you all have instincts from when you were not so civilised but you also bring knowledge from spirit with you because this is the vibration spirit works with in our dimension when we link together. We merge energies but when you enter the earth's atmosphere you gradually lose this memory because you have to learn to live earth life. Gradually this memory is shut down but this continues when you have earth body no more. You have come to earth body for reason so you have to walk earth body path, gradually you lose memory of your instincts from spirit.

I find putting words together not easy because this was not our way, this was not needed, we would communicate on different vibration with each other. Mouth was just used for one or two words or our chants, no need for long words put together to make long sentences. This was before white man came and tried to write down our words. This was not possible, we learned from each other, each tribe had its own way of communicating, Their words were similar but each had their own way. If one from one tribe went to another tribe they would be able to communicate because they would be able to communicate on this other level. It would be easier to learn words that way because they would hear words but also would be able to know what was in the mind. (04.11.97)

A further question was asked 'when they had communication from their ancestors did everybody have the communication on the higher mind vibration or was it a trance speaker.'

I have already explained that our use of words was different from the method you use. We would chant when we gathered together as a tribe, we would sit together and chant because this was our custom. When we sat together as tribe we would wish to communicate with our ancestors, we would not speak to each other with words but we would be communicating on this other level of mind which I have spoken about. We would all commune with each other and we would all know what chant we wished to perform so we would all be together and we would continue calling to our ancestors to join with us. The elder of tribe would be the one who went into deep trance because he had a closer link with ancestors. We would all chant to raise vibration, we would chant to join with them. The elder of tribe would go into deeper trance than others and he would take on voice of ancestor and we would commune with ancestor. Others in tribe would be in semi-trance and they would also be communing as you all commune on this other level. They would be aware of the communication taking place. Younger members of the tribe would sit and take part in chant, in meditation but their role was to observe but as they became older, more senior in tribe they would go into semi-trance. There would always be different stages, those learning, those stepping up to next stage and when the elder of the tribe himself became ancestor the one below him in the tribe would take his place. We would have a ceremony to appoint him as our elder, then others in tribe would step up one place.

E-om-ba was asked to confirm that the words being spoken through the elder were being decoded by the others in the tribe, who were in semi-trance, thus obtaining the full understanding of the communication. Yes, but the elder of tribe would actually speak words. We might ask ancestor for advice 'Should our tribe move to another location? Should we plant seed now? Should we wait? What will happen if we plant crops now?' We may say 'One of tribe is unwell what should we do?' These are examples of the type of question we would ask ancestors. If there was concern over one in tribe, perhaps young warrior was causing concern, we would ask those ancestors for advice. Perhaps there would be problems with animals belonging to tribe, we would ask ancestors advice. So many questions.

E-om-ba was then asked if the communication they experienced was only with their ancestors. We would talk through ancestor to higher wisdom. Our tradition was to respect ancestor, when the ancestor went home to spirit we would revere that one and call on that one but we would realise that our ancestor was not of the highest level but they would act as an in-between. We would call on that one to ask higher ones for advice. We realised there was a higher spirit power who watched over us and would control our climate, our land, our circumstances, our destiny. We realised we had destiny so we would ask our ancestors to intercede for us to a higher spirit. You have evolved and as you have evolved in your human physical body and mind to absorb so much more from different directions so spirit has evolved within you and spirit can now stretch to many directions and contact many more vibrations. I try to give wisdom, I hope you understand. I am now like ancestor as I am calling on others to give me advice. (09.11.97)

QUESTION 101 - Jules answering a question regarding the thought process used in spirit.

Spirit do not think as you think. They do not have a human brain, we do not want human brain! Too much rubbish in human brain! We do not want clutter! We think but not the same process. We are of energy levels, vibrations. I will try and give an example, if you ask question of me, I am not using the medium's brain I just use voice, so you ask me a question now I have to find answer. If it is something I have in my experience I can tell you straight away because it is in my memory and I can tell you, but if you ask me about something which I have no memory of I send thought out to Mafra or whoever can help. They then merge their vibration with my vibration so then I can give the answer. This is how we communicate but you are asking about thinking.

By thinking do you work things out for yourself or do you just merge energy with others who have the experience? - It is mixture, there is so much experience within us from our spirit lives but also experience from our earth lives so we have this which we can call on at any time. Also, there may be something which we try to work out, for example. When you plan for future you have to sit and think 'I am going to do this today, I will do this tomorrow and I will do this next week, then I will have time to do that the week after etc. with all the consequences' this is how you work. We do not work the same as there is no future, there is no past, there is only now. What is future is already planned so we do not sit and work out. We have knowledge of so far along the road but we know that that much further is already planned, so there is no point in worrying, no point in working out, no problem it will happen. Have faith, there is plan, there are vibrations much higher than ours who have it in hand. There is cause and effect, what occurs now will come around again. You attract to yourself what you give out.

If I wish to learn, this is something which I can explain. I am giving an example - I now find myself in spirit and I have to work out what I want to do. I do this by pulling together all my experiences, all my vibrations and finding what from those experiences I have most satisfaction from, what I enjoy. Do I enjoy talking to you, coming back to talk to you? or do I enjoy not coming back to you but working in spirit with vibration, perhaps helping others who have just come to spirit? or perhaps, I am like Hannah, I enjoy being with animals vibrations. Perhaps I want to learn of scientific things. This is how we think not with human brain it is by drawing together all our vibrations and finding what we enjoy, what is the way forward. We do not want to be trapped and have no way forward. I do not want to be trapped and not go forward, some are happy to sit here in spirit and just stay where they are, so they stay. Not Jules, Jules wants to learn but not learn by going to school and sitting with books, learn by merging vibrations and energies. I merge my energies with those in our spirit world but also I come with you and blend with you and learn much from you.

If I wish to learn of something which I have no knowledge of, if I wanted to know how a motor car works I would link with your vibration if you were a man who understood and I would learn from you. If it was something not of your world I would merge with someone in spirit to learn how something in spirit works. This is how I would learn, not by thinking and puzzling, but by linking with an experience that knows. We make affirmatives, for example 'I want to come and talk to those people', I make what you call a thought. I would say I make a vibration to say 'I wish to come to talk'. You would call it thought but I would not I would call it a vibration with an affirmative, or if it was not an affirmative it may be a question. (04.11.97)

QUESTION 102 - E-om-ba was asked 'when you speak of linking with someone on a higher vibration level would we feel an empathy with that person?'

Some people you automatically feel a link with when you first meet and you feel happy with them. Some people you do not feel empathy with but that does not matter you still communicate on their higher level. It is easier for you if they are of the same vibration. You still communicate with those who are not so compatible but it takes longer to 'knock on their door' before they open. Sometimes you meet that one several times but they do not respond to you but one day you may meet them and you will find they are a little more friendly for a particular reason. There may be a situation where someone you meet is not friendly towards you however hard you try, do not be upset just accept them and let them go their way. It does not matter, next time you meet you may meet on a friendly vibration so it will be easier to make the link. If you become angry and upset you will make a barrier so it will be more difficult for you to link with that one in the future. If they are hostile to you do not take any notice. (09.11.97)

QUESTION 102 - E-om-ba telling us about the energy sent out from groups being used by spirit. He was asked whether this energy is for a specific purpose.

It is for all our progress, for your progress and our progress. I will try and explain; you are a group who sit here to learn, you link with us and from this group goes out to many people who need help. Other groups sit like you in other parts of your land and in other parts of your world. Some perhaps, do not sit as you sit but sit in meditation in different religions but they are sending out vibrations to where this is needed. You have been told there is much awakening, many questions going to be asked, already being asked. Your energy, your vibration links with many others. You think of a river in your land, a river starting as a tiny stream and as it goes along more streams join, the stream becomes wider, as more join the stream becomes a river. The river goes out to the sea, sea to ocean. This is to explain your vibration, your thoughts and energy is linking with all other energies that are being sent out to make big body of energy. When there is time of need in your world and our world, because when there are many come over to our world there is much need at that time, this energy is used. We draw from this sea of energy to be able to give help where needed. It is a light, a light which becomes brighter and brighter, it shows the way. This draws a picture for you to help you understand. (30.11.97)

QUESTION 103 - E-om-ba continues responding to a question concerning colour vibration. In particular the colours we wear.
Colour is vibration, vibration is colour. There is no line to divide, colour has vibration. You know when you have a bright colour there is much energy, if you have quite soft colour it is soothing. If you go in room where there are bright walls you feel much energy, if you go in room where there are very pale walls you feel very relaxed. *E-om-ba was asked whether spirit have any reaction to the colours we wear* - When you wear a colour, this colour does something to you because you wear colour you are absorbing colour. This make your energy level at a different level so when we link with you we link with your vibration not with what you wear. Your vibration is affected by the colours around you, what you wear, also the colours which others wear. We link with the 'you' inside, your spirit, your vibration, not with your earth body. You are absorbing colours not only your own clothes but clothes worn by others who are in close proximity to you. If you walk into a room where somebody is wearing a colour which you do not like this makes your vibration different because you shut against that one and this makes a difference to you, you are closing yourself, you are isolating yourself. This makes it more difficult for us to draw close when you close yourself up. When you relax and open it is easier for us to communicate and contact you. When you are very vibrant sometimes this is difficult because you are using much energy of human kind and you are absorbing yourself in matters of your world, which you have to because you are of your world.

The question was then asked 'If we want to meditate would a certain colour be more suitable?' - It depends whether you can shut yourself off from the outside world. You have learnt that when you come here you shut out all outside influences so it doesn't matter if you are sitting in a room which is bright red it would not worry you because you have learnt to shut away. If you were going through a time when you have a great anxiety and you found it difficult to relax and shut away then it would be good to wear a subdued colour, not a colour like grey that is not good. Grey is not a good colour, It is no colour, you need colour as mauve, blue or green that gives energy, grey is no good. It is a 'no' colour. Black is no good for a different reason but grey draws down, depresses, it is a colour which makes vibrations very low. Black is colour which shuts down but if you put another colour against black that colour becomes stronger and gives more energy but this does not happen with grey. Grey makes other colours come down to its own level. It drains. If you are going through time of great anxiety and you have trouble shutting away it may be good for you to wear something of blue or soft colour. Perhaps hold something with colour in your hand, a scarf, handkerchief or something which is a nice relaxing colour. Meditate with this colour between your hands, this will help to relax and soothe you. This is something you could pass on to others who come to you with problems. If it is a condition with nerves green is very good, blue is good for healing of body, yellow is good for stretching out and learning when you are seeking an answer. Red is good for energy if you are very low and you want to raise energy but be careful not too much red as it can cause arguments because of clashes of vibration. Red does not mix well with other colours so the vibration of red would not mix with the vibrations of others very well. This is why you get arguments because colour is vibration. (30.11.97)

QUESTION 104 - *John Lyon explaining how the team in spirit merge their vibrations.*

When you become free of your earth body you take with you of course your memories, your experiences but you become part of a whole, a mingling of vibration. Your human thought is so narrow you think of yourself, your family, the area in which you live but you are part of such a vast universe. You will still be an individual in spirit but you will not stay as yourself you will be part of each other, we merge with each other. This is your progress, when you leave your earth body behind you go to whichever phase of understanding you have prepared for yourself. When you come to an earth body you come from another dimension to take on earth body, when you leave the earth body you return to that level of dimension. I use the word 'dimension' because of your education you understand. You return to that dimension but within that dimension there are many others, if you wish to use the word 'identities, I will use that word, who are on that same level of vibration. If you wish I will use another word 'team', you can be part of the team. That team works together to form the whole because you are on the same level of progression although you have your own memories and experiences, you interchange these because you can share with each other. Also, you retain your identity. I am part of the team but I have come to you as John Lyon because I have touched earth and I have come back as an identity. You are well aware that whoever is sitting here talking to you through this earth body, whatever the questions you ask that one who is speaking to you is able to absorb the experiences, the memories of the others within the team. They can portray these to you through this identity who is John Lyon. For example tonight I have drawn on Hanns experience because we are on the same vibratory level and as I have been speaking to you we have been interchanging. Hanns has been giving me his vibrations and I, as John Lyon, using the John Lyon identity, have been giving these experiences of Hanns to you.

Do not worry you can keep your identity when you join our dimension. When you have been in another dimension for a while and you are free of all earth attachments and conditions you may wish to progress further, you may wish to merge further with higher levels of vibrations. If you wish to return to earth to speak to somebody as I am returning to earth to speak to you, you will perhaps choose to return as the identity you had on earth. You will be able to talk to people, if this is your wish, as this identity.

When you initially go from this body of yours and are free, you will perceive those who you hold dear. They will be perceived as you wish to perceive them. After a while you will learn to mingle your persona with theirs. There will not be any barrier, when you are on earth you have your own identity and your companion has their own identity, you go off to your place of employment and your companion goes off and does whatever they do, you are separated. You may think of each other and you may link in thought but in spirit this will not be the same. When you are in the other stage away from the restriction of earth you can merge much closer, you do not need to be separated.

I will give an example without using personalities, I will use two identities in what you call spirit, a Mr Smith and a Mrs Smith. Mr Smith and Mrs Smith are very close in vibration so they are together and they mingle their vibrations very easily. Mr Smith perhaps, wishes to pursue helping of people who are passing into spirit and he wishes to assist them. Mrs Smith decides she wants to do something totally different, she wants to go and help animals, so they are following their own path in spirit but they are still together. On earth this would not be possible, if one followed one path, the other would follow theirs and they would have to spend time apart but in our dimension this is not so. We are free to follow whichever path we wish but we are still linked, we are still part of same vibration. This is why you are told quite often when spirit return, we can be in more than one place at one time. Our vibrations are able to mingle but still divide. This is very difficult for a human brain to understand because of the limitation of earth life.

In spirit this is different vibration is always moving it is never still, it is always merging with others as a whole. An example is when you see the table move, it is always moving this is because there is so much vibration and vibration is movement. If you imagine vibration as we have explained before, as colour. If you imagine colour as a ball of vibration and this ball of vibration would be forever changing colour. Perhaps subtly but it would be changing because it would not forever stay the same. We would be merging and exchanging. We are never still the vibration is always moving, always growing, always stretching out in various directions, adding to, sending out, drawing in. This may seem confusing but I have endeavoured to find words in a human form to explain something which takes place in our dimension.

You are human and you are on earth for a purpose so you are confined to human thought. Do not worry too much if you do not understand because this is so natural to you, once you are free from human confines you will understand. (07.12.97)

QUESTION 105 - The Doctor responding to a question concerning how spirit communication is effected by the medium's physical condition, especially in trance work.

We are talking of trance communication at this moment. When a person is experienced in availing themselves for trance communication first of all they have to have faith in those who care for them, their spirit companions. They should know who their spirit companions are, they should understand fully the link with their companions and they should have faith that their spirit companions, especially the spirit you call 'doorkeeper'. The doorkeeper is there to look after the medium's body in the medium's absence. In most cases this works very well because there is a trusted companion who is as a shield, a defender for the one who is giving their body and that one is responsible for those spirits that come to the body. The doorkeeper ensures that these ones are of the right vibration, also that they are able to clear the body completely when they have finished their communication.

If there is a medical problem that spirit companion who is the overseer is aware of this problem. Now there may be a circumstance where spirit are able to control the body for that duration of time, they are able to override the physical problem for a short duration to enable communication to flow. There are cases where this is not possible because of the advanced stage of the disease. If trance communication is undertaken too frequently this can happen because the body is not being given time to recuperate. You know yourself, if you have a minor illness if you have what you call influenza type illness and there is something which is vital that you need to do you can overcome the illness for a very short while to ensure that you carry on with whatever task is essential for you to perform. It may be that you are looking after a child and you need to be with that child and to care for that child so you cannot take to your bed and let the illness take its course, you keep your body going for that while and override the illness for a short while until that duty is taken from you. Then your body reverts back to the position it was in before and the infection takes its course. If you are employed and you have a problem at work which you need to oversee, although within yourself you know you are unwell and should go home to rest their is a function built within the make up of your body which can override an illness for a short while and your body can cope and hold the illness in abeyance. It cannot do this for a continuous time, only for a short while. There are instances where someone has occurred an injury to their body during and accident or mishap but it is vital that they complete a certain function before they can have treatment to that part of the body which is injured and miraculously they can cope for a short while but of course the injury means that they then have to revert to the previous position of being injured and the injury has to be treated. So you see there is this overriding function within your human body, your human body can cope for a short while and it can put the illness, diseasement to one side and override but, as I have said, this is only a very temporary measure. There are instances when there is an injury and you would have thought that the injured one would have felt great pain but there is no pain initially, there is pain eventually. There are endorphines which your body creates and this can happen as an in-between process.

So going back to your original question, 'can spirit cope?'. if you are unwell regardless of whether you are involved in spirit communication or have no wish to be involved in spirit communication, if you are unwell you should respect the signs your body shows you. Your body gives you signs whether they are pain, fever or whatever your body gives you signs there is a problem. You should respect those signs and take care of your body. If you so wish to ignore these signs there is this function built within where your body can override but this is only intended for a short while. If you wish to continue with your mediumship and you continually ignore these signs, you can do this for a while but you cannot do this continuously. This is only a back up system in your body, an emergency system which overrides this cannot keep functioning. Spirit can help to trigger this back up system in your body for a short while but spirit cannot override destiny, we are here to assist. If it is your destiny that you have to go through whatever illness or whatever situation although we can be there behind you to give you strength, give you support we cannot wipe this out. The more you battle the more difficult your spirit communication becomes because you are battling, you are creating tension, you are using your adrenaline continuously and this backfires on yourself and rebounds, causing much reflux. So you see, yes spirit can cope but we cannot alter destiny. If you are wearing your body out you are also wearing away your energy. You have physical energy and spirit energy, if one is imbalanced this effects the other, you have to be balanced completely. Your body has to be balanced. Your energy and vibrations link your physical body with your spirit body. When your energy is low this causes an imbalance between the two. When there is an imbalance between the two this hampers spirit communication.

If you would only learn to relax and let spirit draw close and assist this would be of much benefit but the more you battle with the 'I' within you. 'I am going to continue', 'I am going to carry on', the more difficult it is for spirit to draw close and give you that strength and support.

It is not that communication is impossible, it is the way you go about it. If you accept you have an illness, accept your capabilities and your incapabilities you will continue to be aware of spirit, you will have the reassurance of knowing they are close to you and giving you strength. If you ignore all the warning signs and continue in your own exuberance you are blocking out spirit and spirit are unable to assist you. In this way spirit communication is hampered, it cannot take place but if you relax and accept you have a problem, ask for help for that problem. It is no good just expecting spirit to help, you need to be affirmative, accept and ask. Once you have asked you are opening the door and we can draw close to you and assist you. You will be aware that we are there and you may become aware that others are there with you also and spirit communication will flow even though you are unwell in a physical body. As you have accepted this and have resigned yourself to this you are still open to spirit channels but when you battle against this your are closing yourself to spirit channels.

It is a difficult question to answer. No it shouldn't affect spirit communication. Of course it is unwise to sit in trance with certain conditions and if your body in unwell your body needs to rest and recuperate. If you are sensible you will say to yourself 'I am going to have a complete rest, I am resting from my material work so I will rest from my spirit work'. That does not mean you shut out spirit, you can still be aware of spirit around you and still receive from spirit but in a different way. When you are recuperated it is much easier, you come back as if you have been on holiday, you come recharged and your link has not been severed, hasn't been frayed. Whereas, while you are battling this link is tenuous, it is not cut but it is clouded. It is similar to your telephone when you get crossed wires. Vibrations are of an electromagnetic field (we are talking of spirit communication) because of disturbance in your body this electromagnetic field has lost its impetus Because of the electrodes are not charging correctly, they are misfiring, they are not hitting their target. Because these electrodes are misfiring this handicaps when you want to reconnect and continue after your illness, you have to learn again. Instead of just continuing you have to go back to square one and start afresh. You have to undo the damage you have done.

My advice as a doctor would be, if you have an illness however minor heed the signals your body is giving you. Do not override the signals and ignore them, they are given you for a reason. They are telling you there is a problem, you must slow down. They are telling you to seek advice from someone who understands. If you choose to ignore signals they will not go away. Spirit can help with healing, help to alleviate. In some cases the illness can be completely eradicated but as you have been taught it is wise to work with medical people on earth as well as those in spirit. You are talking of a human body in human conditions so you must seek human advice. If you do not like the advice you are given you can ask spirit for their assistance but work together with spirit and the advice you are given. There are many who are given advice by their doctors and they choose to ignore. Of course there are good doctors and there are not so good doctors but do not criticise until you have tried the course of treatment that has been given you. If you have tried the course of treatment and you still have a problem you then have redress. You then have a chance to say 'I have tried what you have given me it has not worked I still have problems'. Then your doctor, or whoever will look in a different direction. When you are a doctor it is not easy there are so many illnesses which have the same symptoms. You treat the symptoms for the illness you think is appropriate but of course they may be symptoms for something else but only by eliminating illness you find the cause. Once you have taken advice ask your spirit friends to help you also and you will be surprised that once you have taken responsibility for your own body spirit can help you a lot more. (You should not be surprised but many people are.) If you ignore the signs in your body it is very difficult for spirit to help you but if you accept responsibility for your body spirit can help.

You are here as spirit within a human body and although you wish not to be part of the human body you wish to be spirit you have a duty to the body you are inhabiting. You have a duty to look after that body. (09.12.97)

QUESTION 106 - Running Bear answering a question relating to close relatives speaking through a trance medium.

Everybody different, every medium different, every spirit entity different. You know when we go home to spirit we are not human anymore but we still take with us part of our character. If we are strong we take strength with us, if we are sensitive we take this with us also. If the medium and spirit are too close in their vibration, if they have inherited too much of that one's character this could cause a problem. Especially if they have inherited the sensitive part of that one's character. You know one of our sitters has two grandfathers who come to talk to you. One comes to talk he is a strong man, the other is strong also but he is a different temperament, when he had a body he was very emotional. Now he is in spirit he has not got the emotion of earth but he is still very sensitive, he feels things deeply, he is not able to put up barrier as perhaps the other grandfather would because he is a stronger character. So he does not come to talk to you because of this sensitivity. He is aware of this sensitivity and when he had a body this caused embarrassment because you do not like men who show emotion, man has to be strong. All through his life he fought against emotion but this was within him, it was part of him but now he is spirit without body he is still very sensitive because he has a very sensitive nature. If he came back to a human body he would feel the condition of a human body whoever's body whether relation or not. He would bring memory of human body with him and he would have this problem with emotion again. That explains the condition of someone who is not a relation but how this can affect.

Now, I will go a step forward to a relation. When a relation comes if the relation is strong, with no deep emotion this is no problem to some mediums because they themselves, although they are caring and loving, they are also very strong. Other mediums are more sensitive and if they link with a relation who also is sensitive and bring memory of when they had a body with them. This sensitivity of theirs links with the inherited sensitivity of the medium who's body they are using. This would cause much emotion and draining of the medium who is giving the body.

When a relation comes to use a relation's body they bring with them their memory of when they had a body. That one who they are coming to also has inherited from many relations different qualities and attributes. They may have inherited something from father's side, something from mother's side. This relation comes and the part of the medium which has been inherited from that one who is visiting the body then becomes stronger because there is a double link. You inherit from many of your ancestors, many things. Some are evident, you will look at someone's face and say they have father's nose, mother's eyes, grandmother's hair, grandfather's ears but there are other things which are not noticed. There are qualities within as child grows they may show they favour doing certain action which you may say they take after grandfather, they take after grandmother because they used to like to do that. Someone might like to sew and you say they take after grandmother, someone might like to bake and you would say they take after other grandmother. This is an example but there are many other qualities, these are material qualities I am talking to you about. You also inherit much more, you inherit the feelings, the reactions of your ancestors. You inherit how that ancestor would react to a certain situation. We have spoken of animals, you may have inherited a kindness to dogs, cats, birds, whatever and this will be from an ancestor but you may not know which ancestor. This is a feeling, a sensitivity you have inherited. You also inherit other sensitivities, how you react to other people. Sometimes you may come across someone who is ill and you wish to treat them in a certain way, another person may come across someone who is ill and they treat them in a different way, one is perhaps kinder, one harsher. This is a different reaction because each one has inherited a different reaction from a different ancestor.

Also, you inherit other things which are dormant, they do not show until there is a trigger and when there is a trigger this reaction comes to the fore. Many times during life you may look at yourself or you may look at others who you have known for a long while, perhaps brothers and sisters, and you have said 'I didn't know they could do that they haven't shown they could do that before but when the need arise they could do it.' This is because this quality has been dormant for all these years but something has triggered and it then comes to the fore. You now understand what you inherit from your ancestors, obvious things, not so obvious things and things which are hidden deep within you these may remain hidden unless there is something in your destiny for which the need arises. You use the word 'DNA' this is a modern word for you but this will then come to the fore.

When an ancestor comes to a medium it can awaken all that is inherited from that one because of the link and if there is too great a link, too many attributes, qualities have been inherited this could awaken something which is dormant. I am not saying a spirit entity could not return but if they did the medium would have to be taken back into a much deeper state of trance so that more of themselves are shut down. We are not saying an ancestor cannot come to one of their descendants but sometimes it is not good if they do because of the sensitivity of the medium.

Each generation back you gain more and more ancestors so if the ancestor is a long way back, their qualities are within the descendent but also there are many more. So the inherited qualities of a distant ancestor would not be so strong as your mother or father because they are very close.

Your parents would have inherited qualities from this ancestor from way back but they would also have inherited qualities of several other ancestors. Although this would not be a very strong inheritance, nevertheless it would still be there and it is possible to arouse. (14.12.97)

QUESTION 107 - George responding to question concerning the advantages of sitting in the dark. A sitter was puzzled as to why after sitting in the dark for a while our eyes do not get accustomed to the darkness and we would be able to see each other across the room but for us the room remains pitch dark.

If the light was on you would see all of you sitting around but you would see a lot of empty space between you. That space isn't space it is filled with us and everything else that is going on. We are not there as bodies we are there as energy but you can't always see this. Sometimes you see colours, lights or movement. Sometimes you see something out of the corner of your eye, you turn to look and it is gone. This is because you bring your conscious reasoning in and you are thinking 'Ah, there is something there, I have got to look'. Once you say that you are shutting the door against this other dimension. I use the word dimension because it is a word you use in your present language.

George, why should we lose it when we look? - You are in your human world looking with your human eyes you can only see human things, you can see the other people in the room with you and you can see the space in between them because you are looking through your human eyes. When you are sitting in the dark you are seeing with your psychic eye, you see into this other dimension that is there all the time but because you are here to use your human body and live your human life you are not really meant to see spirit with your conscious reasoning. You are actually perceiving all the time but it is not coming through to your conscious reasoning. Once you shut your conscious reasoning down, as you do when you are here, you shut out all your worries and thoughts, you open up this other sense and you are able to see things and feel things, it is a sense like a feeling. Sometimes you decode it as seeing, you see a light or you see a colour but another time you just sense something is there. It is similar to when you are in a room and someone walks in behind you, you are aware they are there but you haven't turned around to look at them, you have sensed it. That is the best way I can explain it.

I will now go back to the darkness. You are closing down what you would see with your ordinary senses, your human senses and you are opening up your other senses, call it your psychic senses if you prefer. What you are doing is shutting down your human thoughts and senses and opening yourself up to the spirit senses. If you were seeing with your human eyes after a while this dark room would become lighter to your eyes and you would be able to see each other across the room but because you have shut these senses down this does not happen. You still see darkness but when you start to decode the darkness you will be able to see psychic things in that darkness.

You are opening yourself up to spirit and the room is full of spirit, this is why you get the senses of the atmosphere within the room being dense. This is what we are, we are enveloping you, we are all around you, we are around all the time but you can't see us because you are in your earthly dimension and you have to live your earthly life. When you shut yourself away from your earthly life just for a very short while you experience a little of our reality. (14.12.97)

QUESTION 108 - Mafra explaining about the difficulties of communicating from spirit. This followed an experimental communication from a spirit entity who had not communicated through the body previously.

It is an effort for them also. They have learnt the initial step so next time it will be a little easier. It is just for a short while, just to give experience. You must realise it is quite an achievement to come through, to enter your atmosphere, your earth conditions and then enter into a body. It is totally different from the conditions we are accustomed to, it is a much slower, denser process. Our communication is so fast, so quick. We work on a much quicker, lighter vibration. They also have to learn how to manipulate the body because when they link with the body they bring a certain memory with them. They have to recall what it was like when they had a body, of course this is not their body it is different, they are not thinking through the body they are just instructing the body to communicate. This takes a little while to accomplish because you are communicating with them and they are responding but the response is not coming through the medium's brain. They are linking with you on your higher level of thought but also they are hearing your voice and they are trying to respond to this human connection and it takes a while for them to achieve this.

Initially they start to use their fingers, hands, feet or whatever to get the feel of being in a body and they take on the mannerisms which they recall. They find they are able to move, they do not know what to do with their fingers and then they try to manipulate the mouth, this is not easy. They form words, what is happening they are instructing the body to work. I have accomplished, I can instruct this body to move to speak, to respond but when you first come to a body you think you have to physically do this yourself and you are struggling to find out how to make the mouth move, to form words. You see what is happening now I am instructing the impulses to send messages to various parts of the body to work so I am bypassing the system of making the body work myself. I am using the facilities here which you use yourself when you speak. You are not thinking I have got to shape my mouth to a certain formation to form a word you are telling your body to do this and it is sending impulses through your body and this is the reaction you achieve when you speak. It is like a child learning to talk they are trying to say a word and they have difficulty forming the word because they are copying, a child copies. They look at the parent or whoever and they do the same shape to make word but as a child learns they learn to send a message from the brain to say the word, they are no longer shaping their mouth and copying. When we first come to a body we are as a child, we are learning and we bring with us the memory of our mannerisms, how we used our hands, how we functioned and we are trying to do this in a strange body. You must remember, this is a vague memory because perhaps we may not have been in a body for many of your years, to us it is not time but once we touch earth we are linked to your time. Once we are free of a body, we want to forget body it is a hindrance to us we are free we are not restricted to earth conditions so we do not want to keep body conditions. Of course, there are some on the lower levels who wish to keep to this level but I am not speaking of that level because you have asked to rise above that level.

I have tried to explain to you the difficulties we have when we first come. As you may understand you have Running Bear and E-om-ba who have come to you many, many times now but they still have difficulty speaking fluently as someone of your own nationality or your own continent because their way of communicating when they had a body was much different to our way of communicating. My way is different to yours but there is a similarity, perhaps I put words in the sentence in a different order than you because my language was slightly different. My thought process would be slightly different but I am able to make myself known because our way of communicating was very similar. E-om-ba and Running Bear's communication with their own people was so much different. We have to relearn. Although we bring memory, we have to forget memory and learn again. Imagine yourself, if you were of spirit not of body, and you wish to return to speak through a body perhaps of a tribal man in the African continent, you would have to relearn how to communicate because the way you communicate in your European manner would be vastly different to that of a tribal man in the continent of Africa. There are still tribes in the continent of Africa, many are of a different culture now but there are still some that live in their tribal custom, although very few. (16.12.97)

QUESTION 109 - CHRISTMAS PARTY CIRCLE 1997

To set the scene the occasion was our Christmas Circle Party and the room was decorated in the festive spirit with a living tree and strong smelling sweets. In opening the circle the children from the spirit realms were in particular welcomed to join us and enjoy the sweets and other trinkets around the room. In addition to our regular sitters we had a number of guests who fully understood the circle environment type of communication and were known to have a level of compatibility with the group. Our spirit friends were in party mood bringing us their greetings. A number made themselves known as children, although we know they have progressed in the spirit realms. Hannah, brought a number of friends and relations who were accompanied by pets who shared their earthly existence. We had cats, dogs, a parrot and a horse, all described in detail and the names of the pets given. The horse was brought by Beda (one of our regular communicators), who was her special mount and was of a silver grey colour.

At one point we had three mediums in trance, for a time two spirit friends having a conversation at our level of communication and seemingly thoroughly enjoying the experience. One of the sitters was rather surprised to say the least to learn that one of his companions had been talking through him, a new experience for him in a circle environment.

What was very interesting was the total control of events by spirit and the following given at our next sitting explains what was happening.

George talking about the event - So you had a good time on Sunday, no it weren't Sunday, another day Saturday. Everyday is the same to us, I was here you know but gave the others a chance, only fair isn't it mate, only fair that everyone should get a chance to come. I will just say why we let others come because some of them have only been introduced to you this year, but they have worked very hard so why not let them come when there is a party. They work hard all year when you ask all your questions so why not let them come when you are not firing questions at them ? Make them relax and be happy, gives them a chance. Also you see we were giving others a chance like that fellow who had someone come through for the first time. Their companions do not have the opportunities that we get to pop in every week or whatever, for them it was a precious time. So it was only fair that we stood back and let them have a go because they have people with them that like to come and talk but they don't have the opportunity. Also you see, you know Mafra looks after what's going on, well you see that might seem ever so easy but it's not. It is very, very complicated, balancing the vibrations, and giving everybody a fair chance and fitting the right vibration in at the right time. Mafra knows what questions are coming and he is teaching us as well, teaching a lot of us to come and talk and answer questions. Yes, it is quite complicated. So you see those others who were here, that were having folk come and talk through them, they have also got "doorkeepers", therefore Mafra was helping, not teaching, helping their "doorkeepers", so he was using vibrations to withdraw and then invite another, so it was all very well organised. Mafra would withdraw one and open door for another "doorkeeper" to send someone through their person, so they were not all through together, so for those few moments the energy was concentrated on that one. That was helping that one's spirit companion to make a stronger link, you understand. If they had all come through together the energy would be split and it would not have been fair on those who were struggling to come through because they haven't had the experience so they would not be so strong and they would be floundering. It was a moving around of energies. There were many more here, there was a lot more energy coming, there was so much that it had to be used in the right way.

Christmas is a time of sharing, so why not share everything. Everyone in the room was experiencing things, they may not have realised but they were all having a much closer link with spirit than they realised. So it wasn't just allowing others to come and talk, it was also withdrawing so that energy could go round to everyone so everyone was having a share it just manifested in a different way. In some cases people came through, in others their companions were closer to them than they had been for some while and they were making the link stronger. Even though they did not realise it they were closer and this will help them another time. Each time they make this link stronger it helps to pave the way for the next time the door is opened, it's building up abilities. (23/12/97)

QUESTION 110 - *E-om-ba answering a question regarding auras and colours as to whether spirit can perceive these colours and changes in colour around a human body. He begins by explaining the colours perceived in sunsets particularly when there is a cold climate.*

When you look to sky you see nothing but sky but there is much between you and the sky but you are not able to see this with your earth eyes. You sometimes get a glimpse when the sun is shining low and you see rays of sun and in those rays of sun you see particles. This is just a glimpse but this space around you is very full of us but also of many vibrations. This you do not see with your human eyes. When you look up to sky when your vibrations on your earth are cold you are able to see pure colours. When there is a warmer atmosphere on your earth the warmth from your earth rises, this clouds vision and you are not able to see colours so clearly. Colours are there all the time they are not just there when the weather is cold but sometimes you are not able to see with human eye but because there is no heat rise from your earth due to temperature you will see a lot clearer. This is glimpse of colours we perceive, good colours, strong colours, vibrant colours. If you could only open your eyes and see around you there are many colours also, around trees, flowers, foliage, animals and yourselves, many colours.

Can you see our auras? - Colour you give it name aura because it means all around so you mean colours around you. All of you have colour around you all the time but all the time it is changing. Never one second to next second of your time the same because you change all the time. Colour moves, blends with other colours as your thoughts change so you are sending out vibrations and this changes colour because thought is vibration, vibration is colour. As you listen to what is going on; you listen to music your colour changes and music changes, if you read book you have thoughts and as your thoughts from your words filter through your brain and you think this changes colour. When your human body is working this changes colour, you breathe in you breathe out, you eat food you digest food, your pores in skin absorb from around you and they secrete from body this happens all the time without you knowing this alters colour, Everything is moving, your hair growing, your nails growing all time, your eyes are moving all the time even when you sleep your eyes move within your eyelids, all the time there is movement never still. If you are still that is no good you would be with us! Then you would radiate colour, our colour.

These beautiful colours you say are around, do you see them or do you sense them? - You say beautiful colour, not always beautiful when you have no good thoughts you have no good colour, grey colour. Also you say flowers have good colour but when flowers are polluted by your chemicals or your air that affects colour around flower. Spirit flowers are bright and radiant but your flowers on earth are affected by what is around. You have flower growing at side of road, your motor car goes past, it makes smoke over your flower, poor flower, colours dim. Of course we perceive colour, good colour. We also see when healing is working because we can see the colour of vibrations go from healer, or from spirit to the one who is in need and we can see them absorb this colour and their colour changes because their colour has mingled with colour of healing. You see in your room colour swirling around, you see blues and mauves swirling around, good colours, bright colours. As they leave and go away from you out to those whom you have asked for this colour goes to them. Colour goes from you and goes off away through your walls to wherever, if you could just see you would see the colour going from this building out in many directions, beautiful colour but if you were here and someone was sending thoughts to you, a sitter who is not present sends thoughts to you the colour comes from her into the room to you. There is no need to open door, it goes straight through wall. We do not worry about walls. You think your walls are solid, they are not solid because they are made up of vibration also. All the time moving, all the time not solid, you bang the wall but it is not solid for us just particles joined together, molecules moving, made up of millions of molecules and energy permeates through. (28/12/97)

***QUESTION 111** - Sister Celeste explains what happens with all the prayers that are sent out at the time of the religious festival of Christmas.*
    I bring you blessings. I am always here, I prepare room for you, it is my labour of love, my duty which is no chore I enjoy. It is a privilege for me to come with you and sanctify for you. *You had a busy time before our Christmas party circle* - There was many from spirit here, my friends, it was good. There were many of my brothers and sisters here also from my calling, many of your visitors had ones with them from my calling, not my individual calling but my brother and sisterhood. This is a time when there is much love, many prayers. Many of my calling in your world today are at this time of year on their knees saying prayer and this prayer is going out into the ether with love. This is something we take and we are able to use, there are so many at your time of celebration who need this, so many in your land but other lands also. We do not confine to your land because prayer has come from your land it goes wherever needed. Also, there are prayers all around the world at this time because your religions have travelled to many countries, it is not just your country it is all around the world. You have many hours of earth time with prayers being said because the clock you use in your world varies from land to land so prayers are continuous, they are going on for a long, long while. This is a build up of energy because there is a time when many churches are together in harmony and this is good because this goes on for a long while of your time. We are able to build much from this and we are able to disperse where needed. As you know what goes out comes back so it grows. It starts as tiny thought but it grows and grows and multiplies because, believe me, there is much love needed in your world and also in our world. Those who have come to us from your world need this love too. This is very important work. (28/12/97)

***QUESTION 112** - George explains how they learn in spirit.*
    We don't have lectures like you have lectures do we? We merge energies. We don't sit in chairs and listen to someone talking, we absorb the energy. We have spheres of learning and we humble ones, on the lower vibrations, we are raised to a higher level of vibration so that we are able to

merge our energies with the learned ones, the example you used was the Nazarene. There are others as well on this high vibration. We are lifted to this high vibration and we merge and learn from them because we are absorbing their vibration and energy, we are then able to take this with us when we return to the level we normally reside on. Then we are able to share what we have learnt with others on our level.

Who decides who goes from your level? - It is not a decision, it is what we want. When we want to progress we have a desire within us that we want to go forward and learn something more. It is no good someone sending us like in your schools when you are told to go up to a new class, because that wouldn't be any good. It is no good being forced into something you don't want to do or before you are ready for it because if you try and teach a baby to run before they can walk they will fall flat on their face. If anyone is forced to do anything before they are ready for it, it is a waste of energy. If you are on earth it is a waste of time because you have got time but for us it is a waste of energy because we are not ready. When we have a desire that we want to stretch out and learn we are stretching out. You have folks from our realms who come to join in your meeting who say they have seen your light and are attracted to the light. It is the same we are stretching out, puzzling over things, wanting to learn things and we are drawn by this light and we go to this light. We can't stay the same all the time, we know there is more to learn and as you learn from those who come to talk to you we are also learning from those above us.

At this point George was asked about those who come to earth from different vibration levels Those who come to your world from the higher realms for a particular purpose return to the higher realms when they have completed their task on earth. When you go home to spirit you will go to whatever stage you left when you came to your body but if you have been really good you may go a bit higher! They can't take away what you have got, if you haven't accomplished what you set out to do when you came to earth they would probably send you back to learn again. You have those who you say are evil, they do bad things, sometimes very bad things but inside, although you can't see it, there is a spark of goodness. Someone who comes from a high level in spirit wouldn't come to take on an earthly body and be able to do evil things because their spirit within would rebel. Sometimes people are misguided for a while because of their earthly circumstances, they might have come to this world of your for a reason to learn. There might be someone who has come from a level in our world which is not high or low, but somewhere in the middle, they come and take on a body of someone who is in a family where there are not good things happening. They are brought up with these circumstances around them and because of their upbringing they grow up the same. Perhaps they have come to this body to do this for a reason to learn what it is like to experience this but eventually that spirit within is able to break free and that earthly body is changed. Often you get people who later in their earthly life reverse their roles. The old way of saying it quoting the bible was 'they saw the error of their ways'.

Someone who is perceived to be evil would have come from a low vibration and they may come to earth and create havoc, they may send people home to spirit before their time. So when that one eventually goes home themselves they would go to a very low level in spirit. Whether that one would be sent back to earth, or whether that one stays in that low level, or whether they may be helped out of that vibration by others in spirit I am unable to tell you of a particular personality. There are these three possibilities. They may be sent back to experience for themselves what they created for other people, they may have been sent back to go through a similar experience which they created for others. They may stay in the dark realms unable to see any light. They may be helped toward the light by those in our realms who are specially trained to reach into these dark realms to assist these souls who are really lost. This is a very dedicated calling and not just any spirit can undertake this. The ones who work in these very low realms trying to bring light come from very high vibrations. They are very well trained, they have got protection around them, and they are able to permeate down to a very low level and bring light to try and bring some healing because it is healing that these disturbed ones need.

These are the possibilities you have. We are not allowed to speak of individuals but there are many throughout your history who would be of this low vibration. Someone may come back to right on earth the wrongs they did previously, they may have come back in another body and have been through the mill themselves and through being through the mill themselves they have grown and seen that there is much more to existence than causing evil and havoc. There is more to existence than staying on this low level. Every vibration is different.

Some things that occur in your world are meant to happen and some aren't. Sometimes there is a time when a lot of people are meant to go home to spirit and sometimes there are times when destiny hasn't taken the course it should take and people go home before their time. When this happens there is a lot of souls from spirit are sent to these lower realms to accept these ones who have come home early. You are looking at it with very narrow eyes because you are in a human body but what is destined is destined lots and lots of your time before it happens. There are others who are sent to your world at that time from a very high vibration to try and assist because when history is written through your generations as you live on earth you can see examples of this.

Those in the higher realms of spirit who know what is planned for your earth, and for other spheres for that matter, but we are talking about your earth at this time. As they know your earth is going to go through this upheaval for whatever reason and many of your spirits who are in a human body at that time will be affected. This is what it is, it is spirits from spirit realms who are on earth in a human body they are going to be affected by the circumstances they are going to be placed in at that time. There will be many from the higher realms also placed on your earth at that time in a human body to assist. If you look in your history books at what has happened in the past, whatever time you are studying, there are those who have caused evil but there have also been many others who have been there that have assisted and tried to make calm out of chaos. Those ones have been placed there, they are very evolved souls that have been born to your world, taken on a body in your world, so that they are there when needed. When their job is finished they then return home to spirit. Some return home quickly after the event, others not so quickly they are there to stabilise the situation for a little longer until another generation is born to take over the reins.

George now explains how we can recognise vibrations through looking at people's eyes. There are many who come to your world if you look in their eyes you can see something. You have an expression 'the eyes are the windows to your soul'. If you look at those eyes you will see something coming from those eyes because they radiate, they shine. You can tell a lot from people's eyes, you look at people's eyes, you can tell a lot from them. Some people's eyes are alive and some people's eyes are dead, that is the best way I can explain it. When you look at people sometimes you look at them and their eyes are looking at you but they don't do anything. Another time you can look at someone and their eyes are alive. I don't mean the colour and the physical condition of the eyes. I mean the expression that comes through the eyes. Someone may suffer physically with their eyes and have a human problem with their eyes but even so there is a liveliness within their eyes, a vitality that shines through. You look at some of your handicapped children who's eyes seem vacant, they are not looking at you, there is a lot of life in some of those eyes shining out. You may look at someone who has physical tiredness but if you look beyond the tiredness you see a certain vitality.

In conclusion George returns to explaining levels of understanding. I sometimes have difficulty finding the words to explain things because the levels of vibrations in our world are so different from yours. I will call these levels spheres because a sphere is a circle and this is what energy is, it is a ball of energy going round and round and round. That is probably the best way to describe it. When you talk of levels you usually think of a staircase going up one rung at a time. Going up a different grade of class, Class 1, Class 2, Class 3, until you get to the top of the form. I say spheres because this is what it is, it is a merging of energy, a ball, there is no definite outside to it, it merges all the time. There are not hard and fast lines, like you have doors and walls, we are not like that, we merge from one to the other. As the energy goes out it goes out from the centre and goes all around.

George was then asked if spirit has auras - We all have this ball of energy around us, yours is a different shape because it is around a human body and it has to be the shape of your human body. When I come to see you I come into the earth atmosphere so my colours change because I come into the denseness and slowness of your earth, when I am free of your earth it is a much quicker, livelier vibration. You are in a body but inside your body is your spirit, if your spirit hadn't got that heavy body around it, I am not being personal it is heavy because it is made of earth substance, if it was free of that your colours would be a lot brighter. You are breathing in the oxygen from your world to enable you to live you have altered your vibrations. You should be part of your world because that is what you are here for! (28/12/97)

QUESTION 113 - Mafra explains we are not aware of how far and to what extent the knowledge given by spirit can travel to those who seek spiritual knowledge. There is no way of measuring the extent of love.
You cannot measure how far your energy travels or the extent of your work, you cannot measure this because you do not know. You send your love out for healing, you do not know how far it goes, where it goes you do not measure. You give word to someone who asks a question, they may repeat word to someone else, you do not measure how far that word goes. You may give healing to someone with hands and as that one's health improves they are able to help others, so there again you do not know how far that work goes. You may write letter to someone you do not know how many people read that letter, you do not know where those words go whether they are used for something else. You do not know how far those words have penetrated into the mind of that one who is reading it and what that has done to that one inside. You can not measure. You can measure a message from a platform to say how good it is or how bad it is. You can say 'that was a very good medium I understood all that medium said' but that is one person, the next person that medium comes to may not understand any-

thing. So you see you cannot measure. You may not understand a word that medium says but next week you may understand. You may tell someone something and they may say 'rubbish I do not understand it' but they may come back next week and say 'I asked my friend and my friend said yes, you should have remembered that'. Do not be despondent if one does not shine the same as another. All shine in their own way, some work one way, some work another.

You cannot measure where your love goes which you send to spirit, how it is utilised, how far it travels. You cannot measure how many come to visit you from our world and the progress they have made since they have visited you, you cannot measure. It is not as with your world where you can put it in black and white on paper and write list and tick list when job is done. It is not the same you cannot measure. You cannot mark questions in your exams and say they have nine out of ten, or they have five out of ten, you cannot measure. This is good because you cannot put pressure. When you measure you put pressure on those but when you are open with love and your love knows no bounds there is no pressure.

Someone may come and say I have had healing for ten years and I am no better, so my friend that is God's will. It is not the fault of the healer it is destiny. You must not be upset if people say to you 'this is rubbish' or 'this has no results' because who are they to measure? Can they see what even we cannot see? We can only see so far. There are many things we do not see. We are too busy to worry about how far the snowball has rolled, we just want to get on with next request, or next duty. Once we have played our part in role we hand it on to whoever else. We help where it is needed and then we hand over to whoever is taking reins after us.

When someone comes to realms of spirit and we assist with their entry into our world we surround them with love, we help to make them aware of where they are that they are no longer of your world, they are of our world, we show them opportunities which are open to them. When they have made their wish as to which field they wish to follow we hand them on to next stage. They are then helped, whether it is teaching, or whether it is research, healing, or whatever. We hand them to that area, that field of those ones that specialise. Sometimes they will come back to us and say thank you, sometimes they do not but this is not for us we have done our duty the same as you. Those who are brought to you, you have served them well, you have given them your love, you have given your time. Some have come back to you, some have not. It is no matter you have done what you can. Many you have brushed shoulders with during your walk through your life, some you have kept contact with even though you have not seen them for a long while, some you do not hear about any more but you have done what was to be done at that time. It is good that you realise that you just do what you can and you have no regrets because you have done what you can. You have tried it is up to individuals whether they wish to take advice or not. If they wish to go their own way that is their destiny.

Many who teach tie themselves in knots because they wish to dictate to their pupils and if their pupils have mind not to accept what they dictate the teacher becomes upset and then you have friction. When you have friction you do not have harmony. When you have no harmony you have no progress, there is destruction. You just have to accept that what is right for you may be right for others or may not be right, each has own path. You can only offer your own thoughts and you know you are linking with us and we help where we can. Also we are linking with those ones who are with the one who is asking the question to try and assist them on their right path but there again we have shown light if they wish to take the light at this stage on their journey good, if they wish to go around houses and come back later that is their wish. We try our best. (30/12/97)

QUESTION 114 - A communicator talks about the power of good over evil which affects our world.

At times when there are problems spirit draws very close. When there are no problems we watch, each goes their own way on their path and we stand and watch. We laugh and say 'well' but when we know there is time coming when there is going to be a fight between good and evil, there will always be a fight between good and evil. There are those forces which draw very close to world, very close. We are a team, no one takes a stand, we are a team. We are able to communicate. There has to be a figurehead in your world, someone has to take their name forward but there is team. This is nothing new, this has occurred many times before. Through history spirit has communicated in times of trouble.

You have those who are protectors of your world, ageless. Whenever there is a problem they draw near. You think this is something new, no, this has been in many guises. You have only to read legends of your history books and you find stories which you think are 'fairy stories' they have been wrapped up in tales but behind tales is deep truth. You have legends, each country of the world has it's own legends, own stories handed down before there was writing. These come from source, there are strong powers of protection. There always has been fight of good over evil and there always will be but there is much power from spirit to assist. You have lower forces and higher forces. You say good and evil, we do not like that expression, low forces and lighter forces, darker forces and lighter forces, which struggle for most dominion. One wishes to oversee other but with help of spirit light come out on top.

Your world, as you say, has moved into civilised world these forces have taken names of various religions and sects. Before there were idols to be worshipped there was natural worship and there was the power of your earth but I not here to tell stories of religions way back you have much in your books you can read yourself. When you read these words look deeper than the sentence you are reading. Look what is behind those words, there is deeper meaning. These have been handed down as stories, sometimes to your young ones as fairy stories. Of course, each generation has brought a little bit more picture to the story but if you look deep within you will find a deeper meaning. Go forward in light. (30/12/97)

***QUESTION 115** - Rosa was asked about a instance where injury was caused to a medium when a light was shone on their face whilst in trance.*

It is due to alteration of vibrations. It depends what kind of trance, if it was a trance that created a substance around the face not necessarily ectoplasm but a substance, a vibration. You do not see anything but there is something there. You know that space is not empty there is something there which you cannot see. Sometimes you see swirls of colour or you see shapes, this is a glimpse you get of this 'something' that is there but you cannot see. When in trance this can happen, of course spirit is very close and spirit merges their energy, their vibration with that of the one who is giving their body. Sometimes they come very close and change features of the face and there is this vibration around. The medium who is giving body is very subdued because they have taken a step back to let whichever one from spirit is taking body. The medium is very relaxed, they do not worry what is happening because they have trust in their spirit helpers, they know they will protect so they have no worry. They are very relaxed and shut themselves away from all earth conditions. You have learnt this when you sit, you shut away all that is around you, you do not worry what is happening outside, or next door, or whatever. You are shutting yourself away and putting your faith in spirit to protect. The medium is in this state, they are in trance, very relaxed, no worry what is going on, all their senses are shut down. They are not listening for the phone to ring or waiting for the light to be switched on. The spirit is in their body taking over and talking or doing whatever, as I am doing now.

If something happened quickly, if you put a light on quickly that would cause a disturbance in the energy field around. The medium would suddenly 'come back' because their senses would be awoken. They would come back quickly and this would cause things to happen in the body, it would cause adrenaline to flow quickly because the body would be in a state of shock. In the state of shock the body would produce certain chemicals itself. The one from spirit would withdraw very quickly and so there would be a quick withdrawing of their spirit energy and the substance around. This would cause the very sensitive vibration around the face or wherever skin is exposed to react. It would be as if you were in bright sunshine quickly, if you suddenly put your face in front of fire you would burn your face, it would be this kind of sensation. It would an alteration of the balance of so many chemicals. There would a change in the energy field around the naked face because one minute spirit is over face with all their vibration, their swirls of substance and then the next minute it is gone. With this also the medium coming back to body producing adrenaline and chemicals substance within body, the physical body would be a state of turmoil. If you were in a physical body and you suddenly faced something dangerous your body would react to protect itself. You can imagine the reaction of the physical body coupled together with quick spirit withdrawal this would make extra sensitive condition for physical body and just a light would cause problems.

I cannot understand why in the instance you mention the medium who was in trance, helpers where not there to give more protection. If this happened here this medium would return quickly because she would be frightened for others as well as herself and she would want to assist. She would return quickly, I would withdraw quickly but Mafra would step in, he would control. I do not understand why the doorkeeper did not control the situation and stabilise the condition. We can foresee what is going to happen so the doorkeeper should be prepared take necessary action. You must always ask for protection before you begin your communication with spirit and have faith in those who look after you. You must always sit in controlled conditions.

Many people dabble and they do not understand what they are getting involved in. They think it would be good if they could go into trance but they do not understand that they must put spirit protection around themselves. When you give yourself for trance you are giving your body to whoever. There are many who would wish to jump in at any level of vibrations and talk to you. This is why when you give yourself for trance work you link only with the highest vibrations. It is very silly to dabble and not understand who you are dealing with. Before you go into trance it is wise to know who your helpers are, know who you can rely on, have faith in them so you are completely together in this, a team. Do not just open yourself up for anyone to drop in. It is like opening your front door of your house and saying 'anybody can come in, walk off with this, walk off with that'. You would not do that nowadays. So why open yourself up for anybody to walk in? (04/01/98)

QUESTION 116 - *Hanns endeavouring to explain how spirit utilises molecular structure.*

See Question 110 - Molecular structure is very difficult to describe. So much is thought of as solid, nothing is solid. There are various molecular patterns, not all the same. When we talk of solid substance we talk of a molecular pattern and when we merge energies these have to be compatible. One has to be able to transcend through the other. You talk of harmony, this is good because you have to have harmony in physics. It is not good if there is not harmony of molecular substance. You have to have blending, merging and consolidating. There has to be compatible matter. I am talking about something that is 'no matter' but there is vibration. Vibration is also made up of structure, not structure you can see with your eyes but something not of your world but of our world. You look at space and you see void, within that void there is much energy. Energy is made of components.

When you have energy on your earth it does not just occur it has to be produced through coming together of elements. You have energy produced by fire, by water, by electricity, hydraulics which is water. Our energy also has to be created by the production of a psychic substance. You produce energy from your body, your body creates energy. We talk of a basic human body; your body is all the time creating. Your various systems within your body, your endocrine system, your lymphatic system, your operative systems which make your body function. The more your scientists and anatomist have studied your human body the more they realise there is still more to discover.

Many years ago your medical scientists were very advanced this knowledge was lost. Then your world went into a dark stage where there was no knowledge. When your scientists began again to awaken their senses as to how the human body works, at first they had many peculiar ideas. They did not understand that blood moved around the body, they thought you cut yourself and blood just gushed out from that point. Slowly they relearned what had been in man's knowledge thousands of years previously, this knowledge had been lost. They discovered how they body worked, how the heart was the centre and how heart pumped blood through vessels around body. They learned there were other organs in body that helped body work. They discovered that you breathe through your respiratory system, your nose, mouth, in through your lungs and out again. Then they discovered this is linked with blood in body and oxygen is taken around body in the blood. They then discovered there were other organs, there was liver, kidneys, many other organs but they did not understand that all these systems are linked, one does not work on its own, it has to work with other systems in body. They looked at brain and had many ideas of how your brain works. They do not understand yet how your brain works. Then they thought they were very clever they thought they knew how body worked because they discovered all these organs worked together to make body work. Then they discovered there were other systems within body that were less tangible, endocrine, lymphatic, glands working side by side with the other parts of body, all this controlled by what you call brain. The speed of your body working controlled by your glands, thyroid. hyperthyroid, parathyroid. Your adrenaline, your lymphatic. Your diseases attacking body and your lymphatic glands working as policemen assisting your blood to produce white cells to fight disease, Gradually your men of medicine have learned more of your body but they do not realise there is still much more they have not yet discovered.

With all this there are many things which were known many generations back and this knowledge has been lost.

I have been side tracked, I was trying to explain energy. I have given a pattern of your human body to explain to you how your human body creates energy and how this is relayed through what I call your own 'electrical system' within your body. This is linked with your nervous system which co-ordinates your body. This is how your body works and if you are talking of something which is so heavy as matter but it is so involved. There are so many components that come together to create energy how more involved is the creation of what you call psychic energy or the energy of our realms. How this energy inter links with our world and your world. We take your energy, you take our energy, we merge energies.

I talk of psychic energy this is different from spirit energy. Let me explain. I talk of spirit energy because you are knowledgeable and you understand spirit. Spirit is another dimension, you are spirit within a human body so you understand spirit. Spirit is not weighed down with matter it is free but also surrounded by energy and creating energy of its own. This is spirit energy. You understand human energy and you understand a little of spirit energy.

Now I move to psychic energy. Psychic is something which need not be spiritual. Psychic is another sense which you possess. You do not have to be particularly spiritual to be psychic. To be able to contact spirit you are wise to study spirit matters so that you are able to communicate with the level of spirit which is compatible with yourself but with psychic energy you create for psychic use, you can use this to link with spirit if you are of that vibration. You can use your psychic energy to link human world and spirit world. You are then able to perceive spirit and make link with spirit stronger through this psychic energy because you have attained a certain level. There are many on your earth and in our realms who use this other psychic energy for other things. Some in your world are able to see future, they are not linking with spirit to ask spirit but there is a way of perceiving what lies ahead because there is no such thing as time. All that has occurred and all that is going to occur can be perceived but in your normal function you are only concerned with today. You plan for tomorrow but who knows what happens tomorrow. Although you make pretty pictures of what you plan to do tomorrow, next week, the week after, this all could be altered by destiny for anyone in your world, however powerful that one is. What is going to happen is already planned but is hidden from your vision but there are those who can create psychic energy that can see through this cloud and can shut down the substance of time and look into the future. They do not have to be spiritual to do this, they can be, they may be, but they do not have to be. This is what I term psychic energy. It is the ability to disperse this time capsule you are residing in. It is as if you have curtains over window and you cannot see out, there is a way of creating psychic energy to disperse this and take down the barrier of time and look into the future. Occasionally you get a glimpse of this for various reasons. Sometimes man can go somewhere and think they have been there before, they have not been there before. Some will say 'Ah, you went in past life', maybe, but not always the case. Sometimes without your knowledge you have seen this place, you have broken through this barrier of time, you have seen this place that one day you will go to and when you go there it will seem familiar to you. This is of psychic energy.

I say you create energy. You do not think about creating energy anymore than you think about breathing. It is a natural ability you have but as all natural abilities it has been clouded with time. When you try to analyse you find this very difficult because you have not got the ability in your human brain to analyse something of this structure.

I am trying to talk plainly about something that is very complicated. There is much depth here but I am only skimming the surface to try and give you an idea of what there is around you and how we create energy. I have tried to explain how your human body creates energy to function, I have tried to liken this with us, our spirit energy. How we as spirit without the heaviness of your mortal bodies and your mortal dimension, how we are able to create a much lighter, brighter energy, a much quicker vibration by merging vibration one to other. When you create energy on earth in your earth body you are physically creating it yourself, your body is creating energy naturally to function and then you wish to make more energy. Perhaps you assist your body, you eat special food, you do special exercise, whatever. Sometimes with the help of others you work together, sometimes you do it on your own but in spirit we create by merging our energies. We each have own energy field and I have tried to explain we all vibrate to a different frequency. We vibrate, we are not stationary, we are all the time vibrating, changing, stretching this way, stretching that way but we merge energy with one and another. With this merging of energy, merging of vibrations, we are creating what you would call a molecular structure, another dimension of energy. Similar to your world when you want to move something heavy you cannot do this on your own so you merge your energy with others in team and together you would lift heavy object. This is just a very dense way of creating energy ours is much lighter, much brighter because all the time we are moving, all the time merging, never the same.

I have tried to explain this to you but in the middle of explaining I was side tracked because I did not realise you did not understand psychic energy was something different so I have tried to explain to you a little about psychic energy. Psychic energy is something which is created from within yourself but it can be used on various vibratory levels. It can be used on spirit level and when you use it on spirit level you can again use it in many ways. You can use it for communication, you can use for healing. This energy can be used for different kinds of mediumship. It can used for something as basic as telepathy, which is not particularly spiritual it is something more mundane but it is still psychic energy. You do not have to be spiritual to perform telepathy. When we talk of a spiritual level we also talk of healing but there are so many types of healing.

Once you open up these channels you have to be able to control them. So many open up channels but once opened they cannot control and as with your energy in your world, if you create too much energy you have explosion. If you are not able to shut energy off you have explosion and it is depleted. This is the same with your psychic or your spirit energy, if you cannot control you burn up and you deplete. It is good to open up and the more you perceive the more you create but there has to be a limit. You must realise you cannot do this infinitum. You must be able to shut down. Otherwise you will be depleted. (06/01/98)

QUESTION 117 - Kimyano explaining how to perceive colours
You search, you seek, you stretch but it is natural you do not have to think about colour when you start to think colours go. It is good if you do not think too hard, you are just in the in-between state, just relaxed. You know that colours, spirit vibration is here and you know you can perceive it but you are not stretching out too hard to see because this makes you think of colours from your mind.

There is a good exercise you could do when you are on your own.

You know there is colour all around your hands from the vibrations around your hands. When you are relaxed you sit, put dark colour cloth on your lap, put your hands on cloth, touch thumbs and first fingers and look at your lap. Just drift slowly, no worry, and see if you perceive colour in that space between your thumbs and fingers. When you see this colour look then around your other fingers and see what you can see. You all can do this. Do not stare and stare because you will not see, just look gently, if it is not there look away and come back if not today try another day, do not worry.

So once you see energy from your own fingers this is the beginning. You will then be able to open up and see our energy because this is what you see when you sit in a circle environment. You produce colour because you are vibration and your vibration is producing colour and we bring our colour, this merges, this is why you have swirls of energy and colour. All the vibrations in the room, yours and ours, merge together.

When you are healing you may see a patient who is low in their vitality, they are low in their state of mind, if you could perceive the colour around them it would be dim. Gradually when you merge your energy with them you will see their colour change. This would be good for you because you would know that your healing is working. What a reward to see that one's colour become brighter and lighter. When they walk from the room they take this colour with them, that would be very good for you to see. You must not take their darkness you must throw that away, you must keep your vibration at a higher level than theirs. Do not go to their vibration rise above it. It is good when you finish healing you disperse energy because you do not want to take the patient's vibration with you. (11.01.98)

QUESTION 118 - Kimyano continues her visit by answering a question about the effectiveness of contact to absent healing.
The better you know the one, the more you know about the one, the stronger the vibration because the link is that much stronger.

I will discuss contact healing first. When you give healing to someone who comes to you, they may walk in and they may say 'I have got a pain in my big toe'. If you can visualise toe and the condition of toe, the toe is part of the foot, the bone comes up, it has a nail, and it is fed with blood from the arteries and veins, which in turn goes into smaller blood vessels. This perception makes healing more intense.

If you know much more about the one who is receiving absent healing this would make a much stronger vibration. If you know that one's condition, if you know the person and can visualise them that is good because the link is stronger. If you do not know the person it is good to send your love on the vibration that has made the link. If you think of the one who has given the name, because they know the patient, the healing would go on a stronger link than if you just send the healing out on the name vibration. If you say 'I am sending healing through Mrs Jones to Mr Bloggs' that would make a stronger link. (11.01.98)

QUESTION 119 - George we are told that when spirit communicates in light trance that the words being used are limited to the medium's vocabulary. Is it possible for spirit to link in with others who are sitting, who for example may have a more technical vocabulary?

It would of course be better if the spirit communicator could talk directly through someone who had the required vocabulary. You say the medium sometimes uses words of which she doesn't know the technical meaning. You don't know what is in your brain, you only use a very small part of your brain. There is a lot in your brain of which you are unaware. There are all your memories, your DNA from all your ancestors, there are other things you might have read or seen, not understood at the time but put them to the back of your brain. You might have read something, not understood and not bothered any more, but because it has been read it is stored there in your memory.

Spirit could tune into other vibrations in the room but there would have to be a special link there to be able to do this. It couldn't be just anybody. If it was one of your team that may be possible because you have sat together for a long while and you have established a link between you. If a stranger came in that may be difficult because you wouldn't be on the same level where you interact with each other.

Your visitors from spirit work differently; some of us work on a single vibration at a time, others work with several vibration levels at the same time. These visitors would be able to work on the higher sensory levels. Some work on your thought level, if you were thinking of a particular word they would be able to link this way and use the desired word. Others of us would need to hear the word spoken.

I just talk to you. If you ask me a question and I can't find the answer I then ask somebody who does know the answer, they give me the answer and I find the thought, that finds the word and the medium talks to you. That is the way I work. Someone else may work differently, they work on so may things at once. They answer one question but are thinking about another, and probably having a chat to someone in spirit at the same time. We are all different vibrations but all part of the same team.

There are words in your brain that you don't know you have. If there is something that can be pulled out from memory it will be used. If you are in a room with others who are compatible in thought spirit might be able to use other words from them. The communicator might be able to bring something from spirit also. Someone from spirit who was very closely connected with the medium may be brought to assist and merge their energy with the energy of the spirit communicator. That would be a way of helping.

Do spirit scientists, for example, use knowledge they have gained on earth? You are looking at it with your human brain. They may have been a scientist whilst on earth but when they went home to spirit they may have chosen to continue in the field they had already followed. When spirit comes to take on a human body to follow a certain route, way of life, they might choose something that they had an interest in before they had a body. When they go home to spirit they then might choose to carry on with that chosen subject. It could be healing, it could be teaching, it could be anything. A scientist might choose to continue with science. When they were on earth they would have been very busy writing out formulas and mixing things together in bottles to see what would occur. Can you imagine when they get home to spirit, there all these vibrations just there, they could take a bit of this and a bit of that and mix them together. They can experiment in spirit, they can learn from others in spirit who have learned more than them. It is not so much what they bring from earth but what they have learned since they have gone back home to spirit.

There would be two reasons they would want to return to earth. They might want to return to assist with something particular on earth. They might see somewhere in medicine, for example, which needs some assistance and they would wish to be part of this work. They might want to do something totally different.

When any of you come back to earth you bring with you a certain amount of knowledge but you are only allowed to use it when the time is right. We are talking about someone who has learned a lot in spirit and comes back to an earth body. If the time is right for those who they meet on their earth journey to learn from that one gradually the knowledge they have brought with them filters through to that one's brain and they are able to share that knowledge. If that one has come before their time, before the people who they are working with are ready for this information it would cause too many problems. Can you imagine some scientific knowledge being given too early to your human race, what damage it would do. They have to wait for the right time for this knowledge to filter through. They might just bring a little of the knowledge with them, not all of it, because all of it would be too powerful, too destructive in human hands. They might go through the life of a human, in a human body, and when they came across a problem where this knowledge would help something would occur that would stimulate some thought in the human brain and that would trigger off part of the knowledge being available.

I will give you an example; if someone who studied medicine on earth went home to spirit and learned a lot more about medicine in spirit. They then decided to return to earth, take on a human body, grow up as a child and then decide to be a doctor again, or surgeon, or whatever. They would come to a point where they had a patient who had a disease and no one knew how to tackle this disease. This might be a disease which had caused a lot of problems before in the past to a lot of people, so perhaps in the destiny of your world it was time for some breakthrough in the cure of this disease. This one who had come from spirit with all the knowledge wouldn't suddenly think 'I know all the answers, we will do so and so, that will cure this disease'. That would be too revolutionary a way of bringing this response about. That one would have a little bit of the knowledge filter through and they would say 'if I did so and so, I wonder what would happen'. They would say to those who they were working with 'We will treat this patient in a slightly different way, instead of doing so and so we will do something else. Lets try a different treatment'. That is how it would occur, they wouldn't suddenly say they knew the answer. That would be too revolutionary. Your world has to make changes gradually. (11.01.98)

QUESTION 120 - Mafra explaining why spirit doesn't like to give graphic descriptions of what the spirit environment is like.

Some questions cannot be answered, you understand what you need to understand. This is the reason why we do not like to give graphic descriptions and for you to read many books because once you have perceived a thought you then encase this thought in a vision in your memory. This is how you first understand. When we try to explain something to you when you are in the early stages of learning it would be useless for us to try and explain the deeper meaning, we draw pictures and we talk basically to explain things. A word you use in your language, figuratively speaking, we speak figuratively. In one way this is good because it helps you understand what we are trying to explain but, the problem being, that once you are past this stage you take it literally. This is your first impression of spirit talking to you or reading of spirit and your first impression of anything stays with you.You remember your first lessons at school, perhaps you do not remember all the ones in-between but you probably remember your first few days at school or your first lesson with a certain group in school. The first time you played football, the first book you read, perhaps the first clothes you wore for school, but there have been many others you have worn through the years or many other lessons you learned through your school life, many books you have read since. These just merge into a mass of information but your first impressions you remember very well. Probably the first teacher you remember better than the ones further along your education. It is fertile soil, your mind and thoughts have not been clouded with other substances which cloud vision so your first impressions stay there for a long while.

The first lesson you learn when you are introduced to spirit knowledge makes a deep impression on you. This often occurs at a time when you are very vulnerable. Although you may learn a lot more later you are unable to wipe the slate clean from your first impressions because to give comfort, to give solace perhaps you are told there are beautiful gardens, you will see your dear ones again as you know them, so you become entrapped in these visions you have made for yourself. You then cannot grasp that by this time you should have taken a step forward and realised these are only pictures we have drawn for you to help you understand. Many of your well read authors have also drawn these pictures in their writing of spirit. I do not mean they have drawn pictures in their books, they have drawn pictures through words to explain to those who are leaning the basic steps of spirit's continuous existence. Although those ones who wrote these words were much wiser and could have given a much deeper explanation, in fact they have in other books. In the books they have written for people coming into spirit investigations they have used these graphic terms to try and explain and to try and give food for thought in a way that those who read can understand what is being explained. They are then eager to read more, if they read the book and could not understand they would close the book and say I am not interested I will look at something else. The one who is reading the book goes through the various stages of the book and is able to grasp the understanding, the meaning, this opens doors for this one to investigate further.

The first impression has stayed with many and it is difficult for them to realise that spirit can be in a body, spirit can be in a beautiful garden, woods etc. If you think of yourself on your earth what is beautiful for one isn't beautiful for another. One may visualise a garden as a place of relaxation, beauty but another may prefer to be where there are buildings and hustle and bustle, they would be happier in this position. We give a concept where you are happy in. To walk by the river or by the sea to some it is relaxation but others do not like the sea, it brings panic they do not like water. To some sitting in a garden relaxing is beautiful but to others it means hard work and they would think 'I do not want to be there, I would have to do this, I would have to do that I do not like to see all these green things around me I would like to see some buildings'.

If we had a material dimension similar to your dimension we

would not please everyone. It is difficult to grasp the perception of having different dimensions. Your books tell you of another world, a spirit world, a summerland, a heaven, or whatever the religion you follow, paradise or whatever name they give. It is envisaged as somewhere far away, somewhere you have to travel to but it is not so, it is here with you in another dimension. Your world, our world inter links. You can be in a garden of your world and be in a garden of our world at the same time but it is difficult for you to understand because of our merging of vibrations. We are attracted to light, bright vibrations. Your garden in your springtime is live and vibrant this attracts us in our dimension and the energy from your dimension and our dimension flows backwards and forwards. Of course when you have your other heavier more dense conditions the gulf between our dimensions separates and we draw further away, not further away in our contact with you but our dimensions do not merge so easily. We have to make a different way of linking with you, it is difficult for me to explain. Sometimes there is an abyss between our dimensions, another time there is no distance at all we are intermingled.

This is what we try to develop when we are here communicating with you. We try to link the dimensions so there is no gulf between. We say to shut down your vibrations from your world, shut out your vibrations which make you heavy and dense which draw you down, release yourselves from these vibrations. By shutting these vibrations away you are lifting yourselves to a lighter level. You can easily go from your dimension to our dimension and back again, there is no divide. This is when you perceive spirit, you can see spirit because you are part of our dimension. All you are doing is shedding your mortal overcoat, you are releasing yourself for a very short while from the conditions of your world. You are of your world and you are here to live your life on earth but just for a very brief earth time you are able to step from this dimension into our dimension. Sometimes you may have experienced when you link with spirit in your room, you sit in darkness and you may become disorientated, you are not quite sure how far the one sitting next to you is away from you, who is sitting opposite you, you hear human voices from your friends but it may appear they are not coming from where you think that person is sitting. This is because you are shutting down your earth dimension you are merging your vibration with our vibration and there is no such thing as space, we are together. This is why when you perceive spirit noises one will say 'I hear it this side' but another will say 'I hear it that side'. When you perceive spirit aromas one of you will say 'I perceive this' but another will say 'Oh no, I perceive something else'. You are confined in your earthly world to distance and time but there is not these restrictions in our dimension so entering our dimension you are experiencing, for a while, what our dimension is and how we exist. How you exist without your body. You are just releasing yourself from it.

Of course, you come back and you must come back gently, it is no good to rush back. One minute you are with us and the next minute you withdraw, you must shut down. This is why you must shut down to take yourself back into the heaviness of the earth condition. This must be gradual, do not go instantly, you have a routine where you enter our dimension. When you begin your time with us, you go through your shutting out process, shutting away of your earthly dimension, you open yourself to spirit, you welcome spirit to be with you, you greet them, you say a prayer asking for protection and blessing, this is a routine. As your time span with us has to end and you have to return to your earthly world, you again go through your routine of shutting down the lightness of spirit and taking on the heaviness of the vibration of earth. You physically say this, in your words you say a prayer to say what is occurring. Whatever words you use you are saying that you are shutting down your evening with spirit, you are giving thanks for that evening that you were able to communicate but you now realise that you are returning to earth time and you must take on the cloak of earth. Whatever you say or sing to close down does not matter the choice is yours, but this is what you are actually saying within you. You are aware that this time is precious and this time has come to an end for a short time and you must return to take on your earth vibration.

For those who do not do this they are inviting problems because as you enter into the heavier condition of earth, the lower vibrations that earth contains and you haven't shut down your link with spirit you are drawing to you the lower vibrations of our world. As much as we want to protect you, you are inviting those in because you have not shut down. We cannot do everything for you, we can protect you while you are in our dimension but once you have left our dimension and entered back into your earth condition without closing completely you are saying 'welcome' to whoever wants to come and as you come down the vibration levels you are attracting those in. There are many who are just awaiting an opportunity to come and experience earth again. There are probably things on earth which they left unfinished and they are just waiting for an opportunity to come and take possession of a vibration which they can utilise for their own ends. This is what occurs sometimes, I will not say many times, I will say sometimes.

So many people say 'Why do we have to ask, why aren't spirit there behind us all the time protecting us?'. We can only do so much, you have your own responsibility, also you have your own free will. It the same with healing, people say 'Why do we have to ask for healing, why can't I just be given healing?'. You do not assume, the desire has to come from within the person wanting healing, they have to desire from their spirit within. You can teach a child on your earth, you can take them, you can show them how to tie their shoe laces but if that child does not want to tie their shoe laces, how ever many times you show them they will not learn because it is not their desire to learn. If they really want to learn it will become easier and they will do it simply. It is the same with many things in your world, if you really desire to do something you can achieve it. I am not talking of monetary ideal, I am talking of your abilities in your earth world. There are many who have come from a very deprived background and have not had the opportunities of education. Not so much in your world today although it still occurs but more so in years gone by when there was not schooling and they had to labour and bring income into the family so they had been deprived of education. When there has been desire to achieve, to gain a skill, they have overcome many obstacles and achieved this skill and risen in their material circumstances. They have had a desire from within that has driven them. On the other hand you have had many who have had education, they have had much of your earth world luxuries bestowed on them but they have missed opportunities along the way because they have not had the desire within to achieve. They have an empty soul, they have not achieved themselves, they have relied upon someone else to strive for them.

This is the same with your link with spirit and your desire has to be sincere from within. Whether we are talking about your spiritual progression and your desire to communicate with spirit, or whether we are talking about a health problems and you wish the health problems to be overcome. You have to desire from within, it is no good expecting spirit to say 'Ah well, yes, he has got a sore head I will make it better for him'. You have got to desire help, to say 'I have had enough of this, I don't want this any more, I am going to throw it away, spirit please help me to do this'. Then spirit come in and they are able to assist but just to sit back and say 'Spirit knew I had a headache why don't they take it away?' That is the wrong attitude, that is the wrong way of going about matters. This can apply to whatever you desire. Some will say, you can try many times but you keep getting knocked back why?

This is the reason you are here, you have come to earth to go through these trials and tribulations so that you grow. If everything was perfect in your world there wouldn't be any point in you being here, you might as well not have come. You have chosen to come here to learn and experience and through experiencing you grow, also by experience you are able to assist others who will go through these experiences at a later time. You have to have positive thought. Many times there are hurdles and you stumble but you pick yourself up and go forward. It is not all plain sailing we understand that, we have all walked your path, not your individual path, but we have all walked an earthly path. It is difficult to see with your earthly eyes because you are looking through a mist. You only have perception of a small part of your knowledge, you have deep knowledge within but most of that is clouded from you while you are experiencing your earth conditions. You are thinking 'I know the answer but why can't I get the answer?', This is because you have to work through the answer for yourself.

We know you will ask the same questions time and time again, because until that cloud is lifted and all of a sudden you see clearly, you will still have this uncertainty. It is a conflict because as you progress we don't paint pictures for you, we try to tell you of deeper things, with a deeper meaning and a deeper understanding. If you keep referring back to your basic lessons, as a child would go back to their primary school, they learn 2+2 = 4, so when they graduate to university and they are doing huge sums with lots of figures and then they start reverting back to 2+2 = 4 they are taking themselves backwards. If they were given a large calculation to work out and they went back to their basic principles of adding one figure onto another and drawing a line they would be doing it all day. As they progress they have learnt how to use figures in a different way. You learn to use spirit in a different way. It is like a child holding onto a favourite toy, it is something which gives comfort, gives reassurance. Although that child has grown to adulthood, man or womanhood, they still don't want to lose that favourite toy which gave them comfort when they were small. It is as simple as that. This is the easiest way I can explain. They no longer need the doll, the toy, but it has given them comfort for such a long while they still want it near them.

It is the same with your perception of spirit, when you were first introduced to spirit the first things that were explained to you were in picture form for you to understand. That gave you reassurance when you were very low so you don't want to throw this to one side. You go through the explanations we give you and you understand them to a point but once you have understood them and grappled with them, you then take up your original picture.

We return from spirit to talk to you and we each handle the situation a different way. Some would say 'Yes if that is what you want to believe you go along and enjoy it'. Another would say 'Well that is good up to a point but dig a little deeper'. We are all individuals even though we are a group working together as a team, we merge our vibrations, we merge our energies to talk to you but we still are individuals, an individual basis. This is why we handle things in a different way, as you would on earth. We don't change, as you are individuals in your earth life so when you go home to spirit you take your individuality with you. You don't have the trappings of earth life, hopefully you have learnt to overcome the difficulties, your impatience, your indecision but you still have some who will listen and some who will want to interrupt and say other things, it is all part of individuality. It would not be beneficial to progress if everyone was on the same vibration level. (13.01.98)

QUESTION 121 - In the seance room sometimes sitters are fortunate enough to witness 'spirit lights', small pin point lights darting around the room sometimes coming to rest near a particular person, sometimes appearing to pass through solid objects. Mafra was asked to give an explanation regarding this phenomena.

When you perceive a spirit light you are perceiving true spirit. When others perceive spirit they are decoding spirit and they are creating a body, a colour, or a vibration around that spirit. What you perceive is true spirit. It is difficult for you to reason with your human brain that within that tiny spark of spirit light, which is what we are, is all that we contain. You cannot visualise that all our memory, all our knowledge is contained in that one light. You think of a heavy suitcase and all that that suitcase contains, you could not condense it into a tiny handbag. This tiny spark is what we really are, it is what you are within your body, your light within.

Can you imagine, my friends, I know that some of you perceive that you come to earth several times but even taking into account that situation, for every one who has lived and breathed on your planet who is now in spirit to have a body, although we have a dimension, can you imagine the problem? It is inconceivable, I could not start to explain what it would be like. (13.01.98)

QUESTION 122 - John Lyon explaining that we are spirit within a human body.

You perceive yourself as a human in a human body who has come from spirit. What you do not perceive is that you are spirit that is encased in a mortal body. You are looking at it in a different perspective, you are looking at it as if you are a human first and foremost and you come from spirit and you will go back to spirit. Look at it the other way; you are spirit, which is the most important part of you, and for this very short while you, true spirit, have got the heaviness of earth around you. This heaviness of earth around you clouds your vision to the knowledge that you have without your human body.

For the short while you are here in this room you have shut out your human world. Yes, you are still part of your human world, you are breathing, you are still existing, you still feel the temperature in your room, you still feel the floor beneath your feet and the chair you are sitting on. You cannot cut out the human world completely but you are throwing out the confines of the human world with the worries and the frustrations. For a short while you are releasing yourself from this human overcoat and your spark, your spirit within you is free and is experiencing the vibrations of spirit that you had before you had your human body, before you were encumbered with your human body. When you leave this room you then take on your responsibilities, all your worries and frustrations, and you become mortal again. At this time you are free and this is why you are able to perceive what is occurring around you. You are able to sense and feel, slowly you are becoming more aware of your true self, your true spirit sensations. In your human world you have a fastener which you call a zip, it is as if you have an overcoat on of a human body and each week you are taking the zip down a little bit further. You are then taking off a little bit more of this human overcoat and your spirit is a little bit more free, you are sensing a little bit more. (18.01.98)

QUESTION 123 - One of the sitters brought a photograph that appeared to have some "spirit", extras on the photograph. HANNS was asked if he could advise whether the "extras" on the photograph were spirit or something else. Following Hanns explanation at our next sitting RUNNING BEAR gives an explanation of what was happening.

I want to hold the photograph. Oh, I dropped it. You sit back I can see in the dark so I will pick the photograph up from the floor. I have put my hands on the photograph, there is much energy in this photograph, it is very hot to one side. Yes, there is spirit. I have looked at the photograph but I still want to feel the vibration. I can look and see picture but I need to touch to feel vibration. This is spirit standing beside you when you took picture, over your shoulder. You are in picture but your spirit helper was standing behind camera so there was link from you to camera and they were overshadowing, this is their energy you have perceived.

You are asking who? This is a mixture of vibrations, there is more than one, they are merging energy together. This is an amalgam of energy. You have energy of your own, also they were merging energy from vibration of place where you took picture. They were uniting with energy from that area.

This is what was occurring - you were there to learn, you were there to stretch out to learn. Those who came with you, your close ones from spirit were also learning. They were mingling their vibrations with those learned ones from that place. Over the years there has been much vibration there, this has been a centre for learning but before this occurred there was one who was there who was very wise and his energy is still there. His energy acts as catalyst for all that has gone on since. This is what is occurring, it is your ones from spirit who are close to you merging their energy with those who are already there and this 'extra' you have on your film is the reaction from this catalyst, this surge of energy.

You will not see a picture of a person because it is not a person, its an amalgam. (18.01.98).

Running Bear's explanation on what had occurred - They enjoyed speaking to Hanns, they enjoyed someone a little different. You had a job to understand how this occurred. You want me to explain the reading of the photograph? This was used as tool. We have assisted before with vibrations from paper. This was paper which someone had put their thoughts into as they wrote. They gave much thought to what they were writing so we were able to absorb this from paper. It was not the same with the photograph. The photograph was just used as a link. Hanns was using photograph for own benefit, he was using as a demonstration. There was no real need for photograph but he was making a display. He was handling photograph, also he was seeing photograph but by talking about photograph he was actually linking with the one who had brought photograph. He was making the link stronger.

You say 'Why could that one who brought photograph, not just say I took photograph of whatever and tell me about it?' Yes, my friends that is good but the thought would not be so concentrated, thought would be on other things as well but because there was this two way discussion about the photograph the thoughts were linked directly on the content of the photograph. If it had been a conversation about the photograph the owner of the photograph would have spoken about that photograph and then her thoughts would have wandered to another photograph that was taken on same day, or another day. As photograph was actually here the communication on conversation level stayed on photograph, so followed communication on higher level but on the same vibration. Two way communication was taking place. Hanns was using photograph as demonstration, but he really was not picking vibration from photograph but from the owner of the photograph. By talking about the photograph he was drawing from her the vibration of the event, making the link stronger. If it was just conversation with no actual article the link would not be so strong, because it may have been that picture but it may have been another picture, who knows! There was this intent with the person who brought the photograph, they came with the intent, when she came into the room she had this intent with her, she carried photograph with the thought 'this is what I want to talk about tonight'. If she had not brought the photograph she would have said ' there is something I want to talk about' but it would not have been so intent. She touched it, she felt it, she looked at it, it was much deeper in her mind so Hanns was able to link.

Hanns being a scientist he likes to handle actual article, no vagueness, he likes everything precise. He had photograph so this was precise. It was what he wanted to talk about.

I will now go a step further, he handled photograph. We in spirit are not used to handling a material object, he was not able to grasp, it fell. If you picked up photograph you would have held it tighter, it would not drop, but he was unaccustomed to holding something like a photograph with the medium's hands. The medium's hands were a different size to the vibration he expected from his memory of being in his human body, so as soon as he picked up photograph it fell. Your sitter was amazed that he could go to photograph and pick it up in total darkness. He told you he could see the photograph so he could pick the photograph up. This was said to give simple explanation, what he was locating was the vibration link. He was going to the vibration of the photograph and grasping it. Then when he returned the photograph to the sitter he was going to the vibration of her hand and linking with that vibration to replace photograph. He said he saw photograph but that was his way of explaining, he was sensing vibration.

Hanns enjoyed this because being a scientist he has to have something practical, not vague thoughts, there has to be substance and fact. This is what was presented to him. This pleased him. It is good for you because you are of material world and you live with material objects. For you it makes strong link also, more definite link. (20.01.98)

QUESTION 124 - Running Bear gives an inclination at what happened at the beginning of time on earth.

You have spark within you all and this spark is covered with overcoat of mortal heaviness. You are not just a human who will return to spirit from whence you came, you are actually spirit here and now in a human condition. There is much deeper reasoning behind this.

This explanation goes back to the beginning of time for your universe. It goes back to when your planet was formed and how spirit was working at that time and how spirit formed itself into a materialised form. Within that materialised form there was spirit but this is very deep. It needs someone to explain who has a better master of your tongue than myself and to be given at a time when you are ready to accept in more detail.

When your universe was in state of turmoil and planets were

formed there was much drawing together of particles, substances and matter. You know the history of your plant life and your animals life at the beginning of time and how you had many unusual creations. This was not to be continued, this was only for a while.

Sufficient to say, if this could be explained to you, you would understand why you are spirit here and now. You are just in the body of a human overcoat. Your forebears, going back millions of years have carried a part of this spark of spirit within them, this is what is eternal and this is the true spirit. I will leave this now.

You know now why we worshipped Mother Earth because we are part of Mother Earth. This was handed down to our tribes and many other tribes throughout your world. There was time in the beginning when spirit was part earth and part not earth, they could intermingle. They would not be in a body as your body, they could materialise and dematerialise and shed the heaviness of earth. If you look at legends of many tribes throughout the world you will get a glimpse of this truth. You look at what has been handed down to you from your early civilisations, from Incas also from Greek mythology but behind stories there is a spark of truth. Earth was not inhabited with solid bodies, it was inhabited with spirit who visited your earth and took on form. You are aware that spirit can materialise in your groups by using substance from human. However, there was a time when spirit could materialise without needing assistance from human matter to create the materialised form, and they would materialise and dematerialise at will. Then there came a time when they became a little too clever and decided that they wanted to remain on earth because earth was a new experience, earth was good and this was the birth of your civilisation. Some spirits did not want to return to spirit dimension, they wanted a longer duration with a human body and this was the beginning of time. From these ones came your ancestors, not in the form you are in now, not in the shape you are now.

With evolution man's shape has altered, you only have to look back one or two generations to you see man's shape altering. So in billions of years you can imagine how man's shape has altered. The more of your world spirit became the more shape their form developed.

I am imparting this knowledge to you because you are ready but perhaps others are not yet ready for this information. This happened at a time when there was this massive explosion in the universe and your planet and other planets were formed. This also explains that there is not our world and your world we are all of same world, we all inhabit the same world but in a different dimension.

If you read stories of legends, there are many elaborations on legends but deep within there is a spark of truth. Our stories were handed down by wise ones in tribe and each generation added a little bit more to the story, as you do for your children. You tell nursery stories to your children but each generation adds a little more because your world has altered since you heard the story, so you make the story a little more modern, so that your little ones understand. Most stories relate to good over evil.

A deeper understanding of this knowledge will be imparted when the time is right. (20.01.98)

QUESTION 125 - Running Bear explaining why it is important to have harmony within a group.

You are fortunate to have harmony in your group some other groups do not have this harmony. Lack of harmony not only make communication difficult but it also is destructive. Thoughts have energy and they have to be utilised for good or not so good. Not only does it bring disharmony to group and it affects all who sit in the group, also it sometimes attracts not so good vibrations, so you get interference. Those who are trying to work from spirit, sometimes what they say is distorted because of the vibration. This is what we say, if someone has a question, open mouth and say question, do not sit and think question, throw into room and discuss. Thoughts are very forceful and can cause problems.

Unfortunately there will always be those who cannot be happy. This is a part of their makeup, it is something they have within, it is an imbalance within themselves, their own soul. Until they look inside themselves and are harmonious with themselves they will not be harmonious with others. This is why we say to you, when we talk, look at yourself, be happy with yourself, accept all your faults but be happy with yourself. If you are not happy with yourself there is no point in trying to be happy with others. You love yourself with your faults, so you love your brothers and sisters with their faults. All of us, not only those with bodies, are different, we all have our own way of existing. Some are more harmonious than others. Just because we do not have a human body it does not mean we are free from all vibrations, we may be very evolved spiritually but we are only a small step ahead of you.

Of course, there are many advanced souls who are very evolved and the more evolved the more harmonious they become. This comes through looking within one's self and knowing oneself within, knowing who you are, why you are here, what makes you happy, what makes you sad. Accept that there are things that you cannot alter. We are all different. I am not being boastful but I say this for your information, I have much wisdom through my experiences and the experiences of my tribe, I have been fortunate as I have much wisdom of natural law. I am not saying earth law,

I am saying natural law, because this transcends earth, spirit and universe. Whereas you have Brother John, he is very harmonious, a very advanced soul. He does not have my knowledge but he has much other knowledge of spirit, of harmony, of love, of deep thought and the power of thought. I just give you two examples, there are many, many more examples but I have just introduced two to you so that you can see that we are a little way along the path from you but we are still different from each other, still learning. Still advancing, still going forward, still using the knowledge that we have and adding to that knowledge. We do not say this is old knowledge, it is no good any more, I go forward. It is all part of us so we take it with us, without this knowledge we would not be ourselves, we would be someone else because this has made us what we are. This is what makes you all different, this is what makes me different from Brother John, and Brother John different from me. Without your experience you would not be yourself. It is the same with every soul whether they have an earth body or not. It is no good looking a one of your brothers and saying I cannot understand that one, why does he do this? why does he do that?. He does this, he does that, because he is himself because of his makeup and of his past experiences.

You each have different destiny, because there is no such thing as time this make you all individual. Your past, your present and your destiny. You are all going along the same road but each of you go in your own direction. You carry some of the same 'baggages' with you but some different ones, different 'baggages' from different experiences. Each of you have a different destiny so you travel a different path to reach that destiny, so you cannot be the same as each other. You must accept that everyone you meet, whether they have a human body or not, are themselves and you cannot alter. You can share what you have and they can take from you if they wish but it is their path.

We come back to a group. Within a group you have different brothers and sisters sitting and if you cannot accept that brothers and sisters are different and you try to make them all the same you are going the wrong way. You are going the wrong way round, you must accept each is different, each has own light within and it is not for you to try and change that light to a different colour light, different glow. If it has to be altered, it has to be altered by that one themselves because they want to change.

You cannot force change on people. If someone looks within themselves and does not like what they see within themselves and they dearly want to change themselves, they are going forward. If someone looks at that one and says to that one 'look you are going the wrong way you should do something different' and that one does not accept, or that one does it just to please the one who is suggesting, that is no good because the desire is not from within. Many times people have tried to change because someone has suggested they should and they do it to please, not from their own desire and this has brought many more problems. You need to desire from within, not just to please another mortal, or even to please spirit, you should do it to please yourself. Otherwise there is no sincerity and truth and sincerity go hand in hand. How can you serve others if you are not sincere to yourself?

This is a failing of many prominent people who have walked upon earth. They have tried to show sincerity to others but they have not been sincere to themselves so they are an 'empty vessel'. Those who they are working with can see straight through them. You must realise, you see others with your mortal eyes but you have another sense where you can ascertain the truth behind the face.

This is where it is good to rely on your first instinct when you meet or are brought into contact with someone, what your first instinct is before they are able to 'put their charm on', before they are able to twist words. It is the first impression when you first meet, that first glimpse is very important. You can alter your features, alter your clothes, alter many things of your earth body to try and make yourself look more favourable to others but when it all is said and done it is what is inside that shines out. (27.01.98)

QUESTION 126 - *Hannah answering a question about animal life and do simple forms of life such as insects or even microbes have a continuum?*

Everything that has life has a soul, not as your soul, it is a group soul. Everything that has existence has life and animates, so it goes home to spirit. A butterfly leaves earth but lives again in spirit, it is natural law. Everything has continuum, it goes to group soul in spirit and returns to earth again. There are stages of life, the more advanced the more individual the existence.

Your animals which live in your homes with you have spent much time with you, so they have become a little different from animals of fields, they have closer contact with your level of dimension. Also, when you go home to spirit they have a closer link with you because they have shared their earthly life with you but they go home also to their group. As they have this link with you they are able to leave the group and come to you. It is the same with others, you talk of your animals but some people keep animals which you would not keep as pets. They can also link with their human companions who loved them. However, there are not so many that are loved as your dogs and cats but those that are have a stronger link because they are part of you and you are part of them. They merge energies and vibrations, nothing is lost. Everything that is on your earth continues, it comes to your earth for a purpose but when it has served its purpose it goes home to spirit. Perhaps not the same as your purpose. Your purpose is to advance and to learn. Every insect has purpose on your earth, every creature, it is the law of nature. They serve you, these lower dimensions, they provide service for you, they kill bacteria. Not so much these days in your world, but when I was on earth our animals kept vermin controlled. You do not like it when your cats bring home mice but for us it served a purpose, it kept our food that was precious because we did not have ways of storing food as you do today. If all the mice ate the grain and food that we stored we would have gone hungry.

You think of it as you see with your eyes today, as your world is evolving it is changing but your animals still have a purpose. They now have more purpose as companions, not so much as servers. They still walk with you and give you assistance but in another way. The more your world has advanced the more rushed and frustrated you become. These animals are there to serve you and share with you their love and they help you to take away stress. So you see, they still serve you but they are not here just to serve you, they are also here for a reason, but they are mingling their vibration. It would be very wrong to think you are just the supreme race on your earth and all the others are here to serve you, that would not be the way to think. You are all here to share with each other, you all have your purpose and their purpose is just as important to them as yours is to you. (01.02.98)

QUESTION 127 - A communicator gives words of encouragement for the future.

Go forward. Much goes out from your group, sometimes you think there is no progress when sitters ask the same questions over and over again. If you want to progress go forward you can stay forever asking the same questions, there is no progress in this situation. You have to accept some explanations you cannot understand with your human brain. When there is quandary let go and rise above. You realise that this will all be explained when you do not have your human body, so why worry now?

Different spirit visitors give different explanations, different descriptions of spirit existence there is confusion. Confusion can be destructive, negative, you need to rise above. Accept what is given and accept it is given from the ones in spirit with knowledge that they have at that point in their progress. Do not argue one against another, 'he said so........, but others said so......., it does not agree' This causes disharmony, no progress, pull together.

Go forward do not think back on past problems, use your energy to go forward, do not waste energy on something that has gone. The future is important not the past, build on past for future. Your world has moved on, there are not the same conditions as in the past, your world needs different methods, different explanations, more scientific. What has been recorded is sufficient for the history of the time. Go forward, the future is very important. You are living the future now, those who are recorded in history built for the future. You are living the future now because you are building the future. You do not want to stay in one place and go around in a circle, you want to work forward, progress.

If your religion, for want of a better word, wants to be recognised it has to be credible and answerable to those with future looking brains, no ridicule, no looking back and saying that is something done in old days, no more. You must go forward and build, there is so much opportunity to build for peace. Peace is important, harmony is important. Harmony within each one, if there is harmony within each one then harmony spreads to those around each one, that harmony spreads to that area of town, that harmony spreads to nation, and nation spreads to world. We are striving for peace. There always has been good fighting evil, do not sit on laurels and say 'we know the right way, we have light on our side so we will win'. This is not sufficient, we have to work together in harmony to build harmony. Harmony has to be worked at, peace has to be worked at, make light shine brighter. Bright light will overcome darkness, dim light is not strong enough. Go forward, this is what I say.

Questions, questions, 'Why does this happen? Why does that happen?'. This is negative, accept that it does happen, accept this happens, there is a reason, not for your answer. You have to accept that some things are destiny, you say 'God's will', part of plan. It has to be accepted. If you question, question, you are being destructive and this is not harmony, you need to turn the other way and say 'this happens, what can we do to assist? How can we make this condition better? How can we achieve peace in this condition, harmony in this condition?' Many say your world today is in state of turmoil but your living conditions are much better than many of your ancestors, so go forward.

Communication between our worlds should flow, there should not be a barrier. When there is time of earth problem worlds should merge and draw strength from each other, this should be natural. I am just trying to tell you rise above your petty questions because there is much more to your world than your little nooks and corners which you question, open yourself to a much higher vista. Look above your mundane world, if you stay on this mundane level and ponder on this level, you are confining yourself to this level. You want to rid of this level, you want to go higher, progress, go forward. Do not be dragged down to worry of things which are not for you to worry about. Rise above to greater plan.

Go forward in light. (03.02.98)

QUESTION 128 - Sister Celeste continuing on the theme of progress.
You say 'How can we go forward?'. Do not worry on how you can just know you can. This makes a stumbling block when you say 'how can we go forward?' because you are putting doubt and question, just know you are going forward. It should be natural, there should be no having to plan, it is not a campaign like your army manoeuvres. It is to go forward naturally, it should be a natural progression. Go forward with faith, knowing you are going forward. When you start questioning you are putting halt on your progress, so no questions, know you are going forward, accept you are going forward. There are always times when there has to be a standstill, for whatever reason. Whichever path you travel whether material path or spiritual path you cannot go full speed ahead all the time, there has to be time to stand and reflect before you take up and go forward again. This does not mean you stand still and question and go backwards, it is time to pull strength together, to unite together and go forward together.

Make the affirmative, 'we are going forward, we are going forward in light, we are going forward' so you have affirmative that you are making progress, you are going forward. It is very difficult because you do not want to be too forceful because this would cause a problem, it should be natural, just go forward. As you walk your path down your road, you put one foot in front of another you go forward, it should be the same, no planning 'I am going so many steps today and so many steps tomorrow', just as they come. Sometimes you say 'go forward' and you are looking for something to happen, this is putting brake on. You must believe you are going forward because we go forward together, we are going forward also.

I will give you an example from my life on earth which should help you to visualise your path forward. In my calling, with my sisters, we would each light a candle and walk together, going forward. Our family of sisters, we would leave our cells and we would unite, the holy mother would light a candle and sisters would also light candles and we would go in procession behind holy mother, down corridor, through gate into the church of St Denise. We were going forward to serve. If you can visualise this, you and your family together, linking with those loved ones who walk with you in spirit, each lighting candle and walking forward in procession and you are all walking forward in this light. The more candles that are lit the greater the light and you have those wise ones at head of your column, the very wise ones with very bright lights, your lights are not so bright behind but they are glowing. You are walking together forward in service. Try and visualise this, ask your group to walk forward with those helpers they know they have, those companions, or perhaps some would prefer their loved ones, it does not matter. Try and visualise you are walking forward, you would walk forward with your helpers, companions, others would walk forward with their companions, all with their light, with their candle, you would all unite into a channel of light. You are walking forward together and this light is becoming greater because you are going forward to serve. Not to look either side and stumble but to go forward to the great light of spirit that is ahead, I will not give you an idol, a symbol, or whatever, I will just say the light of spirit. As you all walk together towards this light of spirit, encompassing you all, you all become part of this light. Consciously, leave behind your frustrations, quandaries, throw them to one side because they will be answered later when the time is right, at this time we want you to go forward. When you go forward you will be stronger to be able to find answers to your quandaries when the time is right.

If you visualise one of your cathedrals with the glow of the windows with the light shining through and you are walking down to this, some will visualise a gold cross but this is not essential because this is my faith, others do not have my faith. Walk towards the bright light through these windows and we will walk with you. (03.02.98)

QUESTION 129 - Margarita - a new communicator who talks about learning to communicate.

I learn to communicate, I try hard. We try so much to communicate. There is an expectation from those on earth that when they peceive spirit it will be very positive but it is not always in this form. You can let your mind wander and dream, then it is opening the way for us to step in with two-way contact. If you sit and expect to see a positive form this is not always good, you have to be flexible. If you dream you think you are using your imagination, perhaps at first this is so but it leads on to other things. This is taking away conscious reasoning.

When you are trying to explain to others how to perceive spirit you could use this exercise. Tell them to visualise in their mind somewhere on earth they have visited, perhaps on holiday, somewhere you have walked, something which is of the material world not spirit world and see if they can form this picture in their mind. Then explain to them that this is how you can see spirit, some see spirit very clearly as 'real' people or 'real' objects, but others they will perceive a passing impression, as if you are thinking back on somewhere you have visited and are remember this scene, This is not for them to think they are seeing spirit but it is opening their minds so that they can see something in their memory, then say this is similar to perceiving spirit.

Then they will question how they can define whether they are perceiving spirit or whether it is their imagination. This is something they will develop, they will not know at first. When they see spirit they will know it is different, it is nothing we can explain but when they perceive it they will know it is somehow different. It may be something that someone else in the room can acknowledge but the one who has spoken knows nothing of, so that is proof that it is of spirit.

You think that when someone from spirit comes to talk perhaps it is the first time they have made contact with earth. No, my friend, we come many times before you realise we are here, we spend much time with you. Sometimes we are brought gently with another, perhaps you do not realise this but sometimes when another comes they will say 'come with us'. It is controlled, we do not overlap, it is an experience, because you know we merge energy. The one we come with is in prominence, that is the one who talks and takes control but we just absorb the energy and experience. When we are a little wiser we try to come on our own, sometimes we manage to come and talk but sometimes we are not successful. When you all sit here you do not realise who are with you. All of you have ones from spirit who come and go without you realising, just because they do not speak words it does not mean they are not there. They are there merging vibrations. (08.02.98)

QUESTION 130 - Running Bear answering question 'What is materialisation?'

Materialisation is the manifestation of the vibrations of spirit in a solid form. You sometimes observe the light of spirit or you sense spirit. This is your decoding of a vibration. This is something you would do on your own or your friends would do on their own, you would not very often all decode the same vibration at the same time. If all of your group were fully developed, very good mediums, you may all decode the same vibration at the same time but this is very unusual. Sometimes when you are in a church and two mediums work together they are able to unite and absorb the vibration, one may draw a picture and the other will link with the vibration and explain who this one is. This is an unusual event, when two mediums are linking and decoding the same vibration. Usually you may have many mediums in a room and one will say 'I observe a man', another may say 'I observe a lady', another may say ' I observe a child'. They are not absorbing the same energy, they are each working on their own vibration but when materialisation takes place they all see the same object. This is different from mental mediumship to physical mediumship. What they are doing is they are all decoding this vibration at the same time and this vibration is so strong it is manifesting itself.

Spirit vibration is very fast, we have explained this to you. When we are not here, working in earth's atmosphere our vibration is very quick. We do not have a thought process as you have a thought process, we are able to switch from one direction to another, one subject to another, merge with one energy or another energy. This is not understandable to human mind, you are blinkered you can only look in one direction at one time but spirit can be here, can be there. I can be talking to you now but I can also be talking to my tribe back home, this is difficult to explain but this is how spirit is, a very fast link.

When we visit you sometimes we say to you, when you observe spirit give your first impression because this is fast, first impression that is true spirit, we are fast. The first thing that comes into your head is better than that which you have thought about because this is the quick link that spirit has. If you could observe your room you would see many lights, much movement, spirit dancing here, dancing there. I use the word 'dancing' because this explains, they are moving in every direction.

With materialisation our vibration is slowed down so slowly that you will then observe, perhaps a mist, this is a query because you say ectoplasm, this is different. Ectoplasm is something which is produced by human and we are using this substance to mould our ourselves but this is not used so much in your new modern world. Spirit are turning from ectoplasm, we have evolved as you have evolved and we are able to utilise other vibrations, other substance, which is not tainted with human, this is purer. Sometimes you observe mist swirling, sometimes this is colour swirl, sometimes it is just grey mist. This is a slowing down of a vibration that you are observing, you are decoding spirit that is a slowed down vibration. Instead of observing spirit on a quick vibration that is our natural home, we have entered your earth condition more fully and we have allowed our vibration to be lowered, to be slowed down and by doing this you absorb this mist. You term it mist because this is a word I can explain, it is a condensing of energy. We do not have a body as you have a body but because we are entering earth's heavy pull we are expanding our vibration. It is not quick and vibrant, it is slower and we are allowing ourselves to be pulled by earth's conditions. This is where you observe, perhaps a swirl of mist, or some will observe an object. I do not mean in their mind, I mean they will actually say 'I see a flower, I see a hand, whatever'. This is because spirit has slowed down to a very similar vibration to your earth vibration, not the same but very similar.

You have been told that when you leave your body and go home to spirit you enter a dimension which is very similar to earth's dimension and those who wish can have bodies, they can build house, they can have whatever they wish. This is a similar vibration to this vibration we bring when we lower ourselves to your earth vibration. We cannot be human because we have no skin or bones, but our shape, our vibration is slowed right down and the longer we are here in this vibration the more solid becomes our form. This is when you perceive materialisation. This is why when materialisation is seen there is often a spirit form, but this spirit form is surrounded with a cloak or whatever. This is because this is the vibration that has slowed us down and within this is the pure spirit, and then we are able to take shape of identity we had when we last had a body.

There is a difference between your ectoplasm and this other method. So, 'What is materialisation?' - Materialisation is a slowing down process of a spirit vibration to be compatible with your earth vibration and as it takes on your earth vibration it also takes on a form similar to a human form, not the same because we do not exist in your human world. We do not have bones, we do not digest food, so we do not have earth body but we have earth vibration. This is the moulding is of our essence into the heaviness of earth.

You say 'Why can we not see this all the time?' - This because you are not on the same vibration. You are on a similar vibration but if only we could merge onto the same vibration you would see much more. We come as low to ground as we can, I say ground because I mean pull of ground. We are still not the same condition as yourselves. We also learn, perhaps we need to learn more also. To become closer to earth, even more, then you would all be able to see. You also assist because you are giving out energy and we are able to utilise this energy to assist in making the form, mingling vibrations. We are able to link our vibration with your vibration and by taking part of your human vibration, I do not mean your skin and bones, your slow human vibration, to blend this with our lowered altered vibration and create a form. This is what is occurring in some circles at this time on your earth. Sometimes it is observed as solid form. You may have observed this in other ways, as movement, as physical noises (I do not mean spirit noises). It is a lowered spirit vibration that merges with your earth vibration, because of this spirit is able to make physical noise that can be heard with physical ears. (08.02.98)

QUESTION 131 - *Jules talking about book.*

Spirit are very pleased about book. It means that all the work that we do is for a purpose. It takes a lot of patience, effort to learn how to come to talk, to answer all your questions because you can ask us any question and we are able to answer. If perhaps, you ask Jules a question I might not be able to answer but I will give you the answer because someone is giving me the answer. I am able to pull answer from here, from there, to help you with your question. This takes a lot of energy, work, not all play but this is for a reason, this is good. We are happy this is for a reason, we are not just doing this for nothing.

We like to talk to you my friend, but there is a deeper reason. In some circles people just come and say 'Hello, Auntie Fanny here, Uncle Harry here', but this is not so with this circle. This is here for a reason, not just for communication. We do not have to prove survival, this is for a deep reason, good. This is why we are being organised. We must have an aim, a plan. It is no good just come and wander here, and wander there. It is all right for Jules but not for others. Time is very precious, we have no time, time is nothing to us, but your time is very precious. You say that if you live to three score years and ten that is a long while but in comparison with eternity it is a very short time. Our work is very important, we bring you as much as we can so that it will be here for others. I am not saying you are going home to spirit tomorrow, but I am saying if you live to be 100 it is still not long.

It is good you are utilising all the modern equipment you have, it is being used for good. There are some who will say 'I do not like those words, it is not very well written' but you have to argue both ways my friend. You can write very well but this is what has happened to your many books, your holy bible, it was well written in its time but because it was well written in its time words were altered, sentences changed around. When I come to talk to you I sometimes say words back to front because this was how I spoke in my French language. If you alter my words around the other way, which you can my friend, I do not mind, as long as they mean the same thing. If you alter them and they do not mean the same thing you are wasting your time, my time, everyone's time, the people who are reading, their time.

We do not mind if you alter because we understand that perhaps we are not talking in a way which others will understand. It is easier for them to understand if they are listening because they have the link with us, there is a link on a higher level which is coming to you at the same time and this is helping you to absorb words even if words do not make sense. When you read it on a blank piece of paper you do not have this vibration and you may say 'this is rubbish!' Sometimes it is essential that it is altered as long as the meaning is the same. Even if we spoke to you very grammatically and everything was said very correctly, if you look at your men of words who speak to you on your earth. If you listen with your ears to what they are saying and try to write down what the are saying if would not be as if they had written it on paper. To give a talk you emphasise perhaps some words over and over again, because you want to get your message across. You have your politicians who repeat sentences, bang fists, and emphasise words but when they write on paper they do not do this. This again has to be altered when you write our words because sometimes we say words over and over again because we are talking not writing. If you read, you would say why are they repeating again, again and again? They would get bored, they would say they had heard these words before.

You have to use a little bit of common sense. It is not always good to use the same words over again you have to think what is best for the reader but remember the meaning is important. Sometimes those who come have not been very often, they are not sure what to say and perhaps they start a sentence and then change their mind. You would have a sentence half said and that would make no sense. You have to use a little bit of common sense. You have to understand that they are trying to get their expressions over to you and are trying to find the best way. It is because they do not think.

When you are talking to group of people before you say a word you are thinking of what you are going to say and in your mind you are thinking, no I cannot say that, I have to phrase it differently. We are not thinking, we are just sending the vibration direct and it is being decoded. There is not time for thinking, Sometimes we start to say something and then halfway through we realise this is not what is intended, it is not getting the message across so we stop and start again. This proves genuine mediumship, if it was word perfect you would know this had been thought about before the words were said. Be careful when you have mediums who are word perfect because this could be conscious reasoning twisting words before they are spoken. This has happened in the past. The one who is the medium should not know what is being said until it comes out of mouth. If they are able to think and change then there is a problem, part of their own thoughts are coming into the words.

This is why we say to you, say the first thing that comes into your head, not only when you are in trance but any time. The first things you observe, say, do not try and add or take away. Do not say 'There is a man with a red hat' no it can't be a red hat it must be a black hat. You see how easy it is to change words. Your conscious reasoning is telling you men don't wear red hats, they wear black hats, so you alter. You may think it must not be man it must be lady because a lady would wear a red hat. The first thing you see, observe, feel or sense is what you must say. If after you have said it you do not think it is right it does not matter, you have said it. (08.02.98)

QUESTION 132 - *You have spoken to us many times on the energy that is created by various groups sending out thoughts of peace and healing can you tell us more about this?* - Answer by Running Bear

All energy is used. This is why you have to guard against your thoughts. We are able to utilise your energy of your level of love but other vibrations of a different level are sent by those who are on a different level of understanding. This is why you have to guard your thoughts and just send pure thoughts, pure love. When there are vibrations which are sent on a lower level this causes problems because people send out thoughts which are not good. Those on a different level of vibration than us who work on this level can take that energy and use for not so good purposes.

Also, there are other levels, many levels. There are people like yourselves who are sending love which we use but even those that are accustomed to sending on this level also have times in their existence when they send other vibrations which are not so good. Perhaps there is worry, there is frustration, there is fear, there are many levels of vibrations which are sent all the time. All time of human existence thoughts are being sent from many, many, - all these thoughts are vibrations, all these thoughts are going out into great space. I use the word 'space' as this is the best way I can explain. These are finding other vibrations of similar levels which are being sent by others. One thought on its own, you say, would not do much harm but many thoughts from many sent joined together this is when there are problems. When there are times on your earth when there is much worry, or when there is much fear, this is a time when we have to be very careful because many thoughts are being sent on this vibration of fear. These thoughts are going out but like attracts like and they go together, this vibration of fear can rebound and cause many problems because it is a negative vibration.

I will give an example - there may be a problem when many people may be fearful of an event. These thoughts are sent as I have explained and these thoughts can cause the product which you are fearful of occurring. It can create the problem. There has to be much work with those of a higher vibration in spirit who can calm this energy, disperse this energy, so it dose not create the problem which is feared.

When people from your world send out thoughts of fear these

thoughts are on a vibration, not negative, not positive, but a vibration which is very vibrant, very excitable. It is a vibration which can ignite, can create. Those people are not positively thinking that they are creating the situation, they are not positively saying 'that situation will not occur' but fear is a very emotive vibration. It is a different vibration to that of desire, that of hope, that of positivity, it is different, there is more emotion.

When you are in a situation on your earth where you are in danger your body reacts. I will give you an example from my life on earth. I walked in the forest, I knew forest well, I came to clearing but because of my sensitivity I was able to sense there was danger not far away, perhaps a bear, or another wild animal or something that was going to cause a problem. Because of my closeness to Mother Earth I was able to perceive this danger. Having perceived this danger my human body went into defence to defend myself. My human body would create substances within from adrenaline glands which would make my human body react quickly to avoid danger, either to run from danger or to meet danger face on and attack. My adrenaline would pump around my body and my body would work quick for this self preservation and I would take the action that was needed. Alongside human body is spirit body, this energy which is created with fear is positive energy. Because my body created this adrenaline this had to be used so my human body had to react, I could not return to state of calm. I would either have to attack or run.

So with spirit body fear creates much energy. This energy, as human energy, is pumped on a very quick vibration and this energy has to be utilised. It cannot be dispersed, so when there is fear and alarm this is what is happening you are creating problems with your human body but also alongside your spirit body is creating parallel energy. This energy is going from you out into this big space and when this meets energy from many others you can imagine 'explosion'. This then has to rebound and cause a not so good effect. It may not cause the affect you were fearing, it may cause an affect somewhere else in your world. It may cause an affect in other levels of vibration not just your level in spirit vibration because we are sharing your world with you. Our dimension over links your dimension. So there is rebound of this energy which has repercussions.

I am not sure whether this explains your original question, you were asking what use is made of the energy you send. *People who go into meditation and go into a state of contemplation can you also use this energy?* - As I explained all energy is used but I gave warning of other energy. Energies which are near your earth are base human instinct, and are most vibrant and can cause many problems and repercussions.

We are now talking of a higher energy, an energy where you are leaving your earthly thoughts behind and stretching to link with those of a higher vibratory level. This energy is again going out into this vast space and is joining other energy that is being created by other of a similar vibration, no matter what religion, whether it is Christian, Hindu, Buddhist, those who worship Mother Earth, it does not matter. It is an energy that is above your human energy, you are releasing yourself from your human thoughts and your human vibration and you are able to reach a higher level. This is good because this energy is merging with higher level energy from spirit in our dimension. This is used for many affects, we use for healing, this is what you first think of, this energy goes for healing, which is good. Also I have explained to you other vibrations, those of a higher level in our dimension are able to utilise this energy as a calming affect to diffuse situations which are too vibrant and cause problems. This energy is also used for those in our world who are learning, who are seeking. It is used to show light, to assist with those who are progressing in spirit and as you send this vibration you are linking with them, so you are also progressing. You are merging your energy and you learn from each other.

As we bring those here to you, to learn with you on your earth vibration, we bring those from spirit to join your group, to learn with you because they are on a similar vibration to your earth vibration. When they join us in spirit they are not far distant from your earth vibration so we bring them to you to join with you, to help them step forward and learn, you know this occurs. Also the other side of the coin, when you stretch yourself and raise yourself above human vibrations, and human thoughts, you are able to join with those in our realms who are of a higher level vibration and are learning, you are merging your vibration with them and you are joining them with their lessons and their progress.

Our worlds are intermingled, there is no your world - our world, the dimensions are very close. It depends on which vibration you are on while you are on earth and what vibration those in our realms are, where you are able to merge together. (03.03.98)

QUESTION 133 - We welcome questions from genuine seekers - some friends from Portugal sent us this question which we hope will be of interest to other seekers.

DISTANT HEALING - A QUESTION FROM PORTUGAL

We have been in correspondence with a fledgling group of healers who are working hard to set up a network of spiritual healers in Portugal. While in correspondence our friends asked us to seek some words of wisdom on the question of distant healing. The following was given by Mafra, who of course, when on the earth plane lived in Oporto.

'This healer has much love in her heart. She has many who she wishes to send love to who are not close to her. She is sending love from heart which is good. It is good when you sit quiet and you think of those who's names you have been given who are in need of healing. This healing may be of their body, it may be of mind, it may be that they are distressed, anxious, there are so many reasons to send love. Initially we think of a problem with the physical body but quite often a condition of a physical body, behind that condition there are other contributing factors that have brought about this condition. There may have been stress, anxiety, there may have been bereavement, loneliness, unhappiness, so many reasons. You have to think of the whole person not just the particular symptom you are endeavouring to relieve.

When you think of this person, if it is someone who is known to you personally this makes the connection much stronger. If you visualise in your mind this person, visualise their face, their manner, their eyes, their features. Visualise you are in the same room as them and close to them, you are just looking at them and sending your love to them as if you were talking to them in the same room. Of course there is a distance between you but with your higher sensory perception you are able to link with this one strongly through this energy field, this link you have with them.

Now we move a step further. You may have been given a name by someone else who is concerned of a loved one and they have asked you to send healing to that one. You may not know this one, if the one who has given you the name has a photograph this is good because you can visualise the one who you are sending healing to. A strong link would be to think of the one who has given you the name, use this one as a bridge. Think of the person who has handed the name to you and then think of the name you have been asked to send healing to and that will direct your energy on a stronger vibration. I am not saying that just thinking of the name directly and sending love would not reach that one, it would but it would be a stronger link if you could link with the one who gave you the name and use them as a bridge to reach the one who is in need. That one has given you the name with a strong desire of love and concern for the one in need so you are on a strong vibration.

Once you have made a link with someone whichever way, either on a personal link or through another person, the next time you send healing love this will become easier. Once you have made the link the link is much stronger and it is easier next time to stretch out on that link.'.
(24.02.98)

QUESTION 134 - A communicator gives the following thoughts.
Go forward - Every event is an opportunity, learn from each opportunity. Every event is an opportunity to learn, whatever occurs is an opportunity. Take the opportunity with open hands - go forward. Some events you wish not to experience but each event is an opportunity. When you walk your path in your world some events you wish not to experience but these are opportunities - everything is an opportunity. Turn it around so it benefits you, learn from it, do not say I do not want to experience this, take it in hand this is an opportunity - say 'I will learn from this'. Running Bear talks of paths - If you stood on your path and stayed in the same place not going around the corner, over boulder, through fence, around trees you would not learn anything, you would stay in the same place. It is by going over obstacles that you learn and grow. I experienced this in my earth life, if I could have seen my path I would have said 'I don't want to tread that path' but I could not see so I walked that path and found many obstacles but this was lesson to me. What you experience not only do you learn but others learn with you and those who come after you. - Go forward in peace and harmony (03.03.98)

QUESTION 135 - John Lyon visits our group again and gives yet more information regarding level of understanding in spirit and on earth and how communication takes place regardless of these differences.
As a team we are involved with what is happening now and in the future, we are not involved in what has occurred in the past. It is useful for you to research and to discover for your own information and for your own background knowledge but you must not think that we are living in that era (John refers to the time he spent on earth). We are walking forward as you walk forward, we have to advance as you advance. We have to discover new avenues, new ways of communicating, new ways of using energy, new ways of bringing about peace and harmony. Ways of assisting communication both in our vibration and your vibration, and between the vibrations, between the many levels and various levels of existence. You think of your world, you think of our world and we come together occasionally to communicate but this is just a very narrow view. Within your world there are many degrees, layers of understanding, as it is with our dimension.

I will talk of your earth dimension for one moment, within your earth you have a vast population. If you just think of yourselves, if you thought how many people during your time on earth you have met, communicated with, you would have difficulty recalling all. Each of those, perhaps you have only touched for a minute or two of earth time you have a link with those, you have shared their path for a short time of existence.

Now we go a step farther and we talk of those you know who are no longer on earth, who have become part of our dimension in spirit and you wish to communicate with those ones. How many are there in our world who you have shared a small moment of time with but that link is still there, even though it is just a tiny shred of your existence. You can see the problem of communication. Each of those whom you have met while walking your earth life have been at a different level of understanding at that point in their existence, and as you have walked your path in your life your understanding has altered, it has not stayed the same. You may have met someone when you were a young person, when your concept of spirit, perhaps, was not so high up the progressive ladder as it is now. That person, also may have lived on your earth for many years and during that time they have altered their understanding. They have gone home to spirit, you are still on what you call your earth plane but that one wishes to make contact with you. Now, how can this come about? How can they reach out to make contact with you because the contact you had all those years ago was when your were on a different level of understanding but there is something that has remained which still links you together.

Although you alter, although you change, you become more worldly wise, yes, but hopefully you become more spirit wise. The same thing occurs to others who travel with you along your earth path. Although there are many of your earth years separating you, because at one point you linked at a certain level of vibration, that link was made and you are still able to link if that one so wishes. They may not so wish, but if they do they can penetrate the earth's atmosphere, the heaviness of earth. Perhaps if they are advanced they can do this on their own, if they are not they will have the help of other companions from spirit who can assist. They can search for the vibration that they once knew. Although, perhaps, that vibration has changed there is still an element of all the other vibrations that make up what is now 'you'. You may change, you may alter but within your make up you carry with you all your experiences, good or bad, all your vibrations. Some you wish not to be associated with and you push them to the back but there is still a memory there and that memory creates a vibration and that one from spirit can find this as a key to a door and can home in and make contact with you.

This is just an example I have given of the different layers of vibration, of progress. You can ponder on how many levels of vibrations there are in our dimension. How much understanding and lack of understanding there is when those that travel your earth path come home to spirit. I will give an example, someone from earth will come home to spirit. You automatically envisage when you come home to spirit you will see all those you love, your father, mother, brothers and sisters, grandparents, aunts, uncles, friends, work mates, whoever. Can you imagine how may levels of understanding we are speaking of. Each of those identities could be on a different level of understanding but is it not amazing that when you come home to spirit you can contact them? You do not have to wait until you have progressed to their level. You can make contact, isn't that a revelation? You go to the level for which you are fitted but they can contact you. When you are on earth your companions from spirit, from all levels of understanding come to make contact with you, so it is the same when you go home to spirit they make contact in the same way.

You would dearly love perhaps you meet a great, great grandfather but perhaps that great, great grandfather has progressed to many steps up your spiritual ladder and it would seem very unkind if you came home to spirit and that one you so much desired to meet was unable to make contact because you were of a different level of vibration. You are visualising that because you have just come from earth you will go home to spirit on a mundane level. Of course, this will be the transition period, the time when you become accustomed to spirit but you must not forget that when you left spirit to come to earth you had a certain understanding, therefore you would have been on a level in spirit which fitted that vibration. You had a certain understanding when you took on your earthly body so when you go home to spirit, after your time of adjustment, your time of becoming aware of where you are and your introduction to our dimension again, you will advance to the level which you have worked and striven for. Hopefully, most who travel the earth path come back home a little wiser and a little more experienced and they have been able to share their experiences with those who have walked alongside them during their life on earth.

Some live a very selfish existence on your earth, they do not assist their brothers and sisters, they live for themselves, they live a very narrow existence. When they come home to spirit, perhaps they do have a problem, perhaps they have a problem returning to the same level. Perhaps they chose to come to a body for a reason but when they walked within that body they turned their back on that reason, so perhaps they will return to earth to walk that path of destiny again. I am not here to criticise or point fingers I am just giving examples of what could occur. Those who walk with love in their heart and share what they can with their brothers and sisters, I do not mean necessarily their wealth, the money, it is good if you can, but give of themselves. Giving of themselves, their love, their time, their sincerity. It is very easy for some to give financial assistance to others, they can do this without any hardship to themselves. Some would do it for prestige but within their heart they are not giving of themselves. You must not judge others, you are only here to live your own existence. (08.03.98)

QUESTION 136 - *Our Communicator gives more words of wisdom with particular regard to the knowledge which we bring to the earth world from spirit.*

You do not realise that you link with other groups doing similar work. Your energy goes from one group to another group, you share. It is part of pattern, you are working towards a pattern, structure, not just idle communication, it is deeper education. You are linking with others on a similar vibration and you are exchanging vibrations, merging energies, sending these energies outward for use by those from higher spheres who also bring their energy. This energy is used where much light is needed at this moment.

The destiny of your planet is not to go from one disaster to another disaster so there is a stirring, an awakening of thoughts, a renaissance of returning to beliefs and truths that have long been covered up by what you would call science, but we would not agree. Science is mingled with spirit energy and electro energy from cells within your body and from your spirit within. When you think of science, because of your world, you think of destruction. This should not be so. Science should link hand in hand with spirit because science involves physics, chemistry, atoms, nuclear physics. You think of destruction when you think of nuclear physics but this is because the way your world has trained your mind to think. Your body is made of elements of chemistry, you have magnetism of earth world, also you have magnetism of spirit.

This is not a magnetism which revolves around poles, as your world revolves around poles, north and south. It is a energy that works on attraction, like attracts like. When your spirit enters your human body you bring with you electromagnetism also from spirit to merge with your magnetism of earth. This is how communication takes place on linking on an energy field. Your link with spirit is never severed. You are spirit within human body. You are drawing from your spirit energy, spirit memory, energies which you need to progress.

You walk earth path, you develop earth body, you grow in earth body, you meet along your way others who walk with you, you share your experiences; they learn from you, you learn from them. You overcome problems that beset you, experiences some good, some bad, these are all shared with those who walk with you. You can assist those and they can assist you. Sometimes you may come across a problem which is difficult to solve by human standards, there may be a question arising deep within and you are struggling for an answer. Many in your world today are having this experience, they are trying to ask questions, whys? and wherefores?. What they see around them is material, they have much material benefits but there is still something missing, there is still a need for something, they know not what, within them.

There are many in your world who have a shortage but also, there are many in your world who have more than enough. I speak of those for a moment, they have more than enough but they still are seeking, they are still conscious that there is a gap but they know not what the gap is but there is something missing within them. It is at times like this when you look deep within for an answer, you may go to various churches to seek answers but they are unable to respond to your questions, they give you explanations but they contradict each other and you realise there is no depth. It may satisfy you for a while but you then realise this is not enough, you realise there is something deeper. This is when you have to search within. Those enlightened ones in your world will link with those in spirit to ask for guidance but many have not this benefit, they are not aware. So they look within for their answer for this gap they know is missing. Through much thought and contemplation they can link with the spirit within, the spirit that has come to take on the human form and that spirit has much wisdom and knowledge but it is locked away from the human world. By much contemplation gradually they can find key and unlock, look within and draw from the knowledge that spirit has. Then they can bring back to your world a wiser vision, a wiser knowledge which is knowledge from spirit. The experiences that the spirit within has gained through its evolution. This can only occur if it is destiny because when this knowledge is brought back to your earth world it has to be treated very carefully. Sometimes it is destiny that this knowledge should be made aware and others are informed of this knowledge, this makes a new thought, a new beginning. As all new ideas, thoughts, this is treated warily by those who listen. The one who gives knowledge understands but those who listen treat warily and question. This is as it should be because you cannot accept everything that everyone tells you.

What I am trying to tell you is the link between your spirit existence is not severed, it here with you now and if you go deep within you can tap into that knowledge, that wisdom. Some may not be at the point in their progression to accept this so it may not be meant for everybody, it may be just meant for yourself. This knowledge will only come when the time is right for you to grasp it because it is not knowledge that is new to you, it is just knowledge which has been clouded from your vision for your duration on earth. If you come across a time on your earth where you need answers and answers cannot be found wherever you seek, this then may be the time to seek the answer from yourself.

This method I have just explained is simplified for you but it has been used may times in history. Sometimes for those who have come to lead and show light, to show a way forward. They have been able to tap into this knowledge and bring it to their world to show a light. I am not elaborating because you only have to read history books, we are not here to read history books, we are here to go forward.

This is why I am here to explain. Suddenly in your world you have many people asking questions at one time and it is destiny at this time the new knowledge should come to your world. Not new knowledge but knowledge that so far has been clouded.

I am trying to explain to you that science is involved through your human energy fields, linking with the energy fields of spirit (the spirit which is you). Your spirit within can link with other vibrations in our dimension. There are many vibration in our dimension which if you did not have body you would be in direct contact with through your awareness in spirit. So you see the spirit within you, when it is released is able to send vibrations on this electromagnetic field to the higher ones in our dimension. It is not going along a long line as a telephone, we are together, it is just breaking through the barrier of dimension. It is not sending out message and waiting for the message to come back, it is a merging of energy from one field to another field, breaking down barriers, merging energy and drawing on each others energy. I have tried to explain but it is very difficult, I hope you understand a little of what I have said.

I will explain why I visit you. I am linked with many groups not just yours and these groups are working together, merging their energies, vibrations and wisdom to build an energy force that can be utilised by those in our dimension and your dimension. Those who are seeking and those who are trying to assist the seekers, the enlightened ones. You say 'why do the enlightened ones need assistance because they are enlightened'. This is so, but because many questions are coming from your dimension at this moment your energy is needed to link with the energy from higher levels. It is a drawing together, a merging of vibrations, acting as a link. (10.03.98)

QUESTION 137 - E-om-ba was asked the following question 'We have been thinking recently about the Hydesville knockings, is that method of communication by making knocks the easiest way to communicate and then other forms of communication develop from that method or is this more involved?'

When we want to gain your attention we need to make a noise. It is not easy, nothing is easy when you start but it is a way of getting attention. When we want to communicate we link with your vibration, we use your energy and our energy together because this is a physical noise in a physical vibration. When we want to make knock we have to use our energy with your energy because this is physical. It means we have to disturb energy fields. We have to make noise so that you can hear with your physical ear, this has to be on your earth vibration level. We have to merge our energy with your physical energy. You are all the time giving off energy. You do not realise this not just when you sit here, when you are just existing you are all the time thinking and this thinking makes energy and this energy is going from you. If you could see all around you, you would see much energy coming from you all the time, even when you sleep there is still energy coming from you. Of course, the more rapid your thoughts the more quicker the energy but all the time energy is coming from you and this energy is leaving you and going out. We are able to use this energy linked with our energy to make these noises.

This is very often why you hear of noises and many things happening around young people because young people give off a certain kind of energy, very active energy. This is sometimes why there are problems around young people because others can come in on that level if there is no protection and use their energy.

So you see your question, is it easy to make knocks? - nothing is easy we have to learn. You talk of time a long while ago when there are recordings of what is termed first knockings. This was spirits way of making themselves known. When this occurred, when they first heard knocking this was the result of much practice with those in spirit. They had to learn how to make the disturbance of energy to make sound and this was not achieved on the first attempt. Many attempts were made with others before this family. Although it is written that the spirit communicators knocked and humans listened you must understand this was brought about by their combined energy. Those humans assisted, with their energy that was being sent out without their knowledge. Before this family lived in that house those in spirit who eventually knocked had practised before with other energies but had not succeeded. Eventually they were able to make success of their experiment and then those humans were able to hear the result of the experiment. It was not easy, no communication is easy when it is started.

Each of us prefers to work in a different way. You have got those who speak well to you on your table, you have got those who prefer to come and talk through voice, you have got those who prefer to put pictures in your mind or thoughts in your head, those who prefer to make noises. Whatever communication you have from spirit it is not easy. You say is knocking simple? - it is simple when you have learned how to do it. It is a means of attention for those who know not of spirit, it draws attention. As documented in your history books, this is an opening for them to be aware.

It has to be done carefully because we do not want to make fear because communication should not be fear, it should be love. It communication makes fear this is no good. In the instance you spoke of this was ordained to occur because it was a new opening, a new beginning. As you have now new openings and new beginnings ahead of you so at that time this was the means of opening and beginning, so it had to come about because this was ordained.

It would not be good for us to go around knocking in everybody's house to make them know that spirit is here with them because this would cause much fear and alarm. Sometimes when we know that those living in a house are knowledgeable of spirit and they know that spirit can communicate and spirit lives on then perhaps, if there is no other way of communicating, their loved ones may make noise to let them know they are about without causing fear. If it causes fear this is no good, it is not a good level of vibration, not a good level of communication. If someone mentions to you that they are unhappy because there are noises you must advise them to seek help to close that contact down because they must not experience fear. It should not occur before they are ready. If it occurs before they are ready it is a miscommunication. (05.04.98)

QUESTION 138 - *Again Mafra responds to a question sent to us from a seeker. This inquirer asks a question regarding diet. We hope this information will be of benefit to others.*

You may be concerned that your body is not balanced and in harmony because of your diet and your vibrations are equal. You are spirit surrounded by your human body which your are occupying at this time, you are operating within the confines of a human body and the conditions of that body. As it is human it is prone to variances, infections, illnesses and if there is a problem in one part of your body this affects the energy which travels around the entire body.

If there is a problem it is good to deal with this immediately by your knowledge of spirit and self healing because all bodies are capable of healing themselves. Of course, you must not ignore your medical men and ladies, you must seek their advice and work in harmony with them. Many minor illnesses you can cope with yourself when they first appear because many are caused by stress. Stress is something which you have been taught to cope with. There are ways of withdrawing your energy, going perhaps into meditation or some would prefer other ways of relaxing themselves, each finds their own remedy.

We come back to the question what diet? You may be concerned that you keep your body in working order so that you can work with spirit with healing thoughts and send your healing thoughts to those who need healing and your love to those who need love. You wish to keep the flow of energy pure. We are talking of harmony of your earth body and we are talking of harmony linking with the spirit vibration within but also linking with those who are helping you from the spirit world, your spirit companions. If you are free from stress you are helping your body to function well. Some people wish to follow a diet which is free from animal substance, some prefer not to, this is a question of choice. There is no right or wrong way for us to tell you to eat, you have to define for yourself what your individual body needs. Of course, excess of any substance is harmful, excess of vitamins even, some people would prefer to supplement their diet with extra vitamins. This is good in one way but when you take too many vitamins you can cause damage to your body. I am talking of balance, harmony. As long as you eat a diet which is in harmony with your thoughts and the way that your body works you are continuing this harmonious vibration. If you are eating something which when you have eaten it you feel guilt for eating it you are causing a disharmony. Listen to your body, your body will tell you what it needs. Your body will crave substances in excess, it is the way of your human make up that certain substances are addictive, I do not mean that if your body tells you to eat one box of chocolates after the other you should do this. What I am saying is, if your human body is lacking some substance, vitamin, mineral, element, protein which it needs if you are attuned to your body you will know this, your body will give you thoughts that this is needed. You may, for some reason, think 'I haven't eaten whatever for a long while I think I will try that again', this may be your body saying to you that you are lacking some substance and this is your body's way of telling you. As long as you are eating a healthy diet with plenty of vitamins, plenty of fresh foods, not so many foods that have additives and have been preserved, plenty of fresh vegetables rather than vegetables that have been stored for a long while because they lose their goodness. As long as everything is in harmony with each other, not in excess. Some would say 'I do not wish to drink any substance which has alcohol in it because it is harmful to my body', to some people this may be so but to the person next to them this is not so, as long as it is not in excess. It is when you imbibe in anything to the excess, whether it is food or liquid.

    I am sorry I cannot give you a diet and mention foods but if you wish to link with your inner self and search whether there is anything which you feel you are lacking, explore this. Your body will tell you if you eat something which is not good for you. You will get an adverse reaction. You may not at first realise what that substance is, you perhaps may have a reaction and you will say 'I have eaten so many things I do not know which one has upset me'. The way to discover this is to eliminate all the substances, take note of all the substances you have eaten in that day and do not eat them again until you have introduced each one separately to yourself. I am not saying you should not eat or drink anything at all but take note of what it is you have eaten that on particular day when your body has told you something you have eaten or drunk is not good. Continue to eat and drink but try to avoid those items which you partook of on that particular day and than gradually introduce those items one at a time and if you have a reaction to that particular item you will know that is the item which you reacted against. I am not saying to starve yourself, I am saying to continue eat food that you know you are happy with and the ones that you are not sure of leave to one side and then introduce one at a time and then you will note which one it is that upset you. (07.04.98)

QUESTION 139 - *Mafra responds to question sent by another seeker. This question relates to what is the truth?, why do we get conflicting information from spirit on subjects such as reincarnation, spirit returning by choice and choosing our earthly parents etc.*

What a question, 'What is the Truth?' This is a question which has been echoed through the centuries and will be echoed again way into the future - What is the Truth?

The truth, my friends, is what you perceive at a particular time in your development, in your evolvement. The truth for you is different from the truth for the person standing next to you. The truth for you now is different from the truth that you perceived ten years ago, the truth today for you will be different from the truth you perceive in ten years time. It is puzzlement.

You say that others come and talk to you and you listen, you read and you are given conflicting explanations, this is very confusing. I agree this is very confusing but when those that come and talk to you from spirit, those who you read of in your books and papers who have given wisdom from spirit, they do disagree with each other. When we all go home to spirit, as I have made the journey perhaps I can explain a little easier. You do not suddenly become all wise, you do not know all the answers. We who have taken that step into the other dimension, we are still learning, we are still stretching out trying to find the truth. When you ask us questions we try to give you answers as we perceive the answers to be at this stage in our development, at this stage in our evolvement Sometimes we try and stretch ourselves and draw information from those who are at a higher level of advancement than ourselves and try and bring their wisdom through to you. We ourselves act as mediums.

There are some who are in our dimension but who are not very far advanced in their evolvement and they will give you an answer that is very near the level of the knowledge of perhaps yourself. There are those who come from a higher dimension and they will give you a further glimpse. How many times have you read something yourself and you have thought about it and thought you have understood exactly what this knowledge means. You have perhaps sat and read a book and you have said to yourself 'yes, I agree with that, I understand what that person is saying, that is fine'. You put that book on your bookshelf, you put it away, perhaps in five years time you take that book from your bookshelf again, you open that book and read that page again and yes, you agree with what is written but you see a little bit more that is written in between the lines which you didn't perceive before. You have a deeper truth, a deeper understanding of those words. It is with us also, we are forever evolving and finding more knowledge. We all think we know the answers but at the same time we realise we do not know all the answers, we only know as far along the path of evolvement as we have travelled.

Sometimes when you are talking directly to spirit or you have a medium translating for you, you ask a question of spirit and spirit give you an answer. Perhaps you think, 'yes, that is fine, I understand that but it doesn't answer all my questions. You have answered my questions to a certain extent but there is a little more I still do not know'. Perhaps, my friends, it is not the time for you to know that knowledge, perhaps you need to experience a little more. If that knowledge is given to you before your are actually ready for it you are not seeing the depth of the knowledge, you need to experience a little more before that knowledge is given to you. As I have explained with the book you read and you are not ready for the meaning behind the words.

I understand your frustration with so many different answers. Why does one person give you one answer and one give you another? I am here to try and help, to try and assist you on your path but I am not here to criticise others who come and give information. I am only here to try and assist. When you get information always question, I do not like the word doubt because doubt is negative, but always questions, discuss with others, ask others opinions. Ask yourself and those in spirit who are working on your vibration, send your thoughts to them and say 'I have been given some information I wish to know if this is the truth'. In the quietness of your thoughts you will learn to absorb their energy and hopefully you will be given wisdom from those ones who walk with you because those ones who walk with you are on your same vibration and are there to help, assist and guide you. Rely on them to point you in the right direction.

Sometimes you will hear things, read things and you will automatically think that doesn't sound right to me. This is partly instinct, because you have knowledge within you which you have brought with you from spirit yourself because you are spirit within a human body and you have brought a certain amount of wisdom with you, so you instinctively know that the wisdom you are being given is either correct or incorrect. Sometimes you need to ask those who are your protectors and helpers to assist you in defining. It is not for me to criticise those who come from spirit but just be wary that they do come from different levels and different vibrations and some are more knowledgeable than others. (07.04.98)

QUESTION 140 - *Mafra responding to a question from another seeker regarding calling out names on an absent healing list. Should all the names be called out each time or just the new additions?*

Once you have called a name out from your book you have made an affirmative statement that you wish that one to receive love and assistance from yourself and also from those spirit helpers who work with you, also those who work with that one you are sending to. This is a positive thought and it has registered. As you are aware your love does reach its target and it does go to those who you sincerely send your love to.

When you work with a group, a church, gathering or whatever, you have the ability of attracting many others that know of people who are in need and before you know where you are your list grows and multiplies. It is very difficult for you to say 'this list is so long I cannot read all the names out'. It is difficult for you to say who needs healing and who does not need healing because you are able to keep a check on their progress and you know they are still in need and there are some who have recovered and are grateful for their healing and you can safely take their name off your list. There will be many others who's names you have been given and you do not know whether they have recovered or they are still in need. You feel dutiful to keep their names there and to keep them on your list. This is honourable, this is of credit but we do realise that, of course, this list can grow and grow and your whole evening eventually would be just reading names out.

A word of guidance would be to ask for love to be sent to all those in your healing book but when they are first given to you send their name out that particular time, mention their name. You have no need to mention their condition because spirit will know and spirit can link with the vibration. If you know that one who you are sending to it would be good to visualise them in your thoughts because this would assist with the direction of the healing. If those who gave their names are sitting in your little group, say to them when the name is mentioned, visualise that one and this will assist the healing that is being sent. If you have someone on your list who has been on your list for a while but their condition is not good, they have not made the progress that you had hoped for, say their name again and send your love again. The healing has been sent, do not doubt it has reached but perhaps it has been ordained that this one's recovery is not as quick as you would have wished. Perhaps it is not their destiny to overcome this illness but this does not mean they are not receiving help and assistance. It is wise perhaps, every so often to just say their name again and this will make the link stronger. Especially at times when they are feeling particularly vulnerable, particularly low, depressed, unhappy, it will give an extra boost. Be reassured that as long as you have sent your love on their vibration it goes and if it is destiny that they are helped they will be so. Do not think that because the progress has not been good it is a fault of your own, it is not, it is how things are ordained.

Thank you for the love you send out to others because it is of great value. It does so much good, you cannot measure how much good because it multiplies. You are sending love from your heart in sincerity and not only does it touch those who you are sending to but it also touches many others. (07.04.98)

QUESTION 141 - A new communicator introduces himself, when asked for a name he said he did not wish to give his real name but would use the name "my call" (or if you like Michael). Clearly this communicator is one of the more advanced teachers who says he has been working in the background and it is now time for him to communicate through the trance medium. He speaks in a refined English accent.

I want to introduce myself. You have not seen me before. I have been awaiting my time. I am here just to say 'Good Evening' to you. You have been told to go forward, there is much progress ahead.

We are joining your group and other groups and we wish to progress at the same pace. It is important that there is continuation of knowledge carried forward from one session to the next otherwise we have to recap all the time. This means we are not going forward and this time is precious. It is important that sitters grasp the ability of leaving their worries outside the session, not to sit and let their minds dwell on their day to day problems. When this occurs the knowledge they are hearing from spirit is not being absorbed in their conscious reasoning. When it is being absorbed only in their higher level of reasoning this is no good because for instant recall it needs to be in their conscious reasoning. They then waste so much time trying to find this information before they can go on to next step, we are speaking of something else but they may not understand because they have not understood the previous conversation.

We need dedication from sitters, it is no good expecting spirit to appear and to answer all your problems then going away and bringing some more problems next week and asking spirit to sort those out for you. It has to be together, combined. Spirit gives strength to overcome problem and then when the problem is overcome, forget the problem and look to the future. You are on earth to experience problems, this is why you are here. After you have lived on earth for many decades you should be used to facing problems not trying to find your way around the problems, face them head on, deal with them, then put them away. It is easy for me to say but I am giving you words that are being given to me because mankind is here to travel path, you have chosen your path. If you have chosen path with obstacles there is no reason why you should try to go a long way around to avoid obstacles because you have chosen obstacles to learn from that experience. Sometimes you have an experience which you do not like so you avoid this experience. You have put it to one side and it has gone but some time in the future a similar problem occurs and you wonder why this problem has repeated itself. It has returned because you have not faced it head on. You have thought 'I will sweep it to one side', this is good for the short term but in the long term for your own growth, for your own wisdom you need to overcome and then put it behind.

You must need to know the difference between your problem and the problem of someone else. You cannot take on the problems of everyone in the world. You can give that one strength and support, as spirit gives you strength and support but we do not promise to solve your problems because you are here to learn your own way. It is the same with others you must learn to give them strength and support but you are not there to solve their problems. So why use your vital energy on somebody else's problems, give them your attention and support and then hand them back their problem and shut down the vibration. This is very easy for me to say, especially if you are trying to help someone who is close to you. This is not the way to help that one, you can make them aware that you are there for them with strength and support. Consider my friends, if you had problems and someone told you what to do and you took their advice, then some while later you discovered this was the wrong way to go you would blame the one who gave you that advice. You can only give your wisdom, you cannot solve their problem.

Each one walks their own path, no two people walk the same path, everybody has a different path, no one is the same not even twins they are different, each has own soul and spirit within. Each spirit is different, each spirit has own vibration, knowledge, wisdom. Each one wears a different 'overcoat' of human body, the overcoat may look similar but within the spirit is not the same. However well you know someone there is always something you do not know about them, you cannot know about them because there are things they do not know about their own history. There are things within yourself that you cannot recall, things from your past which you cannot recall, genetic traits you have inherited that you are unaware of. So, if you yourself are unaware of these factors that I have just spoken of, how can you know someone else because they have the same, there are things in themselves which they are unaware of until something happens to bring that to the fore. You have inherited much from your ancestors, you have brought much with you from spirit but you know only at this point in your existence what you need to know from your history.

If you want to discover something else you will have to either take advice from an outside source who can give you this information or you can search within yourself for something that is in the part of your memory which is shut from you and try and bring this memory to the fore. I will give you an example; if you suddenly decided that you wished to paint pictures, up to this point in your existence you may not have done much in this field. You may have dabbled as all children dabble putting paint onto paper but as you have advanced in years you have not taken this option to sit with paint pot and paint brush to paint picture of landscape. If suddenly you decide you want to paint you have options, you could go to a teacher who could teach you how to paint, you could read books or go to galleries and study pictures and you could try to copy these pictures. Having done this you may say to yourself 'in my ancestors there are people who could paint so that inside me there must be this ability, so I will try and bring this ability to the fore. If you are wise you can ask those in spirit to give you assistance but if you are unaware of spirit you could practice and experiment and if there is a deep desire paint, only if you have inherited this trait it will then awaken. Not all in the family will inherit that trait, some will inherit, some will not. Some will inherit and it will become obvious, some will inherit and it will lie dormant and it will need this desire to bring it forward. Others may have no inheritance at all so how ever hard they try they will not accomplish to their wishes but they will not know until they have tried. This is just an example I am using to emphasise the point. (21.04.98)

QUESTION 142 - Michael visits again this time giving words of wisdom regarding our perception of the tree of knowledge.

It is interesting for you to listen to various visitors from spirit because although we are part of team, part of a group, we still keep our individuality. We can each bring you words which have the same meaning but we each bring a different perspective, a different view point. You can take thoughts from us all and filter through which you want to absorb yourself.

I was listening previously on another visit when your friend Running Bear came to talk to you. He gave a very good example; he was standing looking at a tree and he was telling you about the tree, saying to you the tree is straight in front of me and it is standing upright' he went on to describe the tree. He then said to one of your sitters 'if you were looking at the tree you would walk around the tree and you would say to me, "Running Bear you have told me that the tree is erect, it is standing straight, it is perfect but from where I am standing at my angle there is a bough which is broken, so Running Bear you have not told me the truth the tree is not perfect." Running Bear explained the words which we portray to you are a description of the truth as we perceive it. This example of a tree was something mundane, something you can perceive on your earth but was just used as an example.

Each one of you looks at something with a different perspective, each one of you will look at your 'tree' and will see something different in your tree. If there was a tree in the middle of this room, as at times of festivities you do have a tree in your room (Christmas Circle). You have a group sitting around the tree in the centre of the circle each one of you would look at that tree at a slightly different angle, each one of you would see a slightly different vision of the tree.

So it is with the knowledge that we bring to you. We bring you knowledge from spirit, from the wisdom we have amassed for you, to share with you. We bring you the knowledge as we perceive it and each one of us, perhaps, describes it in a slightly different way. Each one of you listens to our words and each one of you takes a slightly different view of the picture we have portrayed with our words and each one of you will take something slightly different home with you, from the picture we have painted of the 'tree of knowledge'.

I have turned your material tree into a tree of knowledge and each one of you are looking at this tree of knowledge in a slightly different perspective. You look at the tree and you see defects, now you must ask yourself are these defects a mirror image of my own, my own lack of knowledge? Is it something which I have difficulty coming to terms with myself? In this perspective of the tree of knowledge I am seeing a defect. This is something for you to think upon.

You will come again on another occasion and look at this tree of knowledge and in that time, perhaps a week in your time span. You have walked your world another seven days, you have had another seven days experience and you will look at your tree at a slightly different perspective because you bring with you a slightly different understanding. Every minute of your existence you are learning, you are changing, you are encountering different circumstances and you encounter different circumstances so your view point changes, so your view point on other prospectus changes. Something which you looked at on one occasion with perhaps shadow and doubt, you now begin to see a glimmer of light shining through. Something perhaps you looked at before which was bright and shiny another time you will look at and see a defect. This is because you are walking an earth path and every moment of your existence you are experiencing your own circumstances and also you are sharing the circumstances of those who walk with you. All the time your thoughts, your perception are changing. (26.04.98)

QUESTION 143 - We have been told on a number of occasions that certain communicators who share their wisdom with us also work with other groups who like ourselves are seeking the truth and energy and vibrations sent out by our group merges with others for progress. Our Communicator gives us further enlightenment on this subject.

I communicated with you recently on your table to try and get reaction from other sitters. I wanted them to contribute by talking directly to me, it was not easy. It is not easy for me to communicate through the table but I tried. This gives the sitters knowledge that I am here.

There is much linking with other groups, not competition with other groups, linking with other groups. Each group has to maintain its own individuality, its own way of working, you cannot interchange your methods. You have your own way of development, your own way forward but can share their vibrations and merge energies because there are a group of us who work with other groups. We bring unity of groups but you each have to individually develop your own way of working because it has to come from yourselves. We cannot control you and take you on path, you have to work yourself and find your own way. On earth you have your leaders who direct you, make laws, legislation, plan the way forward but it is for those who live in the nation to work and keep within those laws. If they decide they do not wish to work within those rules they throw that government out. You will not throw us out but it is for you to work your own way, find your own level, find your own way forward. Your own hopes, your own aspirations put into action. We are here to give support, guidance, strength but it is for you to endeavour. So I say go forward.

There is too much looking backwards. It is good to look backwards at what has occurred but you cannot live in the past, you have to go forward. At this time there is much looking backwards in history. Those who you look back on in history, if you could only see, they are not the same now as they were then, they have advanced and gone forward. So why look back at what occurred then, look forward to where they are now. They are further along their path now. When you look back say 'this was them at that stage, where are they now?' and strive to find where they are on their path now and go forward with them. Where they are now you will be tomorrow, we are more advanced because we do not have the restrictions of your earth. We can bring to you new ideas, new thoughts, this is very exciting but you need to grasp this and come with us not go back with us. Do not get stuck down with history, go forward. Accept what has occurred has happened for a reason and that reason was intended for that time on your earth but that time of your earth time has now gone. You are not in that time any more, you are further on in the evolution of earth so what was right then is not right now.

If this knowledge is to be carried to others who are yet to come you must be working for this, you must be working to bring about new ideas, new energy, new way of working. There is a intermingling of vibrations which should be natural, it should not be something which is special, something which can only occur in special circumstances. It should be a normal event, this intermingling of dimensions, there should be no barrier. You should be working for this, going forward. You look at your past and this was done secretly behind doors because of the laws of the land, this has changed but it takes a long while in earth time for this to evolve.

Many in your world still think this communication with spirit is not good, not natural. This is because of a way of thinking but you must work towards a more open and natural way of working. It should not be something special, only those who are special can have access to this information. All the other knowledge in your world is now available to all. Your children of many lands can now learn with freedom many subjects. There are still those, of course, who are in developing countries but in time they will also have equal opportunity but children, in your so called developed countries, have opportunity to learn so much. This should be the same with the knowledge of spirit, this should also be open to all. There should not be knowledge restricted to just special individuals, this openness is what we are working towards. There needs to be much education but you know many questions are now being asked and this is all part of the plan. Development does not occur over night, there has to be much ground work, much laying down of foundations but we are looking forward to time when this information is readily available.

In preparation for that time there must be a breaking down of barriers, of individuals working on their own. So many groups thinking they are right and others are wrong, there has to be a coming together of those who are aware of spirit and they must learn to work in harmony together. Without this how can they grow? Someone awakening to interest in spirit communication would be very confused because one group does not agree with another group, and that group does not agree with yet another group. They look at these groups and they say 'if they are not in harmony where is the truth?' Before you can open out, stretch and introduce yourself to those who are inquiring you have to learn to work in harmony and put aside your bigotry. You have seen this occur with your orthodox religions and this has been the downfall of orthodox religions. You do not want this to occur with spiritual awareness but this takes time. Personalities have to be removed and this takes time. As you know, when we come home to spirit we still have personality so we can still bring influence to those we have left behind. It is no good saying ' wait until they go home and someone can take their place' because they still can have influence. There has to be a re-education of all, those with body and those who are spirit. There has to be unity and harmony.

This is work which is now taking place. Many events are occurring, some already have occurred, some are still to occur, which will break down barriers and will bring people together. This will touch on emotions and emotively people will come together, they will forget barriers, they will forget which side of the fence they are sitting, they will come together in harmony. Sometimes this occurs through sorrow, sometimes this occurs through joy and happiness. At times of great emotion this can be a time of advancement.

I will not stay too long on past because it is not my intention to talk of past but very, very briefly, the time when I was on earth and the time when I was at my zenith was a time of great emotions. It has been recorded in history that our nation was united, barriers were broken down. This is just an example because I am talking of history and I am now shutting the book of history and putting it on the shelf. Now going forward this is essence of what I speak, the breaking down of barriers, working together for a common good, a common cause. If only everyone who is working for this could see that they could work together and create much more advancement as a whole rather than in their own individual corners. Circumstances are working to change this. Enough said. We go forward together. (28.04.98)

QUESTION 144 - *A fellow seeker suggested we ask the question ' what is the golden band?' The explanation was given by Golden Ray.*

I have come again. Since I spoke last you now see the way forward. You have seen progression, you have seen doors opening as you walk, we told of this. We have been walking with you, we have awaited time to introduce to you new friends. Each step on your path, when you have gone a little ahead we have waited time for you to come to a level and when time was right we have introduced to you a new friend. Much of your "Words of Wisdom" are now being noted, being read. It is part of plan. We told you many times we wanted steady progress, not to forge ahead, go forward steady, build a firm foundation this is the way to go ahead. All in time.

I say 'I am Golden Ray' because this is my vibration but you must think of a golden ray and your path as a golden ray going forward. Starting as a ray and coming out gradually as a ray of sunshine. This is your path going as ray and spreading out little by little, shedding light where there is darkness. Where there are those seeking knowledge they look for ray of light and they see glimmer of your ray and little by little this ray is spreading out to those who are seeking. You must not rush with impatience, take time. Much has occurred since we last spoke. You are now beginning to see a little more of pattern. You started with just a few of my friends introducing themselves to you and one by one more have joined path with you, are walking with you.

Those higher ones are there also waiting their time to make themselves known, some have already joined you realise there is a link between them all. They are working as a golden band. There is a golden thread running through. A golden band linking from very high vibration down through the various levels of spirit evolution. Down through the various realms of our existence, linking down through realms such as mine and down to realms which are not quite so advanced as mine, down, down, to those who are making their first steps on ladder. There is a golden band linking all from the Great Spirit of all. We all have our place in this golden band which has been in existence since before time, before creation of time, and will continue in existence as far into infinity as it is possible for you to visualise, which is not very far. You do not need to grasp further because this is beyond your level of understanding at this point in your human existence.

There is a spark of the divine, light, creation, spirit, whatever name you wish to give the source of all in each soul. So how can you be so different, you all have the same spark within you from the same source. I use the words of one of your other communicators, go forward in the knowledge that you are walking a path of destiny. Those who walk with you share this path, it is their responsibility to take from that path what they wish. It is not your responsibility if they do not wish to take, you show the way, you gently guide, you gently provide information, love and guidance but it is for each individual to take responsibility for their own progress. Each one who walks earth path has an allotted span, to learn as much as they have destined to learn. It is their free will if they take that opportunity, it is precious time to absorb as much information as possible but it is to each his or her own to utilise that time wisely.

No one must feel responsibility or guilt for others, you are responsible for yourself and you must not feel guilt for yourself if you have not achieved that which you have set out to achieve. You can only strive and walk forward, overcome obstacles as you experience them. You are spirit yes, but you are also at this point human and as you are human you are, of course, susceptible to all the human defects. So, of course, you will stumble and you will go from the path. You will experience conditions which you, perhaps, had not desired to experience but this has all been part of your existence and you return to path of destiny in around about way. It is your free will as to which way you walk. So at the end of your voyage you have achieved as much as you can achieve. There is no final closing of book, what is not achieved there is always time to achieve in other ways. You envisage time as a restriction but for us there is no time and as you are spirit within a human body, for you there is no time. You are encased in human conditions. If you look back in history at the lives of those who are written in books. At the end of that life span you will say they have achieved this, they have achieved that, in that life but if you then look beyond that life, and the effect their life has had on the lives of those who follow, you will see in retrospect they have achieved much more than was first envisaged when their life on earth came to a close. I am trying to say to you there is no time.

You judge things in time. You have so many desires to achieve so much but there is no haste, no feverish desire to achieve so much in a short time. It is better to take each step as it comes and to lay foundations than to rush and try and achieve so much in a short while. You are experiencing your life on earth and your circumstances on earth but also you are experiencing the affect of those who walked before you, their lives, both physically and spiritually. You physically experience this through your inheritance of your human body and the connections within it, also you share spiritually with the knowledge that has been gathered by those who have walked your life and passed this knowledge on, and those who are in spirit and are walking with you. There is no beginning or end, this quest for knowledge and learning is continuous, it goes round and round. There are no seams, no joins, it is continuous. There are no highs or lows, there is a continual stream.

My message to you is - go forward in knowledge that you are walking your path of destiny. You are walking in light, you are taking light with you. You have gathered light from those who have shed light to you and you, in your turn, are passing light on to those who are seeking light for their own advancement. Go forward knowing what is occurring, do not be concerned of others, it is for each person to absorb as much as they wish. There is much ahead. You will link with many as you walk your path and many will remember and share this knowledge. Some will not recall whence this knowledge came from, that does not matter. It is important that a word, sign, thought, vibration ignites a thirst for more knowledge and this can be the beginning of others' search for knowledge. Something that is said, thought, some vibration, can set another on their own path of learning, their own path of destiny. They will think there is something a little deeper than what they first perceived and from this they will search for themselves. Once they have put out this thirst, desire for knowledge they are opening the doors for those who walk with them to support them and lead them on to find their own truth.

I hope you have understood what I have tried to bring you this evening. Rest assured everything is happening as destiny has planned. You have seen opportunities come and opportunities open but, as I have said earlier, do not be in too much haste. Take time for events to evolve.

Visualise this gold thread which runs down through many, many levels, many vibrations, which filters through gradually becoming not so bright as it comes farther from its source but there is still much light and energy within. (05.05.98)

QUESTION 145 - *John Lyon is asked the question 'Do spirit think and do you have thoughts?'*

I use the words thoughts because this is a word you can understand. We have energy, we have explained to you that in your life on earth you have thoughts and these thoughts are sent from you as energy. When you wish to link with, perhaps us or others on your earth, perhaps you wish to communicate to your animals, you have thought. When this thought leaves you it leaves you as an energy force. Having understood this perhaps you can understand a little when I say to you, we have thought, we have energy. For me to say to you we have energy this would mean nothing to you. Having energy involves using the essence which is us, we retain our memory, experiences.

When you first enter spirit realms your existence is very similar to earthly conditions. I have been in what you term spirit realms for a considerable time in your time span so I am not at this level. I have risen to a different level where I use energy fields, a blending of energy and vibrations to communicate. I draw from my experiences, the essence which is my pure spirit. I am spirit as you are spirit but your spirit at this moment is enclosed in a case of a human body. My spirit is not encumbered with a human body so I can function on a very quick, lively wave length. If, for instance, I am working as part of your team and one of your team is communicating with you through a voice, that member of the team has been asked a question which is not in their experience they have not experienced this vibration you are asking about. They send a vibration to the rest of the team, searching for one of us who can assist and on this quick vibration, in this instance myself, I can draw from my experience, my essence, the memory which will assist the one who is communicating with you to give the answer that you are seeking.

I use the word 'thought' because this describes this, a word which you can understand. I do not sit here and think 'two and two make four', 'I have got to pay for my house, for my gardener, how am I going to work this out?' This is not thinking. Drawing from experience, from the store of knowledge that we each retain, you retain, we retain. Each individual one retains different because we have all experienced different circumstances and different conditions. Some of our experiences are earthly but we have also experiences on other fields in our realms. We merge our energies with those from higher levels and we learn from those, and we retain these energies and knowledge that we learn from the higher ones and this is stored in what you would say is our memory. There again, if it is ordained that this information is passed on to those who seek we are allowed to pass this information down to another level of vibration but only when this is ordained.

This is a little way of explaining to you when I say 'thought' how I try to explain to you the movement of energy, the linking of vibrations into and energy field that can link different dimensions and different levels. It transcends different levels of evolvement. It is as if you are, on your earth, linking a chain and each one of you is a member of a link in that chain and the energy is passed from one link to the next link, from one length of the chain to the other. The chain is linked, it is a circle, everything goes round. Everything is cause and effect, there is not beginning or end, everything moves in rotation. (03.05.98)

QUESTION 146 - John Lyon answers a question regarding human energy remaining attached to a previous residence.

You are talking of an earthly link not a link with a spirit entity. When you move from one house to another you still have part of you left in that building. Wherever you reside you put so much of yourself into that residence, different level obviously depending on how attached you are to that building. Also what has occurred whilst you have resided in that building, what emotion you have experienced, the more intense the emotion the deeper impression you leave on that building. Of course, when you leave that building you consciously close the door, walk away and in your own knowledge you have left that part of your existence behind, you are moving on and you have to accept this. You have to accept that part of your life has come to an end and you are moving onto another area. Subconsciously you still retain memories and feelings that you experienced in that residence. Usually you can cope with this and after a while your subconscious filters this vibration away and you come to terms with the fact you have moved on and you are now part of another building. You are laying down your foundations and your roots in this other building and your original building is left behind.

Sometimes when you perhaps are in sleep state, when your mind is free and not encumbered with physical body, as we have explained to you on many occasions, you can travel and if you so wish you can in memory travel back to somewhere you have been before. This can be a building, an open area, somewhere you have visited but sometimes when you have left a place where you had deep emotion you travel back with the wish to see this building again. You enter this building in your sleep state. Those who are in this building have no knowledge of this, you do not disturb them. It is partly you coming to terms with the fact that it is no longer your building, you have to see this building, you have to realise that someone else is now living there. You may not see that person but when you enter the vibration of this building you sense another vibration that was not there when you resided in that building. By doing this you have come to terms with the fact that it is no longer your building, it belongs to someone else.

This is a settling of emotions. It is helping you to sever your links and to close part of your life experience down. It does not mean you cannot take the memories with you that you had in that building, they come with you because they are part of you. You cannot shut the door and leave them behind.

Often when you travel on and leave somewhere behind there is much emotion at that time and you cannot cope with it all at once. You cope with the day to day mundane, physical move and you put to one side the other feelings because your mind is occupied with what has to be done and you cope with your other feelings later. This is what occurs later, perhaps when you have settled down in your new building. You then have time to think back and this often occurs in sleep state when your subconscious or sometimes your higher level of consciousness wanders back.

The actual idea of leaving an imprint on a building is another subject. This is something which does occur but we will speak of this at another time. During a traumatic time someone will leave an imprint on a building and in years to come those who are living in that residence perhaps say they have seen this person who lived in the house before. This is a different subject, it is a decoding of a vibration which has left an imprint, as you leave a fingerprint. (03.05.98)

QUESTION 147 - When we come to our earth body why do we not remember what has gone before? John Lyon responds

You come to your earth body knowing why you have come to your earth body but, of course, as you progress and mature into an adult you leave these thoughts behind as you become more and more of the earth. When you come to the end of your sojourn and you return home to spirit you leave behind all the peripheral, you take back with you your memories and experiences. You probably do not wish to take with you much of the dross, the day to day trivia, the petty arguments and disagreements. You take with you what is important. When you return, of course, you remember why you came because you have completed the circle. You pick up the point where you entered the body and you then recall why you visited earth. You then go through your experiences and hopefully you can say you have progressed. You have learnt from that experience and these experiences are the important parts of your duration on earth. These experiences are taken with you because they have changed you and added to your identity.

You have to come to terms with the fact you have come to earth for a reason and not everyone fulfils every reason for their return. You look at your life and have to accept that you were there for a while and during that time you accomplished as much as was possible. There are always regrets but you must not dwell on regrets because this is negative, but build on this. You must look at what has occurred, mark your achievements and look at those other aspects where you have not succeeded as much as desired. Then instead of regretting this event question how you can build on this. Look for the way forward.

You are responsible for your actions and if things have occurred of which you are not proud it is necessary to come to terms with those. You cannot progress until you realise why, there is always a reason why you have not accomplished as much as you would have wished. You do not say 'I have failed', you have to say 'why did I not accomplish as much as I wished?' Then build on this.

We are not talking low levels of existence where someone has come to earth and caused deliberate problems. When they return home there is no achievement, there are only regrets. These souls are on a lower level of vibration and they have to come to terms with their circumstances.

Everyone makes mistakes but you do not have to punish yourself. The problem with religion is it teaches you there is good and bad, no where in-between. You have to accept that you have striven as much as you can during your earthly existence. If you have deliberately gone about your earthly life being destructive, being harmful to others then, of course, we are talking of something completely different. We are not talking of non-achievement we are talking of being malicious and destructive. This is something completely different. When that one returns home they have to come to terms with this and they cannot progress until they have because they are responsible. They have to experience for themselves the conditions they have created for others. If they have spent their earthly life causing many problems, much hardship, many things which are not good, when they come home they cannot progress until they have realised and come to terms with the bad experiences they caused others. They have to live through those experiences themselves.

Perhaps some return to a human body to experience these conditions for themselves and then when they return home to spirit because they have gone through the experiences they have achieved atonement. Others perhaps do not return to a human body but through their experiences in spirit they have been taught. In the lower levels of our realms you can experience conditions as they are experienced on earth. I am talking of the very low levels. There are evolved ones from spirit who come down as teachers to these levels to help these ones explore the conditions they have created for others, experiencing these condition on a different level. When there is a real desire that they wish to progress, to leave these conditions behind they are helped. They have to come to terms with this first.

There is cause and effect which is part of the natural law. Natural law has always been in existence and will continue. Your world changes but natural law stays the same. If you go against natural law you are creating a cause and effect for yourself. You are causing problems in your progression, you have to come to terms with this yourself and realise how you can overcome this before you can progress to another level. It is not as your religion teaches you, there is no one there with an open book ticking your deeds and crossing your misdemeanours, you do this yourself. There is no one sitting on a cloud who tells you whether you are good or bad, this is for yourself to come to terms with. If you wish to progress and overcome your problems there are always those from a higher realm who are there with their strength and guidance to help but you need the desire within to do this.

They cannot do this for you. You have to be stern with yourself and have to be repentant, wishing to overcome your obstacles. There are those there who are willing to help you.

It is understandable that many who come to spirit are in a state of quandary because they are expecting to come to terms with someone who is going to stand there and say 'you have been good', 'you have been bad'. This is how your religions teach and they do not realise they are responsible for their own actions and their own destiny. No one is going to atone them and say 'I forgive you, you have been very wicked but as you have come here I am going to forgive you'. No one is capable of this. Those higher souls are capable of helping you, showing you the light, assisting you but they are not capable of forgiveness this is something you have to do yourself. You have to learn to forgive yourself. (03.05.98)

QUESTION 148 - Mafra explains how he had shown himself earlier in the evening through transfiguration of the medium under normal red light conditions. Then he continues by answering questions concerning the atmospheric conditions.

I am here now, you have no light you cannot see. I am not transfiguring to the same extent, I am moving hands, there are expressions on face but there is not the same concentration of a build up. We build energy around face. There is a concentration of energy, you sometimes visualise us as mist that swirls round, sometimes you perceive as colour. This is a concentration of energy and we endeavour to put this around the face of the one who is sitting and form transfiguration.

Is there a reason why we are all yawning? You have taken a change of energy, it is a different vibration. We utilise the energy for different work, also all of you are experiencing at this time a change in the energy level of your earth condition. Your climate is changing (the weather that day in early May had suddenly become warm and sunny following a long period of inclement weather). Your atmospheric pressure is altering and your physical body is registering this also. You are human and are of the world which you live in. Although you are what you term, civilised, within you have many instincts which go a long way back in earth history to when your ancestors lived on earth and experienced the earth conditions and lived with the earth conditions. Their life revolved around the seasons of the year, the climate, temperature and they were able to foretell for themselves changes in the atmospheric pressure before it actually occurred. They could then make preparations for the changes of climate. You still have this instinct within you but because you are of the 'civilised' world you do not use these instincts but of course, they are still there and are registering. You are not decoding them, you are not reasoning with them but they are still there. As your animals use instinct, so do you also. Your body is telling you there is a change. You can say it is spirit working that is making you tired but also it is your senses within your human body decoding the vibrations of your earth atmosphere.

Do you notice the difference in our weather conditions? It is no different, it is different because you are different, you are more relaxed. When you are weighed down with the problems of your climate, the cold, the frustrations, you are tense. Perhaps subconsciously, not consciously, you are concerned when you leave, is the road going to be icy, are you going to be able to see due to fog. You shut down when you come here but in the back of your reasoning you still have these concerns. When you are more relaxed it is easier for us. The pull of the earth does alter from season to season and as we come in to the condition, of course we sense this also. (10.05.98)

QUESTION 149 - *Another question arrived in a sealed envelope addressed to Mafra from a seeker asking 'What are the "Rules" governing progress to higher planes in spirit?'*
Your human brain thinks along the lines of your human world and everything is governed by rules and obedience to the laws of your country, the laws of your church, the laws of whichever association you belong to. This has to be part of your earthly world because there has to be organisation on this material level.

Yes, in our dimension there has to be rules but I do not like the word 'rules'. There has to be order, there has to be organisation. As you know there is natural law which is part of all life, your life, our life, we are all governed by natural law. Evolution is governed by natural law whether you are in earthly body or you are not encumbered with earthly body.

When you are on earth you are all the time learning, we hope progressing both in your earth world but your spirit is growing also. As you know, your spirit is the part of you that has come from spirit to join your earth body and will return home to spirit dimension when your earth body is no more. Maybe it has come to earth for experience, alternatively it has come to earth to help others. As you develop you go forward as we do in our dimension. You have many who come to speak to you who are from a higher level of understanding but they come to you at a level nearer to your earth to enable you to communicate with them on a level where you are happy to ask questions, happy to discuss, to hold ordinary conversation. They are from various levels in spirit.

You were asking how do they get to these levels? When you return home to spirit you return home to a level which is compatible to your progression. At first you return home to a level which is not far from your earth to enable you to shed your earthly vibration and condition. For those who have perhaps had some trauma, upset, perhaps a illness which has sapped their strength because this saps not only your physical strength but your spirit also. Sometimes you are in this recovery level. When you have shed these earthly conditions you then progress to the level where you are compatible and you are with those who are on the same vibration.

You may then wish to stay on that level where you are happy, but there may be a desire that you wish to progress further. This desire has to come from within, your own desire. There is not someone sitting on a cloud saying to you 'It is now your turn to come up the next step of the ladder'. As it is in your earthly body when you have a desire to progress, you then go through the earthly channels of learning and experience to progress to a higher position on your earth so it is in spirit dimension. You have to desire from within. From this desire you then stretch out your vibration and blend your vibration to those who are on a different level of vibration to yourself. You are then merging your energy and learning from them, they are assisting you to learn whatever it is you have chosen. You may have chosen to learn a little more about healing vibration, you may have expressed the desire to learn a little more on teaching, you may have expressed the desire to learn a little more on the whys and wherefores of philosophy. There are so many directions I have just given you three examples.

So when you truly desire you are opening the door and you are linking with those who are a little higher evolved than yourself and you are learning from them, they are merging their energy with you. You are absorbing a higher level of truth and you are growing. When you have absorbed sufficient to rise to another level of evolution in spirit you are welcomed by those who have been your mentors, your tutors into their level of existence. This does not mean you are then not able to communicate with those who were your companions on your previous level because in our dimension there is much blending, much merging of energies, much linking with others from other dimensions. As a way of explaining; you have your home base where you are existing in a group with those who are on the same level of understanding as yourself but this does not mean you cannot merge your energies with those that are on other levels. Those who were your companions a little time previous before you evolved, you can still link with those and still share your energy, your love, as you can stretch out to those on a higher level of understanding.

All the time you are merging with others, you are sharing with others because spirit is sharing. There is no selfishness in spirit, This is something you learn on a very low level in spirit, you learn there is no selfishness, you learn that you share, there is no envy, there is not jealousy. You learn to blend, you are in harmony, without harmony there is no progress. If I compare spirit dimension to your earthly dimension where your children go to school. In their kindergarten level they learn the basics. When they first go to nursery, kindergarten, whatever you wish to call their first education, they learn many things, how to handle paints, pencils, so many things, but the most important thing they learn is how to associate with their fellow children. It is the same in spirit dimension, when you first go home to spirit you learn how to be compatible to your brothers and sisters in spirit. Those who are not so experienced in spirit as others are taught, you leave behind your earthly jealousies, envies, fears, because fear often causes jealousy and envy. You are taught that there is no reason for this, there is no reason to be jealous or envious because there is love for everybody, every soul is encompassed with love. As you evolve through the various levels of our dimension you are learning more of the harmony, of the blending of energies one to the other and the sharing of spirit. It is by sharing happiness, joy and love that you grow. As it is in our dimension, you progress by merging your energies with those from other levels and you then gradually evolve to another level of our dimension.

There are no hard and fast rules, for example; if you do not learn by a certain length of existence you are not able to progress, this is an earthly concept. Spirit conditions are so different. It is natural law and the farther you progress in spirit dimension the more you learn to blend and share with others.

There are those on much higher planes who share their love with others on lower levels because it is their wish to do so. There are others on higher planes who wish to share their love with those on that dimension and that love is then used for the betterment of progress in general. As you know, there are many plans, there is an order within all existence. We have told you of an new awakening, new happenings. This is an order, a system and there are those ones on the higher levels who have chosen to work for this system, to help bring this system about.

There are no rules, there is natural law and there is a natural progression. If some spirit in our dimension wishes to progress and they find this difficult there is no shame that they are having difficulty, there is no chastisement that you have expressed a desire to progress and you have not achieved. There is just love and encouragement. There is no such thing as time, whereby you have to progress by a certain time because we do not have time, we have infinity. Each works to their own scale of progress. You progress as you wish. You wish to progress and you are striving to progress.

You do not wish to progress then you stay where you are. It is personal responsibility as you know on earth but also this goes with you when you leave earth, it is your own desire, your own wish. (13.05.98)

QUESTION 150 - Another question from a seeker inquiring as to how spirit communication from the time of the Hydesville events developed into the religion we call Spiritualism. This is discussed by Running Bear.

You have to ask question 'what is religion?' It is a belief in something which is beyond human organisation. It is belief in a higher level of intelligence, a spirit entity, maybe you say God if you believe in the church of your country. In other religions it could be their prophets, we worshipped Mother Earth, we worshipped the Great White Spirit.

I will go back to question why was this religion you call Spiritualism created. It was not originally a religion. We are talking of the time of the Hydesville events. This was just a spirit presence making itself known. It was just at first a game. It was not a church, people did not go to that house and worship. As time progressed this developed into what you call religion. This is because people asked questions, 'why is this happening?' At first they took it as a game but then when others became involved, more wiser and educated ones, they then asked many questions. They then became aware that this communication was coming from a higher level, not only this occurrence but other communications came from this.

Hydesville was just the beginning, but as time progressed there was link with other spirit entities, very evolved spirit entities. It became a worship, it became a reverence. It was very slowly evolved. The evolvement from party games to religion was developed slowly and gradually with much progress, much thought, much delving in their minds. There was much comment from outside sources saying this was work of the devil, this was not good. They were told they should not play games, this was termed witchcraft. Those who were involved tried to lift this understanding to a higher vibration and those in spirit were also working to lift the communication from the base level. It was ordained that from these communications much would grow.

So with those on earth and those in spirit working together there was a gradual evolvement to bring sanctity, to bring respect, to bring a reverence, away from what others termed dark forces, to something spiritual, something divine. Gradually they would sing hymns, say prayers, hold meetings in halls and would start the meeting with prayer and singing. From these one night events in various halls this evolved into regular meetings and church then gradually came religion.

It was a gradual development because it started as base communication but gradually became more evolved. It had to come away from all the opposition of being termed the work of the devil. It had to be a higher vibration, a higher intelligence, because many other people became involved they would only become associated if it was something with more respect.

Of course, you are talking of my country and we worshipped with spirit communication many years before these events, but they would not have listened to what the native American Indian had to say. They had to discover for themselves. White men had to have their own religion. There is no disharmony because of this. I appreciate they had their own path to lead and we had our path to lead. There is no thought of one religion being better than another, we all go forward together. (17.05.98)

QUESTION 151 - *A seeker asked this supplementary question after receiving the answer to his previous question. 'What is a Tribune of the Order of the Golden Band and who are the nameless and faceless ones associated with that band?' A detailed response was given by Michael.*

I have come because there is question you require an answer to. Before you read question I will say to you that I will answer question as far as it is fitting to answer at this time

We have already brought to you words regarding Golden Band (Reference 1/144) as to how this band stretches down through the dimensions. At the higher levels there are those who have chosen to co-ordinate vibrations to bring truth and wisdom in its allotted span. There is a destiny that is being experienced and, as you are aware, there is a new awakening. To you this is happening at this time in your existence but the foundations for this have been occurring for a timeless period.

You say 'who are the nameless and faceless ones?'. There is a reason why they are nameless and faceless. These are very high evolved souls with much wisdom. It is a very high level of evolution that they have attained. These highly evolved souls, spirits, whatever word you wish to use to describe these ones, are far detached from your dimension and your earth world. They have no need for names, they have no need of identity as you know identity. They are working as a highly evolved group, the word your friend asking the question has used is 'Order'. So be it, termed an 'Order'. It is an organised band or group, whom themselves, have progressed through many experiences, many dimensions to achieve their position at this level. It is their desire to assist to bring truth to those who are seeking.

Now this friend of yours who is asking this question has had teachings through others on this subject before. I am having a problem finding words because I do not use words. I have not used words for a very long while, I do not like to use the word 'time' because we do not have time as you understand it. When he had the experience of communing with this higher level of existence himself, he was given the word 'tribune' that was used as a description because that was the word that the communicator could find in the vocabulary of the medium he was using. I say he because at that level there is no he or she but I use the word 'he'. So I am trying to make myself known and I am using words in the vocabulary of this medium and I probably would not use the word 'tribune' because it is not to the fore in this one's vocabulary. The word 'tribune' was used as a description of an entity who conveys wisdom from those high ones down to others who are seeking. This is the best way I can describe.

When you talk of an 'Order' in your earth world you think of it as something exclusive that you have to be privileged to join. In the dimension of which I am speaking to become part of this Order one has to be of an advanced calibre, advanced wisdom, one who has learnt to progress to a higher level of understanding and learnt to withdraw from the mundane levels of existence. I am not saying that they are not concerned with these mundane levels because this is the whole purpose, to bring truth and enlightenment to all who are seeking, on whatever level. they exist. No one is barred from this knowledge as long as they are genuinely seeking with a desire from within. They are doing it not for any selfish reason, they are doing it for the good of all. They are doing it because they are genuinely and sincerely desiring to progress themselves, to seek truth in order to bring enlightenment to others without personal egotism. They are not doing it for their own gratification. They are doing it for the good of many.

There is no reason to exclude those of a lower level from these teachings. There are those who, through no fault of their own, find themselves through circumstances they cannot control, in a dimension they do not wish to exist in but they are seeking to be at another level, another dimension that is a higher dimension. If they genuinely wish to draw themselves up from that dimension there are those who are there waiting to help and assist.

So to recap, The Golden Band as you would try to envisage is a group of highly evolved souls who are working in an organised dimension, as destiny ordains, bringing about enlightenment and awakening to those who are seeking truth. To be able to reach those who are seeking truth there has to be other souls who are working between the dimensions. These are ones who have been specially chosen to work as a tribune, a messenger, to relay this news, this message of enlightenment. They, as your friend has perceived, are part of this Order. They have been specially chosen for this work. They have proven themselves capable of this work. It is very important that the right ones are chosen because this is very important work.

I have given you as much as I am ordained to give you at this moment in your time. There is much more to bring at another time but at this moment this is sufficient for your question and for your understanding before you are taken a little bit further along the path and more is revealed. There is much that I cannot explain at this moment. It is difficult for me to find words to explain something that is of such a high organisation, 'Organisation' is a word of your language but this is above organisation, there are no words that fit the frequencies with which we work. (20.05.98)

QUESTION 152 - E-om-ba explains how love that is sent via prayer is directed to where it is most needed.
When love is sent out it comes together to form great sea of energy. When there are problems or if there is need this pool of love can be utilised. When there are tragedies on your earth, people send out their love, this may be too late to help the earthly condition but it helps them on their journey home to spirit. As so much love is sent at one time there will be surplus love which can be used when there are other problems on your earth. This energy can then be drawn to other areas where there is need.
Does the same thing happen to the animals? - Of course there is love for all. People on your earth who send love, they may go to their church and put hands together in position and say prayers for the ones in need but in their thoughts before there are words, before there is a thought form, there is love in heart. This is what goes, the love from heart and the love from heart does not say I give love to people not animals. It is a genuine desire from within to give love to whatever. This love then goes wherever, to people, animals, your plants, trees also those in our world who are in need can share this love because it is not qualified as to where it goes. Love cannot be tied in a bag and kept in one place, if it is genuine love it has to spread and the more it is used the more it grows. When love is sent and it reaches someone who needs that one is thankful, they may not turn round and say 'thank you' but within their heart they are aware that they have received love. In their gratitude they are sending love out. Love grows. You say 'I have got bad arm', someone sends healing to you. You say 'I am grateful for healing' but in your gratitude you are sending love back, so it goes on and on. Maybe not to the one who gave you love but to someone else, and then their love will go on to someone else, it grows. (24.05.98)

QUESTION 153 - E-om-ba continues by answering another question this time 'Do you know when each of us is going to pass into spirit?'
We know so far ahead of time. I will not say to you that we know when you are going home to spirit because we do not have time. If someone who we were close to was coming home we would know so that we could

prepare.

There is time in your world but we do not have time but we know the condition of the body. When there is transition sometimes it is sudden transition and this is different. If it is a gradual transition, although that one breathes their last and that is the time when they go home to spirit, there is time before when that one is preparing to go home and we are very close. Quite often when someone has not got much of their time span on earth left they are aware of others near them who are no longer on earth, they will tell you they have seen their mother, their father, whoever. This is because gradually they are preparing and spirit are preparing and drawing close. However, spirit can not do this when there is a sudden departure because that one is consciously not aware of what is going to happen.

Do not be alarmed if you become aware of your mother and father near you because they sometimes draw near when you are unwell, or your energy is low. It does not mean that if you are aware of them near you are going home now. It is a different vibration when they are preparing.

If someone has an accident and passes to spirit is this preordained? - Sometime yes, sometimes no.

Would they have loved ones waiting for them? - All who go home have loved ones waiting. Destiny usually unfolds as it should but there are times when this does not happen through circumstances because you all have your own free will. This is not usual, when someone goes home it is usually ordained. Sometimes things happen which should not occur. As your loved ones are always near they would be near at that time so there is no reason to be alarmed.

If somebody was contemplating suicide, taking their own life, would spirit intervene? - Spirit cannot intervene. Spirit can guide, spirit can be there to give strength but we cannot alter your free will or destiny. We are there to try and assist, we sometimes will draw close. We have to be very careful because when someone is very depressed they are very low, they are sometimes very tearful, they are very withdrawn into themselves. When spirit draw close to anyone at any time it often happens that you sense spirit and sometimes you become tearful, you become withdrawn because you are sensing spirit near to you. So when someone is very depressed we have to be very careful not to make the condition worse. Sometimes we have to stand back, send our love and strength but not make ourselves too close because this may be just too much pressure and would alter destiny. There are so many vibrations I cannot explain but you must know that we are always near. Not that I am near everyone, every person who walks your earth has their own spirit companions walking with them, they may not be aware of these companions. You may say that one has no mother, no father, they walk the streets, they have no one who loves them, but they do have people who love them, they do have people walking with them. I say 'people' because this is a word to explain. They are loved. They were spirit before they were in that body and they have their spirit family that they will go home to. Their spirit family is always near. (24.05.98)

QUESTION 154 - George was talking about the different way people of varying nationalities think on earth. The question was then asked as to when people go home to spirit do they keep the traits of their earthly nationality?

They come from different lands, different cultures. When they go to spirit they leave behind their earthly conditions. Thought in spirit is not the same as thought on earth. When they come back to earth to communicate they come as an identity so that you can recognise them. If a medium standing on a platform explains to you that a spirit person is with you and describes them so that you could recognise them they would have to take on their earth identity.

When we come as vibrations to you and commune with you on your higher level we are communing in a different way, we are not using the thought process that you use.

You must consider what occurs before they came to earth, they were spirit. Then they came for a little while and took on an earth body. During the time they were in that earth body they were restricted to the conditions of that earth body. To the thoughts in that body, to the characteristics that body had inherited from its ancestors. Once they have left that body behind their spirit is then free to be part of the spirit vibration that it was before it had the human body encumbering it. If that one then decided to come back to make themselves known to you they would have to take on an identity.

I am taking on the identity of George because that was my last body on earth. When I leave George behind I work on a different vibration but I am trying to bring to you my spirit vibration through George's identity because I need an identity otherwise you wouldn't know who is communicating. I couldn't just come here and say 'I am spirit, don't ask me who I am because I am nobody'. I have to talk to you and have an identity. I could come and just commune with your higher level of vibration but your conscious reasoning wouldn't be aware of my presence so the communication would register so deeply.

The answer to your question is when you go home to spirit you leave behind all your earthly way of thinking, you are not English, you are not French, or whatever, you are pure spirit.

I come as George because, not only was George my last earthly identity, but George is someone you can relate to. You don't mind what you say to George, I don't mind if you are cheeky to me, I don't mind if you do not agree with what I say. If someone came with a different vibration you may be careful what you say in case you upset that visitor. You know I do not mind if you upset me I can give back as good as you send. I hope you like me coming as George.

George was then asked if those in spirit have a record of all that has happened to them in their past existence. - Every spirit entity has a history and in that history is all its evolvement, all its development, not all its trivia. You carry things that have made you what you are, all your experiences. You don't want to recall when you had a disagreement with your neighbour and slammed the door in their face, that is trivia it is not something which made a difference in your life. You would not want to carry the memory of falling over and hurting yourself, that would be trivia unless by doing that you learnt something very special or you met somebody very special who made a difference to your life. You don't remember everything, only the important things. You can recall things if you want to but most of us don't want to be pulled down with the earthly conditions, we want the lighter, brighter conditions. There are a lot of earthly conditions I no longer need. I only want things that are going to made me happy and make me grow. If I can recall something at one time that is going to help someone else that is different. If I come across a condition where I am asked to help and I went through a similar condition in one of my past existences I could recall it in order to help the one who would be going through that experience themselves but I wouldn't want to carry that memory with me all the time (24.05.98)

QUESTION 155 - Mafra answering the question 'Does the level of knowledge that is brought by spirit depend on which realm that communicator resides in?'

This is why you have conflicting answers. Someone asked a question before regarding conflicting knowledge given by spirit communicators. This is because we are individuals, also because of our evolvement. You are seeing through a mist, I am seeing a little clearer than you but I am still not seeing as clear as those that are higher evolved. We give to you knowledge that is true to our perception. We merge our energies with those who are higher than us to bring you knowledge of higher thoughts.

If you ask a question of one of our visitors who comes to you and they are unable to answer from their own knowledge, they try to blend and merge their energies with those of a higher vibration who have this knowledge. They are then able to bring it down through the various vibrations to yourselves but you must understand that there are so many levels. I am trying to recall an expression in your good holy book, I can mention this because it is the same for all kingdoms of Christendom, 'you see through a glass darkly, it is in the book of St Paul (The First Epistle of Paul the Apostle to the Corinthians, Chapter 13 and start of 14). I am trying to bring to you a passage from this book, it is a very well known reading, It talks of seeing things as a child and then advancing and you look through a glass and the glass is misted, it is clouded but later you see more clearly as you advance in age. This is to signify to you evolvement. If you read this book it explains to you evolvement, it does not explain to you growing from a child to an adult, it explains to you how you evolve and how we evolve. We see things through a cloud when we first start on this path, then gradually this cloud becomes a finer mist and we see things a little clearer, then a little more of the mist evaporates and we see a little more and this is how we evolve. This is condensed into a very short explanation, of course, there are many, many levels of knowledge and many vibrations. All the time we are gaining a little clearer vision. Eventually when we are highly evolved we see bright clear 'sunlight' no mist, I am drawing a picture for you to explain.

Those who come and speak, your visitors, the higher evolved they are the greater the wisdom they are bringing to you. They are bringing truth as we all bring truth but we do not tell falsehoods, but we only tell what we can give you at that time. Those from a higher level can give you a little bit more knowledge than we can. We are all the time stretching and blending with higher levels to draw this knowledge for you. The highly evolved ones who come to speak to you are able to bring you deeper understanding. There are disadvantages and advantages because the higher level they are the less easier it is for them to speak to you because they are so detached from your worldly atmosphere and conditions. Although they have all this knowledge they have problems communicating it to you. This is why we try and raise and stretch ourselves absorbing this knowledge from them and bring it down to your level of understanding. This is why we on the lower levels of evolvement can bring from those that are higher.

As with all messengers we have to be careful that we do not distort the message. This is why sometimes you have conflicting words given to you. We are just messengers, as you are messengers to those on your earth who ask you questions and you, as an earthly breathing person, answer their question. Perhaps you give them some of the knowledge that we have given you and you are trying very carefully not to distort that knowledge. It is possible that you do because you use your own words not our words. As we draw knowledge from those from higher realms, we are not taking words from them but we are taking vibrations and merging our vibrations, part of us is blending so we have to be very careful that we are giving you pure knowledge and not distorting the knowledge.

This is part of the reason we bring to you also many who are training because they are training to be teachers, teaching truth. They are bringing truth but in bringing this truth they need to blend with others at a higher level and they again, have to learn to shut themselves down to bring the truth through them as a true vessel not as a messenger who adds part of their own theory. It is all part of their learning. This is why we are training teachers. It is not just to open mouth and talk it is very much more involved. We are teaching them to communicate from a higher level. At first they will talk to you and I will be standing here (I say standing for you to understand) and I will be giving them words to say. They can rest assured that my words will be easily absorbed because I have had experience of this. At first they will be literally taking words from myself and giving to you. Then gradually I take step back, gradually, gradually, and they will bypass me and draw from someone higher but this is a very gradual process.

You have witnessed this with E-om-ba, for one example, but there are others but we will talk of him. When he first spoke he had difficulty even finding words, so I was helping him find words. I was not helping him bring truth from higher levels because that would have been too complicated at that stage. I was just helping him find words, just to say 'hello, greetings, my name is E-om-ba'. This was my task at first, just to be able to persuade him that he could speak, he could talk to you and he could relay words. I was giving him words and very slowly as he became more confident, because it is confidence, I was there sliding a little bit back, a little bit back, so that he was absorbing a little less of my energy and using energy from other sources. First I was filtering as it came through but gradually as I stepped back he did not need me. This is good he has learned to become a teacher and perhaps in time he will teach others. There will be many other groups who will need teachers. I will not say that he will leave you but there will be other groups and there will be time when you are not here and he may wish to attach himself to other groups. So you see a little how we work.

Each has their own vibration and each as they draw wisdom from a higher vibration try and connect with a vibration which is compatible. As you are aware, we are a group but we are individuals within that group. So you see how important your work and our work is, working together, bringing knowledge to others but we have to ensure that we train our teachers because this work is so important. We cannot have them talking 'rubbish' because it is important that they talk truth. (24.05.98)

QUESTION 157 - Jules talks to us about harmony

Harmony is very important. So much of your history the problem has been there has been no harmony. I talk of history of lands, nations but also I talk of history of people. People in their own lands, in work conditions, people in churches, in schools, in shops, in offices, on roads. This is problem all the time, there is no harmony. Everyone wants to be a little better than the other one. Everybody wants to say 'I am a bit more clever than the other one'. If someone knows something that the other doesn't know, so what, you know something they do not know! Why become worried? There is no problem, just be happy for each other. You cannot progress if you are not in harmony with each other. You have to be harmonious. You have to accept that each of you here are human, so because you are human you all have faults. If you had no faults you would not be here on earth, you would be with us! You must not expect each other to be perfect, you have to accept each other as you are. Do not worry, just be harmonious.

If someone believes something that you do not believe, so what, that is their way. You believe what you know to be right for yourself and if you are harmonious with yourself that is good. If you are not harmonious with yourself you have got a big problem. You cannot expect to be harmonious with others if you are not harmonious with yourself. I do not mean things like being impatient with yourself, you all get a little worried if things are not going as you wish. Slow down, there is no rush, it will come when the time is right. You have to accept that some things you can't do, but some things you can do. Others can do something better than you, but you can do something better than them.

You all must have your good points and join together and use each other's good points, do not look at bad points. As a team each can contribute something different to the team. This may be in your group here, or other groups that you are part of. The most important thing is to learn to live together in harmony.

Coming back to groups. In groups it is very important, if there is one in group that causes problems you might as well shut doors and say 'no good'. If there is not harmony in group you will not go forward. You might as well bang your head against that wall. If there is problems sit down, discuss problem, overcome problem. I am not saying there is a problem in your group but I am saying 'groups' as an example. Each of you in a small group, you are all part of bigger groups. You are part of group here but you are also part of many more groups. These other groups must be in harmony also. If you link with other groups you must not think 'they know a little bit more than me about something so I must be careful because I must not tell them I do not know or they will think I am stupid.' There is no **worry**, no problem, they do one thing one way and you do one thing another way, so be it, no problem. Just be harmonious that they can do that because you can do something else. What they can do now you may be able to do tomorrow. No problem, why rush?

Harmony is so important. Once you start not having harmony you have a big problem. Whatever you do, whether it is spiritual work, or material work, or just lazing about doing nothing, you have to be harmonious. Your world should be in balance, it should be in harmony but alas, it is not. How can it be when there are so many who are unharmonious with themselves? If you are unharmonious with yourself you cannot be harmonious with others. So your groups are not harmonious, your countries are not harmonious, your world is not harmonious. It must start with the individual.

Sometimes you think everything is fine and happy then something happens and all of a sudden where there was harmony, that harmony has gone. You try and carry on but you must think it is not good trying to carry on, you must find out what has happened to make this disharmony. It may have happened for a reason to make you think. Turn around and look at it a different way. You look all the time from one view point, sometimes it is wrong, sometimes it is good to turn things around and look at them in a different way. (31.05.98)

QUESTION 158 - *A conversation with Mafra regarding organisation. The question being 'We tend in this earthly world to think we are very organised.' Mafra's reply 'You think you are organised!' When Brother John was talking about your group being called upon to do specialised work how does that happen? Is there some sort of higher level which is organising what you do?'*

Of course we all have someone higher than us, there are higher vibrations, higher levels. If I say 'plan' you will think someone is sitting there making great plan and that is all they do. No, my friend. We intermingle vibrations, we blend vibrations, it is so difficult to explain. Yes, there are higher levels and vibrations. There is someone who guides myself, as I try and help you, there is an entity who is overshadowing myself and is assisting me. That one has someone that assists them who is even higher. This goes on and on. They try to guide my steps as I stumble, as you stumble. We are all striving to progress, to become more evolved, to become wiser, more enlightened. As we become more enlightened we try to broaden our horizons, we try to stretch farther.

You are limited and confined to your human body and your human world. You are trying to stretch even so, you are trying to stretch to link with us. You are trying to stretch to link with others on your earth who are calling on you. You are trying to stretch to spread knowledge to others. Although you are confined in your human body you are trying to stretch.

We are linking with yourselves but we also have our own group, as you have your group, we have our group who we work with. We also have our own spirit families who we belong to, who we come from. These are those who are overshadowing us and assisting us because they are, perhaps, more evolved than us. We have those who we have linked with in the past, as you have those who you have linked with in the past, You have lost contact with them but you still keep contact in other ways. We also have those who we linked with in the past and at this point in time they are not with us, as so close as perhaps they may have been because their work is elsewhere. We have many links.

I will try to explain this to you. I will come back to your earth life. You are one person on your earth. You have your family which you have grown up with, your earth family. You had on your earth your mother, father, grandparents, brothers, sisters, whatever. Going a little bit further you had great-grandparents, aunts, uncles, cousins. You also had school companions when you attended school. You also had people who lived within your locality. You also had people you visited when you travelled to different places, perhaps seaside or country and you made links there. As you progressed through life you went to different schools, you met different people, you perhaps joined different organisations and met people there. You then grew a little older and left school behind and you went to place of work and you met more people. When you had friends, perhaps they took you to their homes and you met their family, and so on, and so on throughout your life, you have been forever meeting new people, making new contacts. Some of these people you have stayed close to, you have kept contact with them, some you have not, you have lost contact with them. Some you have lost contact with quite happily because you did not want to stay close to them, others you have lost contact with through various reasons but you still think of them in a happy manner and wonder where they are and what they are doing. These are your connections on earth.

Before you came to earth you came from spirit family and you have many contacts from that family in spirit. Some of the people you have shared your earth life with you have been told that you have shared experiences with them in a past existence, this is why you are drawn together again in this life.

It is the same with myself and all the others who are with you from spirit, we have so many contacts. So many contacts; those who we are working with now in this what you call 'time', for us it is a stage in our evolvement but there are many other links which we have. We have those whom we met while on earth, who were in our family on earth, some are with us, some are not. Some have evolved to different areas, some have returned to earth but we still have links. As others call on you for healing, you then send your love and do whatever you can. In a more physical circumstance, you may have a neighbour, brother or sister who says to you 'I need help to do so and so', you will go and physically assist them to do whatever. Your neighbour may say 'Can you help me push my car down drive' and you will go and help him. It is the same with us. We are a team, we work with you, we try and assist you on your way, we try and guide you, we try and assist those who come to you. We also have other links and sometimes one of those links may send a vibration to us, they know our work, they know our circumstances and they may send a call for help to us and we will go and assist.

Yes, there are those above us who plan and organise but also we have free will, as you have free will. We have other links also. As you are becoming known for your work, we are known for our work. If we can assist someone we will be happy to go and assist in that area. If someone is in need of, perhaps, enlightening, education, we will go and assist if we can. Perhaps they need help in another way. We help in many aspects not just teaching. We are here to teach because this is the purpose of your group and we have chosen to assist your group but we have other ways we help. The primary function of your group is to teach but you are also involved in healing. It is the same with us, if there is need we can go and assist somewhere else. We do not leave you, we are only a whisper away but we know that if there is a problem you will know we are there to assist. We also have others we help, we are not limited as you are limited.

You are limited to being in your room in your building and you cannot be somewhere else at the same time. In your sleep state your thoughts can go and wander. You can sit in your armchair, you can sit in your office and be there physically but your mind can be somewhere else. It is similar to us, we can be with you but also we can be somewhere else. I have given you this description just to help you a little, to explain how you can be one place and somewhere else. For example; if you are sitting in your office and you are sitting looking at papers but your mind has wandered and you have gone somewhere else, someone may come and talk to you and you are instantly there again, you have not left you are still there. It is the same with us, we go but we are still there. It is a puzzle but I hope you understand.

Yes, there is a destiny, there is a preordained plan but we have free will, as you have free will and there are no hard and fast rules as you have on your earth. You have to take this path and you have to do this before you can do that. It is not the same, we are more free and the more evolved we become the more we can spread. As I have tried to explain to you, when you are a child you have your family and as you grow and evolve your family grows, your contacts grow. I am trying to explain evolvement to you. The more evolved you become the wider your horizons, the more you reach out, the more you stretch out. (02.06.98)

QUESTION 159 - Running Bear gives wisdom on the subject of Truth.
We are just messengers, we do not matter it is truth which is important. It does not matter from whence the words come because truth outshines all. Truth opens doors, truth shines light on path. As you walk path you have many lights shining, many lights which attract you, go to this light, go to that light, but some lights soon flickers, some lights do not last, truth outshines all other lights. Truth endures much hardship, much distress, much worry but truth still shines. Sometimes you cannot see truth because there are clouds obscuring your view but truth still shines through. When you have strength to move clouds you will see truth is still shining there for you. This is not so for many other lights that you come across during your path, they are there for short time and vanish, you try to glimpse again but it is not good they have gone. They attract and lure you for a little while, tempt you entice you and you think this is good, I will go towards this because it is good, but when you have found it is not a good light you come back to path and truth is still there shining.

Truth endures beyond all distractions. You seek truth and you will find truth. You must test truth to see whether it is truth. There are many false truths on your way, you have to test to see what is truth. Truth cannot be manipulated, cannot be altered, truth outshines. You cannot change truth to fit circumstance which you wish to put forward. If it does not fit it is not truth. Sometimes when man travels path he faces truth in face but does not like what he sees so he tries to alter, to adapt, to something which is easier. Truth is not an easy path to tread. Truth has obstacles, truth has hurdles but by overcoming hurdles and obstacles you grow and your light becomes brighter. If you try to take easier path, try to alter truth to fit easier path you are not gaining, in the end you have to come back to path and you have made your journey longer and more difficult by taking other route. Sometimes this is good because you have learnt through taking other route that there is only one truth.

Man makes truth very complicated. Truth is sincere, truth is goodness, truth is love. Man tries to put conditions on truth - 'You can only look at truth if you do so and so' - 'you have to believe what this one says otherwise you are not able to glimpse truth'. This is making difficulties, truth is open to everyone. Everyone is entitled to truth from humble to mighty. Those who follow one religion or another religion, they each have truth. Each religion dresses truth in different clothing but if you can discard clothing, I do not mean clothing you wear, you will glimpse pure truth.

There is no need to dress truth in fine robes, truth is free, it is not conditioned by money. Sometimes money clouds truth, you cannot see truth because of your earthly conditions. Sometimes those who have not the benefit of your earthly goods and shackles have a better view of truth than those who are well endowed with earthly goods because their view is clouded, because they only see through their earthly condition. Those who are not surrounded with so much their vision is often clearer. You take joy at sunset, forest, waters, hills, flowers, trees, you can see truth in all these but some seek to see truth through their material conditions and this is where they have problems. They are clouding their vision, they are making truth too complicated, they are putting too many conditions on truth. There are no conditions, truth is free for all. You cannot say 'I give you truth if you agree to follow my words'. How can man put these conditions on something that is so spiritual? Each one that walks is a spirit, they are spirit within, they are part of Great Spirit, so how can another man stop them from seeking truth because it is their right, their heritage. Man cannot make conditions of spiritual matters for others.

Truth is free, truth is there for all. You do not have to be of high status, or highly educated, or of much wealth, truth is there. Quite often your young ones see truth a lot clearer than older ones because they see naturally, they do not question, put conditions, scheme and plot, as those older ones would. Their perception is pure, they trust. Have the trust of a child and you will see truth. Put your wisdom in the vision of a child and you will see truth.

This is just to give you words to think about. I am not directing your thoughts how you should think because this would be contradictory to what I have just said. What I am saying is, I am giving you some thoughts for you to think on, for you to ponder, for you to explore, and then you will find your own truth, on your own path. It is not for spirit to tell you which way to walk, it is for spirit to be there to give you strength, to give you wisdom of spirit but it is for you to seek for yourself. Too many rely on spirit to show way, this is no good. Yes, ask for help, guidance, strength and protection but the impetus has to be from your own being, the desire must come from within yourself.

I leave you with blessings from spirit. May your words be of wisdom, may your eyes be open to clear vision, and may your ears only hear the song of spirit. (23.06.98)

QUOTATION

"*Which brings me to my conclusion upon Free Will and Predestination namely —-let the reader mark it ———that they are identical*"

Sir Winston Churchill

CHAPTER THREE
PSYCHIC WAYS

There are numerous ways that communication is established between ourselves and the spirit world. Together with variations on a theme. This chapter is therefore not an exhaustive list but aims to explain in basic terms the types of communication we have been privileged to witness or experience first hand.

TAPPINGS, this includes bangings on the floor, walls or ceiling, even footsteps, within the environment of a properly organised and controlled circle, normally sitting in complete darkness. The spirit people are able to communicate by harnessing the energy of the sitters and moving the atoms of the atmosphere. During this type of communication it is important to establish the code being used (one tap for yes etc.), and to ask questions. From our experience the sound of the tapping, the rhythm and opening code relates to one communicator and becomes their "Hello". Great care must be taken not to be fooled by creaks in old buildings and other sitters moving in their seats, all communication of this nature should be intelligent communication. However, like all communication it develops and early experiences may be of an experimental nature. If tappings are heard outside the controlled conditions of a circle it may be spirit but treat with the utmost caution.

APPORTS, being the materialisation of a solid object from one place to another. The phenomena of apports relates to the fact that all matter is a group of minute vibrating atomic structures that are attracted together to form a mass, or as we term it a solid object. It may be the hardest metal or the softest plant, even our own bodies. Therefore any matter can be disintegrated and reformed, moved through other matter, if the vibrations are compatible. We are given to understand that this is how apports are possible by the actions of our spirit friends. The objects that appear, we are told, come from where they will not be missed and are of little or no material value. They come when we least expect them, but there is some message relating to the object, which may be a trifle obscure.

One morning Ellen found a small package of faded tissue paper, in her make up draw. This package contained a rather nice St Christopher pendant. The next morning another apport appeared in the same place, this time a lapel badge that was issued to people involved in civilian war efforts c 1945. On another occasion I went out to our garden, which is rather secluded and this part well away from any other gardens, and discovered a perfect lemon on the grass. There was no logical explanation, a lemon could not have been carried by the squirrels or other animals. These three apports were later confirmed by spirit as there intervention. On the other hand we do seem to "lose", little things, despite our searching, we can only wonder who has been the lucky recipient of our junk.

MENTAL PHENOMENA, this being where the medium decodes pictures "clairvoyance" or words "clairaudience", from those in spirit, or a combination of the two. In addition the ability to "sense" the communication "clairsentience" without visualising or hearing spirit is difficult to describe and it all comes down to the confidence of the sensitive in accepting the message being passed on. The major problem with all mental phenomena is knowing when the message is from spirit, this is because the medium, by training tends to become very sensitive, picking up peoples vibrations or the vibrations in the immediate environment. It is vital that the sensitive learns how to control the communication, when to switch on and off. On occasions it is not unknown for spirit to "jump in", with guidance when there is a need, and the time is right. When communication is taking place from our experience it seems that the thought transfer is a total vibration rather than a complete story. For example a perfect rose may indicate that the communicator was a grower of prize roses rather than a person who liked their garden. It also seems that names are of little importance in the spirit realms and they are identified by their unique vibration, therefore some communicators have a problem with their earthly names, especially when they have been in spirit for many of our years. When communicating especially in a public demonstration, communicators often give the physical condition of their earthly body when they passed. This has been explained as the effect of the spirit energy coming into contact with the material world and the last experience in the mortal body coming to the fore.

DIRECT VOICE, this has been witnessed in various forms, with the medium in a deep trance, where the medium has no knowledge of what is happening. A light trance, on the other hand, is where the medium knows what is happening, but has no control over the words and actions taking place. Then there is direct voice produced by spirit without the use of a mediums vocal chords, this may be through a trumpet which amplifies the sound vibrations or seemingly from a corner of the room. The latter requiring the room being used for communication to be completely dark and with a group of sitters who fully understand and are sympathetic to the event. With Ellen the direct communication allows her to be aware of what is taking place. The visitors who communicate through her vary considerably, in some cases speaking their mother tongue, they always give us a deeper understanding in their own particular way. Most of the communicators are happy for us the record their words, after asking for permission, which allows Ellen to hear the communication for herself, which is often very amusing. Never think that those in spirit don't have a sense of humour, they enjoy our fun and chip in with their own "funnies", even the more serious communicators.

TRANSFIGURATION, we have witnessed this phenomena of spirit friends being able to build up a memory of their features on a sensitive's face in the light of a ruby lamp. It is evident that not everyone watching this phenomena observe the same thing. To some it's very clear and others fail to see anything. This seems to be partly where the viewer is sitting and partly their aspirations of how clear they expect to see the face. Care must be taken in not confusing shadows formed by the rather dim red light in a darkened room. However, spectacular proof of the presence of spirit has been witnessed with this form of communication which in some cases is linked with direct voice.

AROMAS, we have been fortunate to experience our spirit friends generating a vibration which has the affect of producing an aroma. In some cases this has been a smell particularly associated with the person communicating, such as the smell of a pipe. In other cases this has been a perfume that identifies with the communicator. When a special perfume is generated it can be for a specific purpose, for example a citrus smell for cleansing the mind giving clarity of thought or for healing reasons. As with colours to fully describe an aroma is not easy, but it does appear that all the sitters smell the same scent, irrespective of whether they have a sinus problem. Aromas generally come in a darkened sitting but it is not unknown for this phenomena to happen when you least expect it.

TABLE MOVEMENT (also known as TIPOLOGY), TRUMPET MOVEMENT, RINGING OF BELLS, BANGING OF DRUMS etc. etc. this phenomena has been witnessed within the confines of a "circle", environment. The sitters all being aware of the presence of spirit and enabling energy from the sitters to be manipulated by spirit to effect the movement of solid objects in a controlled manner. We have heard bells being rung and drums played in time with singing. Drums beating out a tempo, that is beneficial to the healing process. The movement of the table and trumpet being visible by small fluorescent markers on the objects, with the table and or trumpet being moved under the direction of spirit to give intelligent answers to questions asked by the sitters, either mentally or verbally. We are fortunate to be the custodians of a small bamboo table which is said to have been imported from the U.S.A. many years ago where the phenomena of table movement was developed, This particular table being the first table to be used in the United Kingdom to demonstrate the phenomena. We are told that the construction material is not too important, and we have used plastic, wooden and wood tables with a steel support underneath. However, the bamboo is a fibrous wood which is not a dense material, allowing easier movement.

AUTOMATIC WRITING, this comes in various forms. It may be what is termed inspirational without the writer being aware of help from spirit. Other times is may be a sensitive writing at incredible speeds, with words of philosophy, poems or even music. Some sensitives use a "planchette", a heart shaped board on wheels with a pencil attached,that allows spirit writing to take place with one or more sitters fingers on the top. We have also seen spirit writing where a sheet of paper is left in the centre of the darkened sitting room with a stick of charcoal. In this case it has been a single name, a word in another tongue written in ancient script or even pictures.

PSYCHIC DRAWING, there are a number of forms of this phenomena that we have witnessed. There are mediums who are artistic and are able the draw an image of the face they are perceiving at great speed, then there are mediums whose hands are guided by spirit to draw an image of the spirit person wishing to communicate. In Ellen's case the drawings of spirit faces and in some cases symbols are drawn with her left hand with the "operator", finding the right colour pencil. These drawings take about ten minutes, and we need to seek advice as to who they are, they may be spirit helpers, friends or family, of people we are going to sit with, in a few days hence. (It should explained that Ellen is right handed and is not a skilled artist in any way.)

SPIRIT LIGHTS, this is a rather special phenomena where in the darkened room where communication is taking place, one or more pin pricks of white light can be seen by all the sitters, moving around the room in diverse directions, and then seemingly entering the head of the medium before communication takes place.

CHAPTER FOUR
THE LEARNING SYSTEM

The following has been explained to us as the system of learning and how we fit into the scheme of things.

The **HIGHER ONES IN SPIRIT** plan and appoint a
TRAINING GROUP - consisting of spirit and human resources to train and develop those in spirit and in earth environment.

The **Training Team** of spirit helpers as a group energy but each with their own personalities and individual expertise.
The team can be as small or large as needed.
Mafra is the Father Figure

Spirit training as Teachers

Spirit gaining learning & experience

PROVISION OF KNOWLEDGE RELEVANT NOW AND FOR THE FUTURE

Spirit from other groups seeking special experiences

The **training distributors** on earth - communication direct from the Training Team in Spirit

Seekers - needing knowledge

Hint takers who seek at a later time

Learners - wanting knowledge

We are told that the higher ones in the realms of spirit planned a group dedicated to training. The group "in spirit", many of whom are known to us provide guidance to us and those who sit with us through the words we hear but also matters of a higher level of knowledge directly into our spirit energy. We are told that many from the realms of spirit join us in our communications with spirit to also learn, from the questions we ask and the information given. We have visitors from other groups. who come to gain experience, where perhaps there own group do not have the same resources as our group.

We are told that our Circle is the only group on the earth plane that the group in the spirit realms work through. However, we are of course one and the same group, just that we wear the "earthly overcoat". Although we have visiting spirit friends who come to experience being with us in at least in one case we know our visitor also visits and teaches with other groups.

For spirit to develop we are told that they need the experience of our questioning because their gaining of knowledge is a merging of energies from one spirit energy to another. In some cases spirit need to experience coming through a communicator to realise that their existence in spirit is different and to make them fully aware they are in a different dimension.

We are told that the opportunities for spirit to develop by working with us on the earth plane is limited, and therefore a precious commodity.

Clearly we are only on the fringes of understanding the Grand Plan, but planned it is!